WITHDRAWN FROM
CALARTS LIBRARY

WE GO POGO

Great Comics Artists Series

M. Thomas Inge, General Editor

We Go Pogo

Walt Kelly, Politics, and American Satire

Kerry D. Soper

PN
6727
K4
Z87
2012

University Press of Mississippi   Jackson

CALIFORNIA INSTITUTE OF THE ARTS

www.upress.state.ms.us

The University Press of Mississippi is a member
of the Association of American University Presses.

Copyright © 2012 by University Press of Mississippi

Unpublished interviews and other materials from the Walt Kelly archive at Ohio State University,
copyright © Okefenokee Glee & Perloo, Inc. Used by permission.

All rights reserved
Manufactured in the United States of America

First printing 2012

∞

Library of Congress Cataloging-in-Publication Data

Soper, Kerry.
  We go Pogo : Walt Kelly, politics, and American satire / Kerry D. Soper.
    p. cm. — (Great comics artists series)
  Includes bibliographical references and index.
  ISBN 978-1-61703-283-7 (cloth : alk. paper) — ISBN 978-1-61703-284-4 (pbk. : alk. paper) — ISBN
978-1-61703-285-1 (ebook) 1. Kelly, Walt. 2. Pogo (Comic strip) 3. Cartoonists—United States. 4.
Satire in literature. I. Kelly, Walt. II. Title. III. Title: Walt Kelly, politics, and American satire.
  PN6727.K4Z87 2012
  741.5'6973—dc23   2011041673

British Library Cataloging-in-Publication Data available

TO LISA

CONTENTS

ACKNOWLEDGMENTS

There are a number of people to thank for their help in creating this book: Allen Tullos for his mentoring as I first wrestled with the complex issues of race and Southern identities in Walt Kelly's work; George Handley, Stan Benfell, Matt Ancell, Kristin Matthews, and Phil Snyder for reading drafts and offering essential advice; Carolyn Hone for bailing me out on numerous occasions; John Rosenberg, Greg Clark, Scott Sprenger, Ron Woods, Jared Christensen, Mike Call Sr., and other people at Brigham Young University for providing generous resources and support (this includes the people in the College of General Education whose Alcuin Fellowship helped pay for critical research trips); Taylor Ball-Brown, Ben Tingey, Kirsten Steiger, Shannon Dame, Rachel Gilman, and Jaime Bingham for their stellar work as research assistants; Lucy Caswell and Jenny Robb for their patient aid when I spent time at the Billy Ireland Cartoon Library and Museum; Pete Kelly (the epitome of generosity), Carolyn Kelly, Bill Crouch Jr., and Steve Thompson for providing useful leads, corrections, and critical help in shepherding this work into print (Steve Thompson deserves a special thanks, in fact, for working so tirelessly, for so many years, in doing foundational research into Walt Kelly's life and work—I look forward to reading his definitive biography of Kelly someday); Walter Biggins, Seetha Srinivasan, John Lent, Jeet Heer, Judith Yaross Lee, Thomas Inge, and all the scholars in the Comics Section of the Popular Culture Association for their interest and faith in my work; Lanny, Shirley, and my parents for their generous support; Haley, Devin, Taylor, Emmy, Stan, Cammy, Holly, and David for taking an interest in what I do even when it isn't very interesting; and Walt Kelly, of course, for creating the best comic strip to ever appear on the funnies page.

WE GO POGO

Introduction

In 1952 a political rally at Harvard University overflowed with enthusiasm and eventually turned into a mildly violent carnival:

> A crowd of 200 gathered in Harvard square . . . As the restless crowd grew to 1,600, 3 police wagons, 8 patrol cars and 25 policemen arrived, and in the ensuing mêlée 28 Harvard students were arrested. (Boatner 90)

We don't often associate early 1950s college campuses with political agitators, and so it is difficult to imagine what caused this rowdy demonstration. The answer, at first glance, is surprising: the students were there to greet Walt Kelly, the creator of a cute comic strip 'possum named Pogo—a character then engaged in a mock-presidential campaign. The mania, moreover, wasn't isolated to Harvard. Kelly's playful "I Go Pogo" campaign was a grassroots craze, prompting students at 150 colleges to endorse the character as their official candidate—and producing 50,000 requests for Pogo buttons and dozens of invitations for Kelly to speak at college rallies.

This Pogo-mania may sound silly to those unfamiliar with Kelly's comic strip; but longtime fans of *Pogo*, named for its lead character, would understand that real ideological issues propelled this passion. Indeed, after developing an ap-

Figure 0.1: Walt Kelly at college *Pogo* rally, 1952. Copyright © Okefenokee Glee & Perloo, Inc. Used by permission.

preciation for Kelly's comic world—a pastoral swampland where comedic types in animal form deconstruct and satirize American culture through wordplay, vaudevillian slapstick, and folksy philosophizing—one can see the deeper layers of sincerity and significance to this comic strip craze. To be specific, *Pogo* resonated so well with college students and intellectuals in the 1950s because it playfully attacked brands of divisive and reactionary politics in its comedy and satire, and articulated an alternative ideology—a spirit of communal inclusivity, tolerance, and healthy self-criticism—that matched well the spirit of mid-century, Cold-War liberalism (figures 0.2 and 0.3 provide an example of this contrast at work in the strip). In other words, it was a rare work of popular comedy/satire

Figure 0.2: Walt Kelly, "Hey, Deacon!" *Pogo*, 19 May 1953.

Figure 0.3: Walt Kelly, "Decided I'd go fishin' after all . . . ," *Pogo*, 20 May 1953.

that served as a "nexus through which ideologies may be actively reorganized"— a vital cultural product that helped a generation of college students, liberal intellectuals, and many everyday comics readers to shape their political worldviews (Woolacott 217).

Comics scholars and mid-century historians have documented well the high point of Kelly's career—the period in the early 1950s when he and his strip challenged the conservative rhetoric of the age; but less well understood is how Kelly got to this point in his creative life: how he gathered, constructed, and reworked the ingredients of his mature comedy and satire over many years as an animator at Disney, as a political cartoonist for a big city newspaper, and as a comic book artist. By digging into these earlier phases of Kelly's career, we realize that

Pogo was not simply an unremarkable comic strip thought up by committee, or thrown together on a whim by a young, aspiring cartoonist; it was instead the end product of nearly two decades of labor by an auteur who wouldn't achieve serious success until his mid 40s. Moreover, it was a work of popular culture that emerged from a complex hybridization of comic mediums: from dialogues between high, folk, and popular culture—and from syncretic confluences between African American and Anglo American cultures.

In this comprehensive study of Kelly's career I will not neglect the high point of his achievements as a satirist—that period when he was able to comedically undermine the dogma and paranoia of McCarthyism—but I devote a significant bulk of the work to tracing the rich veins of comedic tradition and genre conventions Kelly first appropriated, and then modified, in the years leading up to those signature achievements. Ultimately this emphasis on the genealogical history of Kelly's work allows one to understand his mature satiric methods and core ideologies with greater depth. Just as importantly, it also allows one to explore some of the complexities of a mid-century American culture embroiled in debates over high and low culture, the moral obligations of popular artists, exchanges between dominant and minority artistic traditions, and the relationship between popular and political cultures.

This introductory chapter lays the foundation for exploring Kelly's work and career thusly: it establishes the different mediums that intersected in his art, shaping his aesthetics, comedy and satire in profound ways; it touches on the variety of folk and popular comedic traditions that shaped his work; it explores the significant cultural roles he played, including cultural critic, auteur, and poplorist; it summarizes his overarching cultural significance into our time; and lastly, it lists a brief outline of each chapter.

The Mediums that Intersect in Kelly's Work

While Kelly is most commonly perceived as a comic strip artist, he wore numerous hats in his long career simply as a result of having tried his hand at so many different journalistic and artistic fields: at various times he was also an illustrator, political cartoonist, designer, animator, storyboard man, comic book writer and artist, pundit, columnist, and lyricist. In addition, he was well known among peers as a superior public speaker, a gifted stand-up comedian, a creative and generous correspondent, a stellar chalk-talker, and an incorrigible pub-crawling prankster. All these facets of Kelly's career and character made a mark on the dynamism and complexity of *Pogo*, but three roles in particular—as animator, political cartoonist, and comic book artist—had an especially profound impact on his work.

To begin, each of these career phases is inherently interesting, and revealing about Kelly's character, because of the general creativity, energy, and humor he brought to each. But instead of treating each of these creative periods as simply colorful but inconsequential episodes, this study will approach them as essential building blocks in Kelly's construction of a comic strip that transcended the rules and limits of its medium. In other words, because Kelly tried his hand at so many different crafts, a cross-fertilization occurred in his work between several popular mediums and satiric/comedic discourses that ultimately expanded the possibilities of both his particular venue—the funnies page—and satirically charged popular culture in general.

To briefly expand on this idea, let's highlight some of the aesthetic elements and comedic conventions Kelly encountered in these other mediums: his first "real" job was as a storyboard man and animator at Disney working on *The Reluctant Dragon*, *Fantasia*, *Dumbo*, *Pinocchio*, and various shorts. While his output there was not exceptional, Kelly's time at Disney was a productive period of training and education for an artist who had never attended college. As an animator, Kelly learned how to stage visual and verbal gags; to create a cinematic backdrop for comedic action (see Figure 0.4); to give stories an engaging narrative arc; to create vivid characters with high visual appeal; and to add dynamism, heft, and anatomical realism to cartoon bodies. Informally, Kelly and his fellow animators also reveled in the comic traditions of vaudeville, blackface minstrelsy, and musical theater; this was apparent in their extracurricular pranks, chalk-talks, and musical jams, but also in their animated work, such as the "jive crows" segment in *Dumbo*. That fascination with black culture—as filtered through popular representations—would persist, in muted but significant fashion in Kelly's mature work.

Finally, the signature "cuteness" of Disney aesthetics made a big impact on Kelly's later work; for example, his principal character, Pogo, had the dimensions and overall circularity in his features of Mickey Mouse. Much has been made of the universal appeal of Mickey's visual construction, and thus those same arguments can be applied to the resonance of Kelly's leading character. In addition to infusing comic strips with the energy and aesthetics of film animation, Kelly enhanced the layeredness of his satire with a general "Disneyfication"

Figure 0.4: Walt Kelly, "Look at that art work!" *Pogo*, 8 March 1964.

of his work. Specifically, the cute aesthetics and dynamic shenanigans in Kelly's animal allegory served as a surface sweetener (or strategic distraction) from layers of topical, and sometimes biting satire coursing beneath.

The satiric seriousness of Kelly's comic strip grew in part out of another phase of his career—his work as a newspaperman. As a teenager he first labored at a newspaper in Bridgeport, and later in 1948 he served as a jack-of-all-trades employee at the *New York Star*, an idealistic, left-leaning daily, where he did design, spot illustrations, political cartoons, and a comic strip—an early version of *Pogo*. Despite some significant accomplishments as a political cartoonist with the *Star*—such as creating the icon of Thomas Dewey as the "mechanical man"—the medium was never a perfect match for Kelly's talents. For example, editorial cartoons lacked the narrative continuity and character complexity that would allow Kelly's array of comedic gifts to shine; the field did, however, train him in methods of taking on topical and cosmic targets through caricature, allegory, and aesthetic economy. In a broad sense, he carried away from this work in newspapers the democratic and progressive responsibilities of good satire and journalism; as a result, he entered the comic strip world intent on being both a comedic artist *and* a principled cultural critic.

Kelly's mature comic strip was also shaped by his nearly decade-long stint in the 1940s writing and drawing comic books for Dell Publishing. This work included an *Our Gang* series (based on the classic "Little Rascals" film shorts), and animal stories that borrowed from the trickster tales popularized by Joel Chandler Harris early in the twentieth century. The *Pogo* of the 1950s and 1960s resembled these stories in terms of vivid comedic character types, foundational trickster tale conventions, and sustained and farcical narratives. But a comparison of Kelly's work in these two mediums (comic books and comic strips) reveals he benefited from what might be seen as the limitations of the funnies page—in particular, the reduced space, certain editorial constraints, and the comedic, gag-oriented arc of the medium's limited frames. These pressures and strictures ultimately refined and focused Kelly's satire and comedy: the gags got tighter, the dialogue snappier, and the aesthetics more polished. In addition, the kid-oriented trickster tale knock-offs of the comic books gave way in the comic strip to Freudian-themed tales, pastoral comedic conventions, deconstructive wordplay, and topical satire.

Comic books continued to haunt Kelly, however, in profound but less direct ways through the 1950s, as advocates of comic books and comic strips emerged as opponents in a public war over the morality of comics. Because both were often conflated in the public's and critics' minds, Kelly and his fellow members of the National Cartoonists Society mounted a sustained critique of the rowdy and sometimes lurid content of its sister medium. These efforts at distancing and distinguishing the two professions in the public's eye culminated in testimonies delivered by Kelly and his peers at a congressional hearing in 1954 on the relative depravity, on one hand, of comic books, and the wholesome goodness of comics strips on the other. While this crusade seemed like savvy medium-marketing at the time, it unfortunately entrenched comic strips in editors' and readers' eyes as a highly family-friendly medium that should be aggressively mediated in terms of content, language, and tone. In attacking the carnivalesque excesses of comic books, in other words, comic strips further lost their own connection with the more positive aspects of the carnival: dialogical, multicultural subversive comedy; challenging satire and adult-oriented subject matter; and a general lowbrow irreverence. The full implications of this split would become apparent in the 1960s as the youth culture went one way—toward the irreverence of *MAD* magazine and the dialogical vitality of rock and roll—and Kelly and the comic strip world went the other: into quaint stasis and a general decline in cultural importance.

Popular and Folk Traditions in Kelly's Work

The comic strip, like jazz, is an American invention that embodies the dynamism and flexibility of early to mid-twentieth century popular culture. Through much of the first half of the twentieth century the rowdy, multi-voiced carnival that was the funny pages exploded with vernacular inventiveness, outrageous slapstick, playful visual gags, and quirky aesthetics; to create this vibrant mélange, artists borrowed bits and pieces of artistic and narrative convention from other mediums, various cultural traditions, and each other. Some of that fluid invention gradually tamped down as the medium gentrified and became regulated as national syndication (beginning in the late 1910s) transformed it into a big business, but some vestiges of its riotous innovation lingered through the 1950s.

Perhaps no strip reflected that jazz-like dynamism and sampling better than Walt Kelly's *Pogo*. Here are some of the ingredients that Kelly gathered, magpie-like, in his brilliant collage of comedy, art, and satire: the verbal and visual slapstick of the vaudeville stage; the hammy music, settings, and themes of blackface minstrelsy; the character dynamics and satiric subtexts of African American trickster tales; the philosophical undergirding of pastoral drama and poetry; the resonant symbols and tensions of popularized Freudian theory; the allegorical layeredness of literary satire; the narrative complexity and continuity of rollicking, picaresque novels; and the playful, visual dynamism of Disney aesthetics. And then, of course, there were the bits and pieces Kelly picked up from great authors such as Mark Twain, Charles Dickens, and Lewis Carroll, or from master cartoonists such as E. C. Segar (*Popeye*), George Herriman (*Krazy Kat*), and Al Capp (*Li'l Abner*). The point here is not that Kelly was unoriginal—that he borrowed everything he used—but rather that his work represented what makes certain works of American popular culture especially vibrant, flexible, and resonant: a democratic, unapologetic melding of influences and currents into a work of syncretic originality.

While it is easy to defend or celebrate the general practice of borrowing, melding, and reconfiguring aesthetic and narrative ingredients, Kelly's particular amalgamation is not without controversy. In particular, his debts to trickster tale conventions, African American dialect, and blackface minstrelsy are inherently problematic. The early twentieth century is replete with animated cartoons, comic strips, vaudeville acts, popular songs, etc., that either mock black identity in denigrating ways or borrow African American folk forms in opportunistic fashion. But within that racially exploitative history there are also works of popular culture that either reflect a more conflicted amalgam of abuse and tribute or that even transcend the racist roots of the imagery and conventions to become something almost wholly sympathetic or progressive.

Kelly's work in its most mature form ultimately represented a progressive channeling and creative reworking of the subversive energies of African American mores and images, but there were certainly missteps and awkward stages along the way that resembled more closely the more conflicted treatments that coursed through the popular culture of the 1920s through the 1940s. There were the racially charged jive-crow characters in *Dumbo*, for example, and early comic book versions of *Pogo* in the 1940s that featured a young black boy named Bumbazine, a "little black Sambo" or pickaninny type who interacted with animals and sometimes spoke in a comic black dialect. In addition, early versions of *Pogo* in the late 1940s, as it was transitioning from comic book to comic strip, seemed to borrow heavily from the Uncle Remus adaptations of traditional African American trickster tales. The fact that these trickster types and story patterns had already been borrowed and ideologically softened in opportunistic fashion by another white writer, Joel Chandler Harris, already made them inherently problematic when Kelly channeled them into his own work.

To Kelly's credit, even these most awkward representations and borrowings were more complex and sympathetic than similarly racially themed texts from the time, and Kelly's liberal politics, which included a consistent championing of black rights, shaped the well-meaning intentions and tone of this work. He may have been naïve and slightly patronizing in some of these meldings, but he was never callous or malicious. And his integrity is perhaps further salvaged by his more ideologically progressive and original channeling of these forms in the mature version of *Pogo*.

Two theoretical concepts I use in this study as criteria for judging the relative levels of opportunism or sympathy in the representations and borrowings of Kelly (as well as other comedic poachers such as Harris and Mark Twain), are Gene Bluestein's notion of poplore and the idea of cultural syncretism. The concept of poplore helps to differentiate between mass-produced popular works that are formulaic and cruel in their appropriations of minority voices, forms, and traditions—and those popular texts relatively true to the folk forms' original uses, intentions, and energy. Among other qualities, poploric texts, like many traditional folk forms, achieve a breadth of popularity through grassroots means and revive "stylistic elements and values from the matrix of traditional culture. They also often articulate a brand of democratic, progressive politics usually associated with working class culture and folk forms (Bluestein 6–10). Syncretism, a closely related concept, is a brand of cultural fusion in which the resulting cultural product is an innovative and original blend of those components—synergistically more than the sum of its borrowed parts. Kelly's work, as I will illustrate, fares well when judged by these criteria. Much like Twain, he channels the dynamic energies and subversive functions of African American dialect and folk forms in syncretic and poploric fashion.

Walt Kelly's Cultural Significance

With that brief introduction to some of the complexities of Kelly's work and career, one is better prepared to understand his status as one of the great comic artists, auteurs, popular satirists, and poplorists of the twentieth century. In addition, we can describe Kelly's significant influence on later generations of cartoonists, on the field and business of newspaper comic strips, and on the landscape of liberal politics today. To begin, one could argue that Kelly is one of the top artists to ever work in comic strips. Richard Marschall, a comics historian, refers to him as a "monumental talent"—one of the greatest cartoonists of the last century; and another scholar, R. C. Harvey, asserts that he achieved a "zenith of high art" on the comics page (Marschall 255, Harvey 185). His only peers at this level of aesthetic achievement might include George Herriman (*Krazy Kat*), Winsor McCay (*Little Nemo in Slumberland*), and Bill Watterson (*Calvin and Hobbes*).

Kelly's journeyman experience in other artistic fields before landing on the funnies page prepared him to realize the full aesthetic potential of comic strips. His training as a storyboard artist and animator at Disney, for example, helped infuse his strip with cinematic complexity, dynamism in terms of body and facial construction and movement, funny visual gags, and lively brushwork. Further experience in newspaper design, comic-booking, and political cartooning nurtured additional qualities: an eye-pleasing range of values from brilliant whites to silvery grays and solid blacks; effective caricatures of recognizable political figures; distinctive and elaborate typefaces for different characters' dialects; fully detailed but unobtrusive settings; and logically and elegantly composed frames. While it is possible to isolate and admire each of these aesthetic qualities in the strip, *Pogo*'s real artistic greatness is that the average reader is not consciously aware of any of these qualities. In other words, Kelly does such a good job of taking all these elements and subsuming them to the core objectives of the strip—making the reader laugh or ponder a satiric point—that the end result is a highly entertaining, thought-provoking, completely absorbing comic world.

In addition to being a great artist, Kelly was a superior verbal comedian, storyteller, self-promoter, and businessman. In fact, he performed the many roles associated with the traditional auteur (a creator of a popular text who controls the production of his or her work to such a degree, and in the face of intense institutional and economic pressures, that he or she could be considered the "author" of their work). Wearing many hats is the norm among comic strip creators, thus justifying the application of this most common definition of the term. But the secondary meaning of auteurship—that of being able to create a distinctive, independent voice, and a potentially counter-discursive body of work within the intense economic and institutional pressures of industries such as Hollywood or the comics page—can only be applied to a few iconoclastic figures in the medium's history. These funny page auteurs might include George Herriman, Al Capp (*Li'l Abner*), Garry Trudeau (*Doonesbury*), Berke Breathed (*Bloom County*), Bill Watterson (*Calvin and Hobbes*), Lynn Johnston (*For Better or Worse*), and Aaron McGruder (*The Boondocks*).

Common to all of these figures was a willingness to work within the editorial and economic restraints of the medium, while also fighting against oppressive business practices or editorial meddling that might compromise their aesthetic or satiric vision. Some of these cartoonists such as Trudeau or Watterson leaned fairly far toward resistance and rebellion, but Kelly favored a more diplomatic mix of compromise and principled protest. As a longtime newspaperman, he understood the virtues of self-promotion, tasteful merchandising, and the courting of sensitive editors. However, he fiercely protected his right to include difficult satire in his work. Kelly thus sought out and achieved auteur-like control over his strip and career through two means: he built a broad readership (thus protecting his work from cancellation or too much editorial meddling); and he literally acquired ownership of the copyright to his work (an anomaly within the field at that time).

The clout and independence Kelly achieved within his field were critical to his accomplishments as a satirist. Indeed, he would not have been able to follow his own maxim—that "good cartoonists are subversive—they are against things"—had he been unsuccessful protecting his own voice and art from censorship, cancellation, or blacklisting (O'Sullivan 93). In other words, surviving and thriving in a highly mediated entertainment industry was prelude and precondition to survival in an oppressive political landscape as well.

Beginning in the early 1950s, Kelly consistently used his highly popular strip as a vehicle for pointed, topical satire. His most consistent target for several years became the communist witch-hunts conducted by Senator Joseph McCarthy and like-minded politicians and cultural guardians. While most journalists were content to observe and report on these events in a detached manner, and many entertainers or comedians were hesitant to raise a dissenting voice out of fear of being blacklisted by conservative critics, Kelly bravely entered the fray. His caricatures may have been coded into an allegorical comic realm, but to any informed reader his points were clear; and he backed up his layered satire with essays and television interviews where his criticisms were even more explicit. It turned out that his satiric attacks on McCarthyism—a political system especially effective at silencing any *overtly* critical voices by labeling all opposition as traitorous—was the ideal rhetoric for surviving and thriving in this oppressive media and political landscape. In effect, Kelly could avoid outright censorship while speaking for a diverse readership of college students, liberal intellectuals, and far-flung everyday readers who were opposed to the reactionary spirit of the times.

Kelly has rightly been credited, then, with providing in his strip and through his public persona a rallying point around which like-minded people could gather. But he attracted more than just college students and intellectuals; fan mail and newspaper polls revealed that Kelly's work drew in people from all walks of life unhappy with the paranoid tone of the cultural discourse at that time. While a critic of communism himself (he featured a pair of dogmatic cowbirds in his strip who represented the myopic, doctrinaire, and oppressive attitudes of a typical devotee of the ideology), Kelly defended the right to adhere to a wide range of political values or philosophies. He also forwarded an alternative worldview that emphasized caution, tolerance, moderation, self-criticism, and humility. This liberal ideology both reflected and shaped the political orientation of a generation of left-leaning thinkers seeking a middle path between an old-school leftism that was dogmatic and sometimes violent in its methods, and a far right conservatism equally rigid and arrogant in its assumptions.

In sum, Kelly's popularity as a satirist and prominent cultural critic gave him an unusual level of prominence and cultural influence within 1950s society. Through his comic strip, college rallies, television interviews, and newspaper essays, he reached an enormous and diverse audience with his politically charged entertainment. Beyond achieving the status of an independent-minded auteur, Kelly could also be described as a sateur and poplorist—designations that help set him apart from typical cartoonists and entertainers. By sateur, I mean he was a popular satirist who achieved a certain degree of economic and institutional freedom within his highly mediated and commercialized field, and then leveraged that power to engage in principled social criticism (this can stand in contrast to the basic auteur who uses that position simply to create a distinctive aesthetic or narrative vision).

As a poplorist, Kelly achieved a breadth of popularity through grassroots means, and engaged in a collaborative "call and response" with engaged readers that allowed him to address their ideological interests and psychological needs in resonant ways (Bluestein 6, 8–9). The designation of poplorist is primarily applied to popular folk singers in the 1960s such as Joan Baez or Bob Dylan, but it works nicely for Kelly as well, setting him apart from most mainstream cartoonists and comedians. Indeed, Kelly's productive relationship with college students and other engaged readers gave him the status and aura of a media-age folk storyteller who was both entertaining and ideologically engaged. And his channeling of both the form, and some of the political functions of early trickster tales and playful dialect comedy, allowed him to channel the subversive energies of unruly folk forms. In sum, giving Kelly the distinction of poplorist is helpful in describing his cultural significance because it illustrates how he and his work were unique at a time in American cultural history when entertainment was highly mediated—in terms of both content and form—by powerful institutions, and indirectly censored by reactionary cultural guardians.

Kelly's resonance and unique position in the cultural landscape shifted in the 1960s. With the collapse of McCarthyism and the dissolution of many oppressive entertainment entities (such as the old Hollywood studio system), left-leaning audiences were not as starved for popular texts that spoke to them in honest and entertaining ways—they could be found in a variety of other places in the media landscape. Audiences came to expect, moreover, satire and comedy that was more direct and openly subversive to a conservative status quo: the irreverent nose-thumbing of MAD magazine, for example, fit the bill. The layeredness and genteel ironies of *Pogo*—its celebration of contemplative, "horizontal heroes," as one critic put it—made Kelly's satire seem old-fashioned (Berry 196). Moreover, his clubby, old-boy-network style of dealing with cultural guardians, editors, and colleagues was a mismatch with the times; it seemed stuffy and bourgeois in comparison to a new wave of folk heroes like Bob Dylan, the Smothers Brothers, John Lennon, or Jules Feiffer.

Despite this loss of cultural significance, *Pogo* can be seen as a pioneering text of the countercultural movement, and Kelly as a satirist who inspired or opened doors for other left-leaning dissenters such as Mort Sahl, the Smothers Brothers or the cartoonists of the underground comix movement. And within the field of comic strips, Kelly still influences subsequent generations of creators determined to realize the medium's full potential. Indeed, he set a standard of greatness in several aspects of the field's history: auteur-like courage and independence; aesthetic complexity and polish; narrative richness and verbal inventiveness; resonant character construction; and satiric integrity. Other iconoclastic cartoonists who benefited from his pioneering efforts and example include Garry Trudeau, Berke Breathed, Nicole Hollander (*Sylvia*), Bill Watterson, Lynn Johnston, Aaron McGruder, and many other figures in the alternative press such as Jules Feiffer, Tom Tomorrow (*This Modern World*), and Matt Groening (*Life in Hell*).

Kelly's firsthand familiarity with other popular comic mediums (animation, comic books, vaudeville, blackface, political cartooning, etc.) and love for works of "high" literary comedy (Twain, Carroll, and Dickens) also expanded notions of what a comic strip could be. Rather than simply a series of frames featuring a throwaway gag, a strip could feature a novelistically complex, allegorical world that includes parody, folklore, visual and verbal slapstick, cosmic philosophizing, and topical satire. A cross-fertilization of those mediums and influences occurred in Kelly's work in other words—expanding the visual, comedic, and satiric vocabulary of the funnies page.

Finally, Kelly effectively communicated a vision of the cultural importance and potential of the comics page that can stand as an ongoing challenge or inspiration to creators and mediators in the field. He stated:

> A good many editors still believe that the comics page is the playpen of the newspaper, or a sort of inert baby sitter for the brain, whereas it could be just the reverse. It could be the most stimulating section of the paper. (Kelly, *Ten Ever-Lovin' Blue-Eyed Years with Pogo*, 135)

The idea that the comics page can be both intellectually stimulating *and* entertaining is especially significant at this cultural moment as the comics industry struggles with shifting media paradigms and a declining readership. Some syndicates and newspapers have responded to these shifts with a greater variety of voices and modes of representation on the comics page, but the funnies are still generally far removed from Kelly's vision of their being the most stimulating part of the paper (or the Internet, as syndicates are only tentatively taking advantage of new modes of distribution and formatting). This lack of dynamism within the field is due, of course, to the chronic constraints placed on the medium: claustrophobic dimensions, superficial popularity polls, and draconian rules about appropriate content. Combined, these strictures have largely succeeded in eliminating what might energize and attract new readers: sophisticated verbal irony, complex art and narratives, and topical satire.

Immersing ourselves in Kelly's work and vision thus reveals that the present state of the comics is not natural or inevitable. Indeed, Kelly inspires us as an artist who defied the culture's low expectations of the medium, who navigated his way through oppressive mediations, syncretically fused cultural traditions, and operated as both a comedian and cultural critic. Perhaps this study of Kelly's career—that explores both his great achievements and significant missteps—will provide some direction and inspiration to cartoonists and editors interested in once again making comic strips and the funnies page a viable and resonant medium in the cultural landscape. In addition, perhaps it can inspire artists and satirists working in other fields or cultural frames in which oppressive political, institutional, or social strictures exist. They may benefit from following Kelly's model of creating a popular text grounded in a resonant folk tradition, that retains its sharpness and integrity in the face of intense mediations, and that effectively communicates its potent criticisms through allegorically layered satire.

Chapter Summaries

The first chapter discusses Kelly's biography and the general arc of his career. Beginning with his colorful lower-middle-class upbringing in the 1920s in Bridgeport, Connecticut, it charts the building of his political worldview and comedic sensibility through family, school, and work experiences; it also highlights his early entry into the world of journalism. His first real job beyond his hometown—with the Disney Corporation—is given special attention as it was there he developed some of his core aesthetic and narrative sensibilities. The next stage of his career, in comic-booking, is fascinating as well, because it was there Kelly introduced an iteration of *Pogo*—a fairly traditional trickster tale setting in which a young black boy, *Bumbazine*, also featured prominently.

Kelly's job with the *New York Star* in 1948 is also explored in some detail, as it helped him to solidify his political convictions and conception of himself as a cultural critic and political cartoonist. He also launched the comic strip version of *Pogo* while working for the *Star*. After the dissolution of that newspaper, Kelly entered into the world of comic strip syndication and experienced a rapid rise to popularity and cultural significance. A number of strips and storylines from the height of his career—from 1952 to 1965—are featured, highlighting especially controversial episodes. Discussions of other aspects of Kelly's career in the 1950s—college tours, work for the National Cartoonists Society, and interaction with family and friends—are also included in order to give a complete portrait of his life. Finally, the chapter charts *Pogo's* gradual decline in popularity and cultural importance in the changing social and political climate of the late 1960s.

In the second chapter I explore the most apparent keys to Kelly's success as a cartoonist: the resonant setting, lively comedy, and engaging satire of *Pogo*. To begin, the narrative functions and cultural meanings of Kelly's setting—the swamplands of Southern Georgia—are explored by looking to the philosophy that undergirds the settings of both trickster tales and pastoral comedies—two major paradigms that intersected in Kelly's work. In addition, the appealing symbolism of a frontier backwater is explored in relation to anxieties that coursed through a mid-century, suburbanized and corporatized, mainstream reading audience.

Secondly, I discuss in this chapter how *Pogo* works as comedy and satire, first by connecting the comedic elements of the strip to established comedy traditions in other entertainment fields, which include narrative conventions, dialogue, verbal jokes, slapstick gags, and character construction. Then, while conventional treatments of Kelly's work fixate on the strip's topicality as the "serious" matter that lifts his work to greatness (distancing it from its home medium) and compensates for the seemingly gratuitous wordplay and cute aesthetics that otherwise dominate the strip—I make the point, in contrast, that the "silly" matter in the strip is an integral part of the satire. Specifically, the relentless wordplay and dynamic aesthetics have carnivalesque and deconstructive qualities that both reinforce Kelly's topical attacks as well as articulate a larger cosmic critique of dogmatism, hierarchies, and scapegoating. The comedy and satire of Kelly's work, in other words, are inextricably intertwined—and the lowbrow status of his medium, moreover, is ultimately a key factor in Kelly's power and significance as a cultural critic.

In the third chapter I cover Kelly's negotiations with the commercial and institutional mechanisms that undergirded and sometimes shaped his art and satire. This discussion includes an analysis of how different mediums—with their accompanying industry pressures and genre conventions—allowed Kelly to engage in different kinds of art and satire—at times limiting, and at others expanding, his array of tools and methods. In particular, I look at how the commercial and institutional limitations of several related fields—animation, political cartooning, and comic books—compare to those of comic strips. The fact that Kelly worked in each of these fields, eventually became a strong critic of one (comic books), and emerged as the industry representative of the final one (comic strips), gives this analysis a greater significance and complexity.

In this chapter I also explore Kelly's work as a businessman—an aspect of his career that may seem, at first glance, to be less interesting or critical than the art or satire of *Pogo*. I make a case, however, that the auteur-like independence Kelly achieved and practiced through negotiations with his syndicates, struggles with newspaper editors, and collaborations with fans, was simply another facet of his success as a great satirist. That clout was a precondition, in fact, to his ability to construct such a distinctive aesthetic and consistently sharp political vision in *Pogo*.

And so attention is paid to several facets of Kelly's work as a businessman: his forward-looking approach to contracts and advocation of a variety of other artists' rights; his methods of self-promotion, both resisting and sometimes pragmatically compromising with newspaper and syndicate editors; and his work behind the scenes of the industry as member and president of the National Cartoonists Society. This last facet of Kelly's business life—his engagement with the NCS—is especially interesting because this organization was so backward in its professional and political vision during Kelly's tenure. Indeed, it was largely an old boys' "chowder club" in the 1950s with generally sexist and self-serving practices. Surprisingly, Kelly's work in the organization was not always as a progressive as one would expect (given his forward-thinking vision for the funnies page); at times Kelly was simply content to reinforce the conservative status quo. An attempt is made to explain this seeming disconnect or contradiction in light of Kelly's working class background, early work experiences, and devotion to an overarching ethic of "professionalism." Nevertheless, Kelly's work and vision as a business-minded cartoonist can be seen as progressive, creating standards and ideals that have inspired many of today's cartooning sateurs.

In the fourth chapter, I explore one of the more complex and controversial aspects of Kelly's career: representations of black identity in his work, and the influence of African American folk forms and dialect in his comedy and satire. While in the mature version of *Pogo*—with its generalized animal allegory and playfully ambiguous dialects—Kelly seemed to have erased all specific markers of race and ethnicity from its visual contents, the satiric discourses of the strip were still grounded in comedic types and conventions that grew out of early twentieth-century ethnic comedy, and one could still trace the general spirit, character dynamics, and setting to their earlier functions and resonance in the African American folk forms and vernacular speech (as filtered through popular culture) that Kelly so admired. For example, the influence of vaudevillian blackface, in all of its conflicted comedic complexity, can be identified in Kelly's mature work; and the setting and character dynamics of *Pogo* were born out of African American trickster tale conventions (as filtered through Joel Chandler Harris and Mark Twain).

In addition, the inventive dialect of the mature strip has its roots in the deconstructive powers of black dialect and oral comedic discourse. This chapter explores these issues of representation and cultural fusion by tracing Kelly's lifelong fascination with black cultural forms; by charting his cartoon representations of blackness from Disney days, through his comic book years, and up into the mature comic strip; by tracing the evolving use of trickster tale conventions in his comedy and satire; and by appraising his treatment of these issues in contrast to similar borrowers of black comedic forms such as Joel Chandler Harris and Mark Twain. The concept of poplore and syncretism—the melding of existing forms and traditions to create a cultural product both unique and progressive—is used as a criteria for judging Kelly's sensitivity and success in channeling these images and forms.

The fifth chapter explores Kelly's accomplishments as one of the best artists to ever work in the field of comic strips. First, the origins of Kelly's aesthetic sensibility are explored, tracing the look and structure of *Pogo* back to his training as an animator at Disney, to his work as a comic book artist, and to his tenure as a political cartoonist at the *New York Star*. The influence of his animation training is given special attention because so many of the cinematic and character-building effects of animation are on display in *Pogo*, setting it apart from more statically constructed comic strips. Then the different facets of *Pogo*'s aesthetics are discussed, which include composition, line/brushwork, character construction and movement, caricatures, typefaces/lettering, and panel construction. Finally, I explore how Kelly's complex and cutely Disneyesque style eventually began to feel disconnected from the cultural spirit of the 1960s, ultimately becoming overshadowed by emerging styles in animation and comic strips more minimalistic and geometrically stylized in look and spirit.

In the sixth and final chapter I consider Kelly's significance as a poplorist who borrowed and channeled many of the conventions and political energies of traditional folk forms. Building upon the earlier explorations of the folk origins of Kelly's work—in African American trickster tales and black dialect—I turn the focus to other aspects of Kelly's poplore such as the dialogical nature of his comedy and satire, and the collaborative call and response relationships he developed with his readers. Archival data drawn from fan letters, college newspapers, and correspondence helps to support these discussions. I explore, as well, the carnivalesque aspects of Kelly's college rallies—using that paradigm to revisit and interpret more closely the Harvard rally described in the opening pages of this introduction. The chapter concludes with comparisons between Kelly and mid-century folk revivalists and poplorists working in other fields such as Pete Seeger, Bob Dylan, Lenny Bruce, Mort Sahl, and Al Capp. The comparison between Capp and Kelly proves to be especially effective at highlighting both Kelly's occasional failures to fully exercise the clout and independence of a principled auteur, as well as his enormous success at becoming one of the most important satirists and social critics of the mid-twentieth century.

CHAPTER 1

Walt Kelly's Biography and a General History of *Pogo*

Walt Kelly lived much of his adult life in the public spotlight, reveling in his celebrity as a premier cartoonist and satirist of the 1950s and 1960s. Indeed, one can easily follow the trail of his whirlwind professional career as he appeared on talk shows, rubbed shoulders with politicians and movie stars, traveled the world as a pundit, toured college campuses, and performed chalk-talks or roasts that resembled vaudevillian stand-up routines. It is more difficult, however, to document his childhood and young adult years for two reasons. First, Kelly was self-effacing about his significance as a cultural figure worthy of a biography or academic study. Like many of his pre-1960s cartooning peers, he saw himself as a working class newspaperman who had succeeded in a generally underappreciated field through sheer hard work and luck. When an academic approached him in 1959 with a proposal to write a book similar to this one, Kelly articulated this modest view of himself as he gently but firmly declined to participate at any level:

> [As] much as I hate to discourage you, the project you propose staggers my imagination. In all truth, you must realize that what you have in mind is a dissection of Kelly from age two months on. A person such as I is elusive, cranky, impatient with talk about himself and thoroughly unreliable. Your idea suggests much too irksome involvement for me and too little reward for you. My education and training has been completely informal and I am afraid has not prepared me for the other end of this particular saw. Sorry. (Kelly "Letter from Feb. 2, 1959")

The second challenge in documenting Kelly's early life is also indicated in this letter: he was "elusive" and "unreliable" when describing his upbringing. Irritated, perhaps, with the serious, self-aggrandizing tone of most memoirs, Kelly chose to write autobiographical sketches featuring silly exaggeration and self-mocking comedy. For example, referring to his high school accomplishments, Kelly claimed that he was "the only man in the Senior Class who could take apart a ukulele blindfolded. No useful purpose has ever been discovered for blindfolding a ukulele (they are not skittish like horses), but the information is there—so we set it down" ("The Land of the Elephant Squash," 49). In other passages Kelly may have included a few small bits of fact among the silliness—as with this passage on the childhood traumas he endured: "He had survived fire (fell into the coal scuttle with a jack-o-lantern in 1919), flood (homemade boat struck swimming duck and splintered, 1923), starvation (lost the lunch on a fishing expedition with father, 1924), savage beasts (rabid rabbit shot to death on other side of town, 1924), disease and pestilence (Chicken Pox and Mumps, 1918), and education (6 years of grammar school)" (Kelly, "Autobiography," 9).

Despite this irrepressible silliness, one can still cull certain vivid information about his upbringing from facetious memoirs and other contemporary sources. It is clear, for example, he was of Scotch-Irish-English-French-Austrian descent and that he was born in Philadelphia in 1913, and named Walter Crawford Kelly, Jr. He had one sister, and his parents—Walter Crawford and Genevieve MacAnulla Kelly—raised him in a relatively happy, if somewhat impoverished household. What his parents lacked in money, they made up in creativity and encouragement. For example, his father—a scene painter for a time with theatrical production companies in Bridgeport, Connecticut—taught his son how to draw and encouraged him in his "rainy day" daydreaming of someday becoming a rich cartoonist ("Walt Kelly Exhibition Guide," 1). He also instilled in Kelly a love of African American trickster tales and playful dialects (which would become elements of his mature work as a professional cartoonist) by performing Uncle Remus stories for his children in what was euphemistically described as "fun talk"—the exaggerated black vernacular so popular in regionalist humor and vaudeville in the early decades of the twentieth century (Beiman, "Walt and Selby Kelly," 29).

Kelly may have also gravitated toward the solitary craft of cartooning in his early years as a result of severe childhood illnesses that kept him at home, convalescing, for long periods of time. As a small boy, he suffered from a debilitating paralysis to his left side and later struggled with acute articular rheumatism and rheumatic fever—illnesses that permanently damaged his heart and kept him out of military service as a young adult (Horn 41; Marschall, *America's Great* 257). Serious illnesses, in fact, would haunt him throughout his life, with chronic heart problems slowing down his whirlwind schedule at the height of his career, and complications from diabetes overshadowing his final days. The fact that Kelly drew so little attention to these real ailments over the years—choosing instead to joke about fake traumas or everyday mumps and measles—highlights his unsentimental, self-effacing character.

Bridgeport, Connecticut, Kelly's childhood home, played a profound role in shaping his politics, worldview, and satiric methods. In the 1920s Bridgeport was a busy industrial town with an active seaport, weapons industry, and other manufacturing plants; as a result, it attracted many working class, immigrant families, eager for the steady jobs. Kelly recalled:

The First World War brought to Bridgeport many strangers to work in the factories. The people later settled there, along with the Kellys, and we found ourselves
living cheek by jowl with the Dzumaties, the Slaernos, the McKedricks, the Kilroys,
the Luchtenbergs, the DeFeos, the Zadoffs, the Colemans, the Duffys, the Vander
Kruiks, the Klespers, the Zizmans, the Ostrofskys, the Kekacs, the Grietches, the
Seresins, the Varjabedians, the Marchands, the Budas, and many more. We children learned more unusual phrases in foreign tongues by the time we were ten
than most world travelers learn in a lifetime. (Marschall, "Walt Kelly Remembers,"
8A)

In this case Kelly is not exaggerating the multicultural nature of the city. In the
early twentieth century the town had "seven different newspapers published
in Italian, three in Hungarian, and one each in German, Yiddish, and Slovak;"
one observer noted that "Bridgeport has so many ethnic groups that the joke in
Boston was, 'They don't speak English there'" (Grimaldi 43, 31). While these immigrant groups were patriotic and grateful for their opportunities (committing
themselves to home-front war efforts in the 1910s), they were adamant about
their rights in the face of poor working and living conditions. As a result, Bridgeport became known as site for union organizing and labor unrest; in the summer
of 1915, for example, over one hundred strikes swept through the city (Grimaldi
40).

Kelly later celebrated the politicized, multicultural mix of his hometown as a
seedbed for a brand of "natural" liberalism—a community of colorful dialects,
casual tolerance, and working class solidarity. As a successful adult, Kelly explained that

> Bridgeport was a good place to be brought up. We neither preached nor practiced
> tolerance; we were just too ignorant to know there was anything to tolerate. Miss
> Blackham [his grade school teacher] never tried to harness compassion, as I see
> political parties doing. She just used it, constantly, casually, and some of it rubbed
> off . . . Bridgeport . . . was more flower pot than melting pot, more by-way than
> highway, maybe even more end than beginning. (Kelly, *Ten Ever-Lovin* 6)

As a teenager, Kelly relished the opportunities Bridgeport provided to develop
various talents and shine on a public stage. Friends remember him as a tall lanky
kid (a "stringbean") who was polite, eager to please, and smart (graduating from
high school before his seventeenth birthday). His family were active Methodists
and he was highly involved in the local church's youth program; friends from the
group remember he had a "flair for the dramatic" and often spearheaded the production of variety shows (Anderson 69; Crouch, "Ray Dirgo," 70). At Bridgeport's
Warren Harding High School, Kelly also participated in glee club, theater, and

blackface performances (a practice surprisingly common in the 1920s) (Thompson, "Returning to Our Gang," 4). This appetite for the stage would persist throughout Kelly's adult life; indeed, as an animator and professional cartoonist he relished any opportunities to perform in roasts, chalk-talks, impromptu musical jams, or amateur vaudeville-style productions. The characters in *Pogo* too would reflect Kelly's love of theater, as they enthusiastically put on their own dramatic productions, musicals, and spontaneous concerts.

Kelly's avid social involvement in high school went beyond the theater department; he also worked on the yearbook staff and was a reporter and cartoonist for the school newspaper—serving for a time as a teenage correspondent on sports and school news for the city's big paper, the *Bridgeport Post* (Crouch, "Early Kelly," 157; Crouch, "Walt Kelly in High School," 65). During these years Kelly avidly pursued his childhood dream of becoming a famous cartoonist like his idol, Bud Fisher (*Mutt and Jeff*). He spent numerous hours perfecting his cartoon craft—working hard, for example, at mastering the block lettering featured in comic strips in those decades (Crouch, "Ray Dirgo," 70). The *Post* rewarded his talent and determination, eventually hiring him as a crime reporter after he graduated in 1930 from high school; given the small scale of the paper, he was also able to become a one-man art department, doing spot illustrations and editorial cartoons. One of his more interesting pieces published in the *Post* during this time was a fairly elaborate comic history of P. T. Barnum, another famous figure to emerge from Bridgeport (Crouch, "Early Kelly," 157).

Kelly was so enamored with newspapering during these teen and young adult years that he recalls having "printer's ink" in his blood—a "condition that so affected his veins that friends called him Zebra Kelly" (Kelly, "Promotional Material," 1). This general devotion to journalism would become an ongoing theme in Kelly's life; as an adult he constructed and nurtured a persona as a "newspaperman of the old school" who relished the "stereotypical cigar-chomping, saloon-haunting, deadline-crunching" life of the reporter (Chute 1; Marschall, *America's Great* 257). Even after the monumental success of his strip in the mid-1950s, he still half-jokingly asserted about himself (in the third person), "Were he truly deep he'd be an editorial man, winning Pulitzer Prizes, fame, and the favors of politically-awakened females" (Kelly, "Promotional" 24). In sum, those journalistic aspirations—and that newspaperman's identity—shaped his politics, comedy, and methods in significant ways, steering him toward a brand of topical satire that combined the crafts of both pundit and cartoonist.

Lack of familial resources prevented Kelly from going to college, so he tried a number of odd jobs in the years following high school (Kelly, "Letter to Donald Clarke," 1). In 1930, before landing the job at the *Post*, he worked briefly at an art store ("most of which time was spent hunting rats in the cellar"), and then as a sign painter and floor sweeper at a local factory that made ladies' underwear (Kelly, "Autobiography," 9; Kelly "The Land of the Elephant Squash," 141). Given

Kelly's track record for exaggerating his biography with funny details or asides, the information about the items produced by this factory could be suspect, but it does make for a funny image, with one imagining Kelly working on large paintings that might have featured a woman's girdle or some other awkward undergarment. After the newspaper job, he worked as an investigator for the Bridgeport Welfare Department—another job title that begs for greater detail. Finally, in 1934, he moved to New York City in an attempt to break into the field of professional illustration.

This ill-fated excursion to New York was in 1934, at the height of the Great Depression, and Kelly must have been daunted by the challenge of starting a career with only a high school education and a smattering of on-the-job training in newspaper illustration. He does not go into great detail about why or how he failed at establishing himself in New York, but it is clear that a lack of serious training and general naïveté conspired against him. For example, he reported in an unpublished autobiographical sketch that he succeeded in selling only one illustration to a magazine titled *"Old St. Nicholas"*—a periodical that unfortunately went under after Kelly's work was published (he feared that there was a connection). About the quality of this lone published piece, Kelly simply stated, "It was to laugh" (Kelly, "Unpublished Autobiographical Sketch," 3). The only other paying work he was able to secure was in window painting—a notoriously rough and tumble field of working class art. He described one disastrous department store job in which he was duped by an opportunistic and unethical employer: the man falsely claimed that Kelly painted a Santa on the wrong window in order to get him to paint it a second time on another window with no extra pay. Kelly had no choice but to comply, but he had the satisfaction of leaving the head off of one of the Santas, thus forcing the store owner to hire a less capable artist to complete the head in a "sickly" fashion (Ibid. 4). Kelly reported that this window-painting fiasco had a big impact on his worldview, cementing his disillusionment with the big city and burying his dreams of becoming a wealthy illustrator. The fact that Kelly's later satire would celebrate pastoral life, far from the corruptions of big city politics and business, suggests how deeply he may have been traumatized by some of these early encounters with the competition and corruption of a cosmopolitan world.

Kelly at Disney

Kelly's first big professional break came in 1935 when he took a train to California and secured a job working for the Disney Corporation. The circumstances that brought him to Disney were unusual: his initial motivation for heading west was to pursue a girl with whom he had fallen in love in high school choir; her name was Helen DeLacy and she had moved to California to take a job with the National Girl Scout organization. According to Bill Crouch Jr. (one of the most avid collectors and organizers of Kelly's papers and work), Helen wanted to shake off Kelly's attentions because she felt that his age—several years her junior—made him an unsuitable match (Andrae and Blum 131). Kelly's persistence in following her across the country apparently paid off, nevertheless, since the two were married in September 1937. Because Kelly would later divorce Helen and remarry twice, his autobiographical writings tend to gloss over his early years with Helen. One can discern, nevertheless, that they had an awkward home arrangement in California, with Kelly working in Hollywood and Helen working in Oakland. They did not have their first child until 1942, a year after returning from California to Bridgeport.

Once in California, Kelly was eager to find a "real job" with which to begin a marriage and family, so he sought and found work with the Disney studios—a thriving company that was considered the "WPA of the cartooning world" during the Depression (Andrae and Blum 131). According to Kelly, this meant that "anybody who owned his own pencil and could get to the studio, clothed and in his right mind would be given a 'tryout'" (Kelly, "Unpublished Autobiographical Sketch," 5). Kelly's talents and experience far surpassed that threshold, of course, but like many of his fellow aspiring animators, he lacked a complete liberal arts education. Walt Disney, who insisted that his animators achieve unusual levels of quality and realism in their work, remedied this situation by setting up in-house programs that would expose his employees to classical literature, art history, and various cultural traditions. These courses may have been more superficial than those found at traditional liberal arts colleges, but Kelly appreciated the opportunity, asserting that Disney "truly offered a free academy to young American artists for the first time . . . [I think] he deserves a plaque for that despite parts of *Fantasia*" (Ibid. 7). Later in his career Kelly communicated that gratitude directly to Disney, stating that ". . . I, for one, have long appreciated the sort of training and atmosphere that you set up back there in the thirties. There were drawbacks as there are to everything, but it was an astounding experiment and experience as I look back on it. Certainly it was the only education I ever received . . ." (Barrier). The fact that Kelly's later work would become so densely literate and full of parodies and allusions to great authors such as Mark Twain, Lewis Carroll, and Charles Dickens suggests how well-read he had become as an adult—through both his own efforts and this liberal arts training at Disney.

Kelly originally sold himself as a gag and story man at Disney, and was thus assigned to the storyboard department. He worked here for several years on a series of short pieces that were never produced. It is not clear why his work was passed over, but in 1937 he was transferred over to the animation division. Here Kelly excelled at creating clever visual gags, but struggled with the "in-betweening" assigned to junior animators. "In-betweening" required that he refer to model sheets (the template of how a character should look and move in various situations) in order to imitate the style of the senior animators, and generally make the figures move fluidly. Almost invariably his work would be sent back by the directors and senior animators with a note attached, saying, "Have Kelly clean these up and make sure they follow the model sheet" (Andrae and Blum 135). Kelly's professional struggles at Disney may have been due, in part, to a lack of ability, but it probably had as much to do with his independent disposition. Kelly disliked the conformity of this workplace and the monotony of the tasks assigned to him. Eager to put his own personal stamp on his drawings, he would often change the look of characters to fit his personal style and comic sensibility.

In a company that emphasized conformity and toeing the line, Kelly was also somewhat of a maverick in the clothing he wore and they way he acted. While others dressed down for the California weather, Kelly wore three-piece suits and bow ties. The formality of his outward appearance belied a trickster's heart, however. He quickly gained a reputation as one of the biggest practical jokers in the company. For example, he and several other artists such as Fred Moore and Ward Kimball entertained themselves by messing with the lunches and desks of more stuffy colleagues and by passing around satiric sketches of daily events and the general workings of the company. Kelly was especially admired for his ability to draw these gags quickly and accurately, creating devastating caricatures of his peers (Kimball 9). This group would also play impromptu games of touch football in the hallway, meet in the men's restroom for tin whistle jam sessions, and aggravate colleagues with amateur renditions of old-time blackface songs. The joviality would persist beyond the workday as they headed off to local bars to drink, joke, and grouse about their working conditions (Andrae and Blum 132–138).

Although Kelly never fully adjusted to the corporate climate at Disney and failed to master some of the technical tasks of animation, his friendship with senior artists such as Kimball and Moore earned him a place in their ranks. Officially, he was Fred Moore's assistant, but his humor and general talent at creating fluid, dynamic drawings allowed him to make a significant contribution in *The Reluctant Dragon*, *Fantasia*, *Pinocchio*, *Dumbo*, and several Mickey Mouse shorts. In light of the subsequent arc of his career, Kelly's most significant piece of work in this body is perhaps his work in *Dumbo*. In this film, Kelly collaborated with another artist on executing the infamous musical scene in which the crows speak and sing in an exaggerated African American hipster dialect. Given the combination of Disney's poor track record with ethnic stereotypes at midcentury (think of Uncle Remus in *Song of the South* and the Native Americans in *Peter Pan*), and the growing discomfort among critics and audiences for ethnic-infused comedy in post World War II culture, it is no wonder that this *Dumbo* bit has been disparaged in some circles as another instance of jokey, insensitive racism in pre–Civil Rights popular culture.

In chapter four I delve deeply into issues of black identity and cultural borrowings in Kelly's work, both complicating and challenging charges of racism in the *Dumbo* scene and other ethnically charged work. At this point, however, it is sufficient to point out that Kelly approached black cultural forms and identities while at Disney, and in subsequent years, with a complex mix of condescension and sincere admiration. During his post-Disney years as a comic book artist, Kelly continued to feature black characters and forms prominently in his art. But then in the mid-1940s, facing pressure to eliminate the most ethnically charged aspects of his work, he moved away from explicit representations of black identity, language, and culture. Nevertheless, traces of trickster tale themes, characters, and dialect—as well as blackface tropes—persisted in allegorical form in the mature version of Kelly's comic strip. One is generally inclined to forgive Kelly's missteps in these borrowings for several reasons: the ultimately syncretic originality of his mature strip; his left-leaning politics, which advocated tolerance for racial and ideological heterogeneity; and a career-long championing of African American rights in his satire and commentary (he deplored, for example, any mistreatment or derogatory comments directed toward blacks, and in the late 1950s and early 1960s, he was one of the few mainstream cartoonists who spoke out in public and in his satire in favor of desegregation, interracial hospitals, and civil rights) (Kercher 61).

Kelly's ambivalent relationship with the Disney studio came to a point of crisis in 1941 when the junior animators went on strike. The causes of the strike ran deep into the company's history, stemming from old grievances such as the illegal firing of union organizers, a lack of screen credits for animators, arbitrary bonuses, and the bilking of overtime pay for junior artists who had worked on *Snow White* (Sito 1). The final triggers, however, were related to financial pressures created within the company as a result of World War II. The closing of foreign movie markets in the face of war in 1941 severely hurt the Disney studio. In an effort to avoid financial disaster, Walt Disney decided to reduce the already low pay many of the animators received and asked his employees to work overtime without extra pay. For senior animators this hardship was manageable since they earned substantially more than their juniors (close to $25,000 a year), but for the men and women who worked in the "sweatshops," animating backgrounds for $100 a week, this belt-tightening was too much to ask (Andrae and Blum 131). Several junior animators called for a strike, and the company employees divided over the issue between those on Walt Disney's side (most of the higher-paid workers) and the strikers' side (all the lower-paid employees).

As a junior animator earning wages similar to the strikers, Kelly was put in an awkward situation; his sympathies were with his disgruntled peers, but most of his friends were in the non-striking, upper-level hierarchy. Kelly was also concerned about the prospect of financial ruin for his fledgling family. His maverick nature, his need to be his own boss, and his love of the newspaper business may have eventually pushed him away from Disney, but the dilemma surrounding the strike helped him to make an early departure. In order to avoid committing to one side or the other, he initially took a leave of absence, citing a family illness as justification; several months later, he simply resigned and headed back East. In a move that would have probably made him unpopular with the strikers, Kelly secretly crossed the picket lines before he left to meet with Walt Disney himself; in this interview he apparently secured work on the East Coast with the Dell Western publishing company—an organization not directly a part of the Disney corporation, but affiliated through a series of Disney comic books (Andrae and Blum 131). That secret meeting with Disney is especially intriguing to imagine considering the radically different political paths each man followed in subsequent years: Disney aligning himself with the anti-Communist paranoia of the early 1950s, testifying against the animators' union leaders and other alleged Hollywood "subversives," and Kelly, on the other side, emerging as one of the few satirists willing to publicly challenge McCarthy and the general witch-hunting hysteria of those same years.

Kelly's Work in Comic Books

Kelly's official explanation for why he left Disney was much more evasive and jokey than the real story, of course. He stated that after a public showing of the Disney short on which he worked—"Baby Weems," a strange, half-live action, cheaply animated work starring Robert Benchley—he wandered away from Disney in shame and "showed up on the Mojave Desert trudging east." He continued to summarize the next eight years of his career in one flippant sentence: "He got a job doing comic books, fooled around with the Foreign Language Unit of the Army during the war, illustrating grunts and groans, and made friends in the newspaper publishing business" (Kelly, "Autobiography," 9).

In keeping with his other autobiographical sketches, Kelly elides over his personal difficulties during these years. Without the steadiness of a Disney paycheck, finances were often tight, and he and Helen had to move often. Biographers such as Kalman Goldstein have speculated that these financial struggles gave Kelly a special sensitivity to the challenges people face, and that he later translated much of this empathy into his generous humor and satire (Goldstein 91). Perhaps Kelly's sometimes excessive enjoyment of the trappings and privileges of success at the height of his career can also be explained, in part, by his years spent as a struggling, freelance comic book artist.

Financial stress certainly forced him to be prolific in the 1940s. He worked on a number of different comic book stories for Dell, including Disney features, *Raggedy Ann and Andy*, *Uncle Wiggily Animal Comics*, *Our Gang*, Roald Dahl's *Gremlins*, and *Santa Claus Funnies*. He also illustrated cereal boxes, children's books, performed on children's records, and did freelance illustration work for the U.S. Army Education Branch, contributing drawings to foreign language guides. Kelly later pointed to that government work as a significant exposure to the complexities and beauty of both foreign tongues and regional American dialects. He stated that during that period of his career he became especially fond of Southern vernaculars—those of Georgia in particular—and thus chose to feature the voices of that region in the mature, comic strip version of *Pogo*. Given his earlier engagement with black vernacular through Joel Chandler Harris and blackface entertainment, this story of first encountering and falling in love with a generic "Georgia" dialect seems slightly disingenuous—a pat story that attempts to vaguely deracialize those earlier influences.

Kelly's most significant work at Dell were the *Our Gang* adaptations and the *Animal Comics* series that featured early versions of the characters from *Pogo*. In sharp contrast to the factory-like production of many mainstream, mid-century comic books, Kelly was essentially a one-man production unit, both writing and illustrating these tales. This working method allows one to read these texts as almost complete expressions of Kelly's comic sensibility and to identify traces of his mature work in their developmental stages. For example, while the *Our Gang* series borrowed its foundational characters and dynamics from the popular film series, Kelly still infused the comic series with qualities that would also be prominent in *Pogo*: wordplay, ensemble comedy, farcical plotting, and chronic miscommunication. The good-hearted kids vs. corrupt adults dynamic of these stories also anticipated common plot devices in *Pogo* in which conniving outsiders were pitted against the naïve and heroic folk of the swamp.

The *Animal Comics* series can be seen as a more obvious precursor to Kelly's strip work since it featured early versions of Kelly's most famous characters, Pogo and Albert. Tracing the series through the 1940s, one can observe how these characters developed and were refined both aesthetically and comedically. Most significantly, the early stories featured trickster tale dynamics and dialects that seemed derivative and two dimensional, while later installments showed traces of Kelly's true genius and originality: a melding of those trickster tales with topical satire, pastoral motifs, Freudian codings, and existential philosophizing. In terms of aesthetics, Kelly learned to move away from literal caricatures of animal types toward anthropomorphic and stylized drawings that made his characters more emotionally appealing. The same progression can also be seen in the *Our Gang* comics, as Kelly gradually abandoned efforts to create exacting and complicated caricatures of the original child film stars, and moved toward simplified, iconic drawings that were more dynamic and visually potent.

One reason that Kelly's later comic strip version of *Pogo* gained popularity so quickly in the early 1950s was that Kelly had been able to refine his drawing methods and comedic sensibility for over fifteen years—first as an animator at Disney, and then as a freelance comic book artist. This long apprenticeship in cartooning obviously gave him time to improve his storytelling and drawing abilities, but it also allowed him to excise gradually those parts of his comedy that were derivative or two dimensional. In other words, over time he was able to quietly abandon many embarrassing and clichéd missteps from his early work such as unthinking racist caricatures, predictable gags, and tired Uncle Remus-style dialects.

If Kelly had persisted in the comic book field, his career would have been little more than a footnote in the history of cartooning. There were the borrowed aspects to his work that made it somewhat forgettable, but there was also the relative obscurity associated with working on unflashy children's titles. Indeed, although children's titles sold well (Dell moved over twenty five million comic books a month) they were not given much respect by either fans or critics of the medium. The genres of comic books that received the most attention during these years were the more adult—and often lurid—crime, war, horror, sci-fi, and romance genres. Even superhero comics, which were then experiencing a fallow period between their golden and silver ages, had a higher profile among fans than little kids' tales at this time. Perhaps exaggerating generously, Kelly made jokes, later, about the tepid response his comic book work received from children. He related one particularly disheartening interview with a small boy who gave a frank, critical assessment of the *Animal Comics* series: "That comic book didn't have no action in it. Nobody shot nobody. It was full of mice in red and blue pants. It stunk" (Becker 351).

Beyond serving as a bit of funny self-deprecation, this anecdote also effectively communicated aspects of Kelly's core ethic as a cartoonist: he preferred gentle storytelling, slapstick comedy, and cerebral satire over entertainment featuring violence, sexual themes, and punishing humor. At the height of his career these preferences graduated into quasi-political action: he aligned himself in the mid-1950s with critics opposed to the morally subversive content of horror and crime comics, and acted as a spokesman for a media council that educated parents on the dangers of too much television watching among children. While there seem to be traces of traditional moral conservatism and even prudishness in these stances, they have more to do with Kelly's general devotion to progressive politics (shaping solid citizens through responsible entertainment), journalistic professionalism (texts should be thoroughly edited, properly geared to their appropriate audience), and his dedication to creating popular culture that was of high—almost literary—quality. The tag of being a reactionary prude does not fit, moreover, as one examines Kelly's rambunctious personal life, or considers his vision of the comics page as a challenging medium that can showcase satire, complex comedy, and elaborate storytelling.

Kelly at the *New York Star*

In 1948 Kelly returned to his first love, journalism. He was hired by the *New York Star*, an experimental paper that grew out of the famed "ad-less, leftish" paper,

PM, that had run from 1940 to 1948, and was the original home of Crockett Johnson's innovative comic strip, *Barnaby* (Crouch, "What do you know," 10). Kelly was hired to work as an art director, spot artist, designer, adman, political cartoonist, and later, a comic strip artist. A lot of this labor resulted in forgettable works of art, but some of Kelly's political cartoons during this period, such as his depiction of Thomas E. Dewey as a living robot, were excellent and were reprinted nationally, creating a minor political splash (Marschall, *America's Great*, 261).

Kelly's politics were already well left of center before coming to the *Star*. Factors pushing Kelly in this direction included his less-than-affluent upbringing in working class, multiethnic Bridgeport where his family supported a Socialist candidate for mayor; an affinity for the writings of Lincoln Steffens, a muckraker who had explored the corruption of urban governments in *The Shame of the Cities*; and an embrace of New Deal principles when it "dawned" on him that the "old conservatism, the old Horatio Alger formula, was not operative any longer" (Kercher 60). While creating political cartoons for the *Star*, Kelly was able to refine further his political vision, pondering complex issues such as the formation of Israel, the presidential race between Dewey and Truman, and various labor disputes. In a foreshadowing of his later opposition to the red-hunting of Senator McCarthy, Kelly created cartoons in 1948 that sharply criticized the House Un-American Activities Committee probes of Hollywood for "communist" entertainers, writers, and directors (Crouch, "Walt Kelly's Editorial Cartoons," 38–39).

Kelly was especially well liked by his newspaper peers during these years. He relished the life of a hard-drinking journalist, and became famous for holding court during after-hours, bar-hopping sessions. He and his colleagues spent many evenings telling stories and laughing over drinks at bars such as Moriarty's or Costello's. He was also equally admired for his professionalism and fairness during the daytime, within the walls of the newspaper's offices. As one of the older, more experienced (and multi-talented) employees on the staff, he often mentored younger journalists, and one of these coworkers remembered that collaboration fondly:

> During the time that Kelly was running the shop you looked forward to coming to work. He wasn't a boss, he was a teacher. He never gave an order, he suggested. He never said, "you did something wrong." He would show you the way to do it. (Mastrangelo B1)

On 4 October 1948, Kelly first introduced the comic strip iteration of *Pogo* in the *Star*. The only readers who encountered the strip were those that subscribed to this particular paper, but Kelly benefited from the small scale of this arrangement for two reasons. First, like some turn-of-the-century artists such as Bud Fisher (*Mutt and Jeff*) and George McManus (*Bringing up Father*), Kelly was able to develop his strip in the less-restrictive environment of a single home newspaper. By this point, in the late 1940s, most cartoonists were required to develop their work under the strict supervision of syndicate editors who often tried to excise the quirkier or more controversial aspects of a work in order to maximize the breadth of its appeal for a national audience. Secondly, the liberal orientation of the *Star* (it was pro-labor, pro-Israel, and the only New York City daily to support President Truman) made it an ideal cradle for the development of a strip that would both challenge reactionary entertainment and politics in subsequent years, and defy many of the economic and editorial mediations that homogenized satiric, comic art (Ibid. 10).

Pogo's developmental period at the *Star* lasted for only about four months, however, because the paper went into financial insolvency on 28 January 1949. The reasons for this collapse had much to do with the experimental and idealistic vision of the paper's backers; they attempted to create an "independent newspaper, as independent of the tyranny of slogans and colors as it is of vested interests" (Ibid. 10). A publication with such lofty principles and goals would require some kind of private or government funding in order to survive in a market in which most papers were too eager to subsume all editorial goals to the primacy of the profit margin. Marshall Field, a Chicago millionaire, had earlier bankrolled *PM* until advertisers in one of his other papers, the *Chicago Sun-Times* convinced him through threats of withdrawing ad revenues that *PM* was "too liberal." He unloaded the paper on publisher Bartley Crum and editor Joseph Barnes, two men eager to uphold the paper's liberal slant. The odd conditions of the sale included a payment of $300,000, a loan in return for $500,000, and promises of continued financial backing (Ibid. 10).

Even without these added burdens, neither the *PM* nor the *Star* had ever been very successful papers. The first daily to start up since 1924, the *Star* racked up enormous debts with the Associated Press wire service, and it suffered from limited circulation because of its leftist orientation and a binding distribution contract that made it available at only 4,500 of New York's 10,000 newsstands. Considering that Marshall Field had lost seven million dollars on the paper during *his* ownership, it is not surprising he reneged on his deal to continue offering financial assistance to the *Star* under the new owners. So when the promised money never materialized, the *Star* went out of business.

Pogo and National Syndication

Fortunately for Kelly, this brief taste of creating a daily comic strip gave him the confidence to take his work to national syndicates. The fact that he had a track record as a serious newspaperman, political cartoonist, and comic book illustrator—and had test-run *Pogo* with a real audience—gave him added clout and credibility when he initially approached these distribution companies. But they did not immediately see the strengths and potential of his work. For example, the first syndicates he contacted passed on the strip, arguing that there was no room for animal comics on a page dominated at the time by westerns, adventure, crime, and soap opera genres (Horn 332). One editor rejected the strip with the argument that the comics page did not need another "duck" comic strip. When Kelly insisted it was not about a duck, she informed him that it was difficult to tell, since Kelly could not draw animals that well. Several of the editors he met with said that they liked *Pogo* but felt that the dialect it featured was too difficult to read or that it was simply too intellectual; one added, "Try it out on ordinary people—you'll see" (Kelly, "Autobiography," 9). These negative reactions would have discouraged a less mature or confident cartoonist—or convinced him or her to come up with a more blandly marketable concept, but Kelly persevered, bolstered by the knowledge that he had received some enthusiastic letters from ordinary readers and other industry people during the strip's brief appearance in the *Star*.

Post-Hall (later to become Publishers-Hall), the newest syndicate in the field, finally accepted the strip because Bob Hall, the head of the syndicate, simply thought it was hilarious. His written response to Kelly was effusive: "I have just finished reading *Pogo*. Fella, it was terrific. TERRific! I tell you fella, I was knocked cold . . . laughed all the way to Chicago . . . WOW! I tell you, guy, we'll make you a million dollars" (Kelly "Unpublished Autobiographical Sketch" 18). These must have been exciting words for an artist who had struggled with money his entire career, and who had once dreamed as a small boy of becoming a rich cartoonist like Bud Fisher.

The youth and relatively small size of the Post-Hall organization made it an ideal fit for Kelly's unconventional work. Eager to sign someone who was already a polished, experienced cartoonist—an artist who had the potential to create a hugely popular strip—they informally gave Kelly freedom to pursue his vision: an animal comic with dense wordplay and challenging social and political satire. The ten-year contract he signed resembled the rigid documents that most other cartoonists were forced to sign during those years, but it had one significant exception: the syndicate agreed to automatically transfer ownership rights over to Kelly at the end or renewal of the first contract. Kelly ultimately renegotiated this contract before the ten years was up, effectively wresting away complete control of his work at an earlier date. As a result, he achieved a relatively unique position in the field of comic-stripping—an auteur who could shape the aesthetic and content of his work without too much heavy-handed, institutional mediation.

This syndicate's underdog status in the business also prompted Hall and his associates to give special treatment to the few artists and strips they represented. Betting that they had something extraordinary in their hands with Kelly, they promoted his work with "care and ferocity" and generally trusted his judgment when it came to including provocative satire (Marschall, *America's Great* 262). Post-Hall's respectful treatment of Kelly's satire, and its support of the innovative work of some of its other featured artists such as Herblock and Jules Feiffer, gave them the reputation through the 1950s and 1960s as the most progressive, artist-friendly syndicate in the business.

Despite the faith and commitment of his new syndicate, Kelly originally imagined that the most he could hope for was to attract a solid niche audience to his peculiar work. He explained later that he did not have "great hopes . . . inasmuch as it was a talking animal strip (a pet hate of most editors) and when you got past that hurdle you found it was hard to understand the dialogue. Then if you understood the dialogue it was hard to tie the action in with previously accepted rules of conduct in comic strips. There was no attempt at a last panel BOFFOLA and nobody was getting shot" (Kelly "Unpublished Autobiographical Sketch" 20).

Kelly apparently underestimated mainstream readers and editors, for the strip achieved almost immediate success. An early promotional booklet by Post-Hall in 1950 stated that Kelly had acquired within less than a year over 156 subscribing newspapers, and was adding a new one every forty-eight hours ("About *Pogo*,"105). *Pogo's* popularity continued at the same pace over the next couple years, and by 1953 it was one of the top five strips in the country. By 1954, only five years after *Pogo* was introduced, Kelly reached the height of critical and popular success. Book collections of his strips were topping bestseller lists, *Pogo* was carried in over 400 papers, he had received the highest awards in his profession (including the Reuben Award, or "cartoonist of the year," in 1951), and he was elected president of the National Cartoonists Society (Kelly, "Autobiography," 9).

The rapid rise in *Pogo's* popularity can be attributed to several factors. There were, of course, the merits of the strip itself. The funnies page had featured talking animal strips in the past, but none so effectively combined cute, anthropomorphized characters with resonant content and humor. Thanks to Kelly's training as an animator, his characters stood out on the comics page because they were dynamic, had heft, and were drawn with an eye-arresting, dark and fluid brush stroke. His huge cast of hilarious, nuanced characters (more than

Figure 1.1: Walt Kelly, "You stop kissin' me!" *Pogo*, 6 February 1953.

150), moreover, looked funny and real at the same time, and their vaudevillian style verbal and physical slapstick melded nicely with their graphic solidity (see Figure 1.1). In addition, the strip's broad comedy and complex misadventures made it consistently entertaining to read. Finally, Kelly was able to wed a coherent, humanistic vision of human nature and society to an allegorical and often sharp-edged, brand of topical satire. There was something in the strip for adults *and* kids, and even critics and the cultural intelligentsia (such as Carl Sandburg and Edward R. Murrow) became enamored with *Pogo's* world (Marschall, *America's Great* 263).

Post-Hall was effective in courting new papers during these early years of the strip, but Kelly deserves credit for winning over many editors. He was a relentless self-promoter, continually doing favors for editors, writing letters to fans, sending free books, posing for publicity photos with local folk, doing impromptu chalk-talks, and hitting the lecture circuit. His jovial, self-deprecating persona and easygoing, generous manner helped to sell the strip as much as did the comedy and art. On a side note, this willingness to accommodate editors and bend over backwards helped his career take off quickly, but later in his career became a bit of a stumbling block, leading him occasionally to compromise his art and satire.

Kelly as Cult Hero and Auteur

In 1952, Kelly accelerated the pace of his promotions, forwarding *Pogo* as a mock presidential candidate on college campuses. The huge success of this campaign—with 150 colleges endorsing Pogo as their candidate—cemented Kelly's status as a comedic guru for the rising youth generation. Many of the students on the *Pogo* bandwagon seemed to be sincere fans of Kelly's satire, but there was also probably a certain faddish hype in so many students embracing the cartoon marsupial as a hero. Kelly capitalized on the craze by mounting a cross-country tour of campuses, giving funny stump speeches and mingling with students. Before visiting campuses, he effectively built enthusiasm among the student body by sending out free buttons and giving the school newspaper and student governments guides on how to run the campaign and prepare for his arrival ("*Pogo* Campaign Memorabilia," 183). By the next election in 1956, Kelly had further refined his *Pogo* campaign promotional materials—he sent along packages to newspaper editors containing official certificates designating them as "honorary chairmen" of the Pogo campaign in their area, offered to do promotional drawings that could be placed prominently in another part of the paper, and promised to send mock-news release updates on the *Pogo* campaign.

The free publicity and excitement generated by Kelly's aggressive campaigning, sharp promotionals, and speeches to college students and community clubs, helped to establish *Pogo* as the most critically acclaimed comic strip of its day.

This success also brought with it some of the complications of celebrity. Kelly related in 1956 that he was overwhelmed and fatigued from speaking to over fifty civic and college groups each year, and that "mail from enthusiastic readers [was] a major problem, albeit a flattering one." Two stenographers had to work continually at answering mail, clipping drawings, and sending off books (Kelly "Memo to Post-Hall Syndicate, 1954" 1). Still, the relentless schedule paid off, and Kelly was embraced by hip college students and intellectuals, while winning over mainstream editors. The enthusiasm and goodwill generated by these efforts in turn trickled down to the average reader through glowing endorsements by editors, word-of-mouth recommendations from college students, and free books and personalized letters sent by Kelly to fans.

The joviality and generosity in Kelly's character seemed to be a core personal trait rather than just a mercenary promotional strategy. By all accounts Kelly was "gregarious, fun-loving, open, friendly, and best of all, a first rate conversationalist." He also put people ahead of money and belongings. One friend recalled that "Kelly probably made a lot of money over the years, but he didn't care about money, he just gave it away" (Lockwood 48–49). He could get along with people from all social levels and economic backgrounds. A lack of formal college education, coupled with a substantial knowledge gained from self-study, allowed him to go comfortably from lecturing to college students, to chumming with local Rotarians, to bar-hopping with working-class friends. In addition to his generosity with editors and fans, he quietly gave gifts of money to those in need, and fulfilled numerous favors to close friends with sketches, letters, and tributes within the strip. Most famously, he continually renamed the strip's swamp skiff after different friends or special readers.

Kelly was also adept at putting people at ease through easy banter and poking fun at himself; indeed, he was a master of witty self-deprecation. He preferred sharing mock insults with friends rather than receiving praise from admirers, and his most common self-description was that he was "an imposingly flabby man" (Kelly, "Aesop Takes to the Swamp" 113). In personal correspondence and relationships, he combined these character traits with a penchant for absurdist free-association and playful language, creating a loopy, stream-of-consciousness form of discourse that endeared him to colleagues, fans, and editors. Kelly displays this inspired silliness in the following nonsense letter written to Herbert Block ("Herblock"), an editorial cartoonist also working for the Post-Hall syndicate; in it, Kelly parodies the common requests famous artists receive to contribute a drawing for an event or show:

Mr. Herblack

. . . We'd like this in oil, 18" by 56" at once. We'll display it in the lobby where you will get some very favorable, I guess, notices. Also if you can make it up here, most of us would be glad to see you. There's a bus that leaves from Ithaca, overnight, getting here just in time for the evening services. We intend to serve sponge-cake and prunes at about 11:06 p.m. so it will pay you to "stick around." Please do come.

Naturally there will be no pay for this job, but in the interest of being fair, we have arranged with the Playhouse Proprietors that they will not charge you anything for the display.

If you'd like to stay on for the entire convention (it ends in March), we would like to squeeze you in somewhere to say a few words. I am sure that a number of us will be up at that time of the morning and will be on hand to hear your interesting remarks. In the event that there is nobody about at your scheduled speaking time perhaps you could speak rather loudly and awaken your neighboring tent mates. They will be happy to give you some attentions I am sure . . . PS: Many of us here have some other good ideas for you. (Block 216)

On both the inherent strengths of his work and these self-promotional skills, Kelly's strip became deeply rooted in the comics page within just a few short years. Whereas some of the "intellectual" or satiric strips that had preceded *Pogo*, such as George Herriman's *Krazy Kat*, had achieved only a limited cult following, Kelly's strip was truly popular. Polls in 1956 and 1963 showed that his most devoted fans were members of a "media-conscious, college-educated set," but Kelly also received thousands of letters from children and everyday comics fans. In addition, the breadth of his syndication gave him over 50 million regular readers and his book collections sold millions of copies (Candee 332). With so many demographics embracing the strip and editors developing a personal attachment to its creator, it was almost completely safe from threats of cancellation. Those few poor editors who tried to discontinue the strip, such as a fellow in Vancouver, Canada, in 1956, were met with a barrage of phone calls, picketing, reports of wakes in which fans dressed all in black, or complaints by parents who claimed that their teenage children had become "unbearably sullen" after the strip's cancellation ("Possum Attack," 118). A cancellation in Boston elicited a similarly fervid reaction: "We'd never seen anything like it. The switchboard was clogged with *Pogo* protests all day so that we could hardly get a line into the city room. Several of the wives of staff members stopped speaking to them" (Kelly, "Unpublished Autobiographical Sketch 21).

Given the monumental success of Kelly's work and its place as the cornerstone of the Post-Hall syndicate's finances, it is no wonder that by 1955 Kelly was in a position to radically renegotiate an already generally favorable contract. In these contract renegotiations, which Kelly instigated three years before the agreement was due for renewal, he essentially took legal ownership and control of the strip, and ensured that the freedom he had enjoyed as a satirist could continue under a more formal, binding arrangement. It is clear in reading between the lines in the contract that Kelly, by this time, was earning over $150,000 a year and was guaranteed that over the course of his contract his yearly earnings could never go below $100,000, regardless of the performance of the strip. Given that the syndicate readily agreed to this, it is clear that Kelly's star was continuing to rise, and that the syndicate anticipated that the strip's syndication numbers would continue to grow. In effect, the rights asserted in the second contract ensured that Kelly could continue to pursue his genre of comic strip commentary that mixed "cute" characters, slapstick comedy, and pointed satire, without fear of heavy mediation or censorship. Kelly's bold moves in these negotiations also offers a model of how an artist can control and limit the merchandising and commercialization of his work—an example followed recently by iconoclastic cartoonists like Garry Trudeau, Berke Breathed, and Bill Watterson.

Figure 1.2: Walt Kelly, "Don't fight facts . . . ," *Pogo*, 13 May 1953.

Kelly and McCarthy

The beginnings of *Pogo's* prime as a work of pointed and sometimes controversial satire can be traced to 1 May 1953, when the swamp was disturbed by an ax-wielding bobcat bent on taking over the place and rooting out all "Reds," or subversives. In the three previous years the strip had included trenchant parodies of other cultural texts and sharp caricatures of identifiable political and social types, but this character—Simple J. Malarkey, an obvious caricature of Senator Joseph McCarthy—was Kelly's most blatant foray into the territory of topical satire. Although this storyline—and a later cameo appearance by Malarkey—only lasted for weeks and months at a time—it made an immense cultural splash, energizing college students and everyday readers eager for a way to respond to the paranoid and divisive spirit that the senator had introduced into the political and cultural rhetoric of the time.

Malarkey's tactics in *Pogo*—intimidation, subversive-hunting, elimination of rights and constitutions, and so on—were never countered with direct opposition or organized rebellion from the other characters in the strip. As one scholar put it, "The liberal Pogo never defeated Wiley Cat [a predator similar to Malarkey] and the other goons nor mobilized his friends into action . . . the forces of liberalism merely survived—in an optimistic hope, we might say" (Berry 196). It was the innate tolerance and self-mocking humor built into the swamp community that served as a passive but resistant antidote to the Malarkey virus. In cartoons within the Malarkey storyline, for example, Kelly articulated an ethic of good-humored resistance and critical self-examination that contrasted sharply with McCarthy's tack of xenophobic scapegoating (figures 1.3 and 1.4). This non-violent response and goal of mere survival may seem somewhat cowardly as far as political rebellions go, but it was perhaps an accurate reflection of effective real-world strategies. At a time when reactionary politics dominated the cultural discourse and people could be attacked or blacklisted for dissenting political views, a strategy of flying under the radar with one's principles intact was wisely pragmatic. In addition, because Cold War liberals were loathe to forward any kind of equally shrill or dogmatic ideologies of their own—based on lessons learned from earlier brands of leftist radicalism that had failed—it made sense that Pogo the character would not take up arms or engage in direct debate.

Figure 1.3: Walt Kelly, "Phoo! Deacon . . . ," *Pogo*, 30 May 1953.

Figure 1.4: Walt Kelly, "Makin' dern fools of ourselves . . . ," *Pogo*, 2 June 1953.

A year later, on 18 August 1954, Malarkey resurfaced again and attempted to reintroduce his campaign of terror into the swamp. This cameo lasted for two months and included some especially vivid images of the bobcat running through the swamp with a fish-sack on his head, making him resemble a member of the Ku Klux Klan. In 1954, Kelly also lampooned the senator in a short graphic novel based on the Lewis Carroll's court-room scene from *Alice in Wonderland*; this allowed Kelly to satirize McCarthy's antics in front of the Senate committees. Finally, Kelly appeared on Edward R. Murrow's *Person to Person* in

1954, using this venue to elaborate on his critique of McCarthy, and after McCarthy's fall in 1955, Kelly continued to denounce the senator's politics in interviews and written editorials (Horn 46).

The featuring of a recognizable political figure on the comics page produced a voluble response among many newspaper editors and cultural critics for two primary reasons. First, Senator McCarthy was widely feared, and this was one of the few negative commentaries on his behavior at a time when a large majority of cartoonists, reporters, and "editorial pages were notoriously silent" (Denney 61).[1] And second, a backlash occurred because most editors, comics readers, and even a number of fellow cartoonists did not see the comic strip page as the proper place for political commentary.

The editor of the *Newark Star Ledger*, for example, removed *Pogo* from the comics page after the McCarthy parodies and placed it on the editorial page, arguing that politics did not belong with the entertaining funnies (Crouch, "George Ward," 79). Although there is no accurate documentation of how many other editors protested, Kelly and his assistant, George Ward, reported that one Rhode Island paper pulled the strip. At least a half dozen editors complained that Kelly had trespassed "on the editorial writer's preserve" or that this was "improper" treatment of a United States Senator; and, strangely, one editor simply made the decision to have an artist paint white over Malarkey's heavy beard (Kelly, "Walt Kelly Views the Press," 194; Turberville 94). After a Rhode Island paper threatened to drop the strip if *Pogo* featured McCarthy's face on the comics page again, Kelly cleverly responded by placing the sack over Malarkey's head in the second run, evoking the additional reference to the KKK (Kercher 71).

In typically self-effacing fashion, Kelly downplayed his own role in challenging or "bringing down" McCarthy. He later argued that the hype surrounding his heroism as a cultural critic was blown out of proportion, and that his satire of the senator was over-analyzed (Kelly, *Ten Ever-Lovin'* 87). Nevertheless, the fact that Kelly became emboldened by this melding of political cartooning with comic strips and made it a regular facet of his satire ensured a reputation among editors and some conservative cultural guardians as a dangerous subversive. Kelly's third wife, Selby, for example, reported that over the years Kelly received a number of threats "with the removal of his livelihood" and that his phone was tapped. It was also later revealed that at the time, a government agency "was corresponding with a civilian reporter who was sure that the 'lingo' used in *Pogo* was a secret Russian code" (Beiman, "Walt and Selby Kelly Interview" 30).

Kelly's alternative, liberal philosophy achieved a powerful distillation early in his career through his famous maxim, "We have met the enemy and he is us."[2] This pithy slogan was first coined in an introduction written for the strip collection, *The Pogo Papers*, in 1953, at the height of the McCarthy dramas; it originally read, ". . . we shall meet the enemy, and not only may he be ours, he may be us." The core concept was malleable enough to be rephrased and applied over the ensuing years to various cultural ills beyond McCarthyism such as a resistance to Civil Rights, a societal penchant for warfare, and the pollution of the environment.

Another outgrowth of the McCarthy brouhaha was Kelly's emergence as an advocate for the comics page as a venue that could feature challenging "intellectual" strips with social and political satire. For example, Kelly became a sharp critic of comic strip popularity polls that conspired against niche-appeal strips or gave too much weight to the most outspoken, conservative readers (Kelly, *Ten Ever Lovin'* 135). Kelly chastised editors who still believed "that the comics page is the playpen of the newspaper, or a sort of inert baby sitter for the brain." He asserted that "it could be just the reverse. It could be the most stimulating section of the paper" (Ibid. 135). This advocation for a better comics page led Kelly to criticize, at times, brands of satire or comedy that he considered opportunistic of irresponsible. In 1957, for example, he argued that "good cartoonists are subversive—they are against things," and he deplored what had passed for satire in the early years of the medium: the scapegoating of immigrants or facile attacks on "whatever everyone is against" at a specific cultural moment (O'Sullivan 93; Kelly, "*Pogo* Looks," 291).

Kelly and the Profession of Cartooning

A more complicated and sometimes less progressive side to Kelly's professional life can be observed, however, beginning in 1955, when he was elected president of the National Cartoonists Society. Although he was well liked as the leader of this professional organization and generally did an admirable job of elevating the profession to new levels of legitimacy, at times he seemed more interested in partying, resting on laurels, or keeping things peaceful and profitable. Kelly seemed to especially enjoy the clubby, hard-drinking, and sometimes sexist aspects of this organization. He relished the society's dinners, for example, because it gave him opportunities to perform roasts, give jokey speeches, and put on vaudeville-style musical and comedy acts. This was the same theatre-loving kid and Disney prankster with a bigger stage and an enthusiastic audience of like-minded newspapermen.

The organization's festivities featured a deep-seeded sexism, however, that Kelly sometimes failed to challenge. His peers were notoriously slow to treat women cartoonists as equals, for example, and regularly included sexist themes in their shows and created drawings of nude women printed in their program booklets. Kelly was also content, moreover, to see the organization continue on as a sort of exclusive drinking club for successful cartoonists rather than to transform it into something more progressive and union-like.

To be fair, Kelly could not have made radical changes in the organization without causing serious discontent among many of the most powerful founding members of the club. He also had the misfortune of having to lead the society through some especially difficult situations. For instance, Kelly had to keep secret an embarrassing battle between Al Capp and Ham Fisher that included charges of obscene drawings hidden in comic strips, falsified documents, ugly legal wranglings, and a suicide. He also had to represent the field of comic strips at the Senate hearings on the alleged connection between juvenile delinquency and comics. In the first case, the Capp and Fisher feud, Kelly effectively buried the story, preventing it from reaching the public eye and maintaining the professional façade of the organization. At the Senate hearings, Kelly also put the financial welfare and public reputation of his field ahead of any heroic defense of embattled peers. He flattered senators with drawings, trumpeted the family-friendly aspects of comic strips, and denounced the horror comics that were under investigation.

Depending on one's level of sympathy towards the challenges Kelly faced as an industry leader, this behavior could either be cast on the one hand as hypocritical and inconsistent (the opportunism of a successful cartoonist who could have done more to reform his profession); or, on the other hand, it could be perceived as the pragmatic, real-world compromises a mid-century artist in this highly commercialized field might have to make in order to survive and thrive. Indeed, it could be that one key to the success and longevity of Kelly's career was his talent for compromise and flexibility—a willingness to wear different hats to accommodate shifting audiences or expectations. For example, when in the presence of other newspapermen or conservative editors, Kelly would often adopt the pragmatic persona of a working-class businessman—he was just a "good ol' boy" trying to entertain and make a quick buck. But then, if asked to do an interview or speak to a college audience the next day, he could easily modify the rhetoric and embody the roles of folksy, liberal satirist, and high-minded social critic.

One can identify, nevertheless, aspects of Kelly's work and worldview that did not shift according to the moment or the audience. His left-leaning political views, for example, were consistent beyond his satire, as was clear in his advocation of desegregation, civil rights, and a variety of other liberal causes. And by extension, his core convictions as a principled social critic (his adamant opposition to McCarthyism, for instance) were clearly not opportunistic choices adopted simply to please a particular audience. Evidence of this core stability can be seen when he admitted in private to friends such as Herblock, that he detested certain aspects of the business side of his profession such as flattering or socializing with editors who might be touchy about his satire (Block 121). The schmoozing and conciliatory poses, in other words, were sometimes necessary strategies for one utilizing the channels of an inherently conservative entertainment industry for forward-thinking political and social satire.

In the end, there were only a few areas in which Kelly truly seemed to be conflicted in his beliefs and practices, or out of alignment with what one might expect of such a progressive-minded satirist. These flaws included eschewing brands of collective bargaining that might have transformed some of the more backwards aspects of his profession, his penchant for bar-hopping and hard-living that took a toll on his work and personal life, and occasionally his perception and treatment of women. Kelly's retreat from the most radical, union-like strategies for reforming his profession can be explained in part through his impoverished background. As someone without a college degree who experienced the deprivations of the Great Depression, he was loath to challenge his own welfare and security as a star cartoonist. He also loved the bourgeois trappings of that success too much to feel compelled to fully challenge the rules and hierarchies of his field.

The hard-drinking lifestyle, womanizing, and health problems seemed to be interrelated issues. Among fellow cartoonists, Kelly was notorious for his over-indulgent drinking and eating habits. Milton Caniff, a close friend and the creator of *Terry and the Pirates* and *Steve Canyon*, described him as a "Falstaffian character" who struggled with his weight and loved hanging out with newspaper hotshots at bars like Moriarty's, Bleek's, Costello's, and the Pen & Pencil. He would hold court at these saloons, attracting large crowds as he spent many hours eating and drinking, talking shop, and often generously covering his dining companions' tabs (Crouch, "Milton Caniff" 108). Longtime Kelly assistant George Ward remembered fondly that Kelly had "a following of good friends from all walks of life. They always counted it their good fortune to be sitting with him when Walt was in rare form. That is when everybody would just have to break up at Kelly's keen sense of humor and his amusing stories" (Crouch "George Ward Talks" 79).

Close colleagues and friends like Ward focused on the positive aspects of Kelly's excesses—the pranks, the lively conversations, and the entertaining anecdotes, but the late-night carousing and drinking also exacerbated Kelly's health problems. As one friend put it, although Kelly was incredibly fun and generous, he "took care of everybody but himself—that he wouldn't do" (Lockwood 49). Indeed, because of the hard-drinking and overeating, Kelly struggled throughout his career with his weight, developed diabetes, and showed signs of alcoholism. His compromised health forced him to curtail his lecturing and promotional tours at the height of his career and eventually led to a premature death in 1973 from complications related to diabetes.

The drinking and partying lifestyle may have also contributed to what Bill Crouch described as a "wild roll" of romantic flirtations or indiscretions during the 1950s that might have negatively impacted his family life (Crouch, "George Ward Talks," 79; Crouch, "Milton Caniff Talks About Walt Kelly" 108). Like many of the older members of the National Cartoonists Society, Kelly openly enjoyed admiring other women, unapologetically flirted with female dining companions, and occasionally became smitten with a severe case of extramarital infatuation. There is no evidence his behavior went to the extremes of someone like Al Capp (who at one point in his career chased and entrapped coeds while visiting college campuses), but Kelly seemed to possess a libido that became more active the more alcohol he consumed (Anderson 1). For example, Caniff related a story of Kelly developing an embarrassing infatuation with a female dining companion during one evening's carousing. Over the course of a dinner he made his friends uncomfortable with his semi-drunken, maudlin attempts to court the affections of this particular woman. At other times, according to Caniff, Kelly became "desperately avid for a couple of completely unapproachable women. He made no bones that he lusted after them," Caniff continued, suggesting that many of them were flattered by these advances and loved him "for his mind" (Crouch, "Milton Caniff," 108).

None of this behavior was public knowledge during Kelly's life. One would think his opposition to McCarthy would have made him a prime target for the FBI or a reporter intent on revealing a hard-hitting social critic's less-than-upstanding morals and behavior. Kelly's indiscretions, however, were perhaps never bizarre or egregious enough to attract much attention, and it is likely that the old-boy network of cartoonists and journalists protected Kelly from rumors and revelations. Indeed, among traditional cartooning and newspaper men, this type of rowdy lifestyle was perhaps winked at because it was so common in the legend and lore of the journalistic trade. Kelly even joked openly about his carousing habits, claiming in a mid-1950s promotional piece that "When he [Kelly] does stir abroad it is usually with a high school leer and a yen to outdo Carrie Nation in destroying innocent booze" (Kelly, "Promotional" 24).

For the most part Kelly's carousing lifestyle seems to have had little serious impact on his home life. His children recall that their dad was perhaps absent too often—always traveling or at work in the city—but he always treated them with generosity and good humor. His first marriage, nevertheless, may have been a casualty to Kelly's roving eyes. It appears that Kelly divorced his first wife Helen in 1950 after falling in love with his secretary, Stephanie. For several years in the early 1950s Kelly had an unusual set of family relations in which he kept up a home in Connecticut with Helen—giving his children and many neighbors the impression that nothing had changed there—while maintaining a separate household with his new wife, Stephanie in New York City (Block 216). It was only when Kelly was interviewed on *Face to Face* with Ed R. Murrow, and Stephanie was introduced as "Mrs. Kelly," that many friends and acquaintances discovered the reality of Kelly's marital arrangements.

Despite ongoing flirtations with other women, Kelly's marriage to Stephanie appears to have been fairly happy and stable—though marked by tragedy (with two children dying in infancy and one receiving brain damage as a newborn during a difficult delivery). George Ward, Kelly's assistant, suggested that Stephanie and Walt's spats generally amounted to a young wife's inability to understand the mind and habits of a quirky, headstrong "genius" (Crouch "George Ward Talks" 83). The fact that Kelly based his most attractive female character, Mam'selle Hepzibah, on his second wife, also attests to his affection for her. But because Hepzibah was such a two-dimensional shell—possessing only superficial traits of female desirability—one has few additional clues about how Kelly might have cherished Stephanie differently from other women. Indeed, Hepzibah's "va-va-voom" appeal to the male characters in the strip also tends to reinforce the notion that Kelly perceived all attractive women, well beyond the domestic sphere, through an idealizing, libidinous gaze. Stephanie passed away in 1970, and Kelly married for a third time in 1972 to Selby Daley, a fellow artist who had a fiery and independent character. Despite the brevity of their marriage (Kelly died just one year later, in 1973), Selby took charge of his immediate legacy, working to keep his strip going and helping to cement his reputation through book anthologies in subsequent years.

In addition to hiding effectively his personal troubles behind a jovial public façade, Kelly seemed to mask throughout his career a degree of depression that sometimes curdled into misanthropy. Caniff, for example, said, "I always remember him being concerned about something. I never saw him in a state of total happiness." Caniff continued, suggesting that one could always detect a void or degree of unhappiness beneath Kelly's partying: "If you ran into Walt it was his party from then on. There was a certain loneliness about this. He had friends on all levels of society . . . [but] . . . he was expert at letting you see only that portion of his life he wanted you to see" (Crouch, "Milton Caniff," 108). That angst could also manifest itself through Twain-like acerbity or belligerent incivility. Selby reported that later in life Kelly often responded poorly to adoring fans:

> [He] never small-talked and particularly didn't like anyone to fawn over him. When anybody came up and said, 'Oh, Mr. Kelly, I think you're marvelous!' he would just withdraw completely and wilt back down inside himself. As a result, he'd be gruff toward these people because he was embarrassed and ill-at-ease with them, and wanted them to just go away and leave him alone. (Crouch "An Interview with Selby Kelly" 192)

Even among friends Kelly's moods could be unpredictable. Caniff, again, reported that if Kelly were drinking heavily, his mood could become volatile: "You never knew what would happen and you'd better either go along with him or go home" (Crouch, "Milton Caniff Talks" 108). Additional evidence of that grouchiness can be seen in some of the internal communications of the National Cartoonists Society where he shoots down some political/professional concerns of junior members (Kelly, "NCS Newsletter 1953," 2). These occasional jabs could emerge in informal settings as well; younger cartoonists, for example, feared Kelly because he had a notorious, Algonquin roundtable-style "sardonic wit" that he could unleash on dinner companions or advice-seekers (Crouch, "Milton Caniff Talks" 108).

It is possible this mildly depressive misanthropy and low-boiling contempt for less-experienced colleagues also reflected some of Kelly's deeper, philosophical convictions about the incorrigibility of human nature. A vaguely pessimistic view of his fellow man emerged in interviews and in the most broad, cosmic aspects of his satire—in particular, in his view that not only have we met the enemy (us), but that there is little we can do to reform that enemy. He stated, for example, "that very little we do will actually change the kind of people we are . . . we shouldn't ever expect too much of ourselves because we're frail and we're inclined to break very easily" (Kelly "London Calling" 94). That generosity in withholding judgment (or pessimistic lowering of high expectations?) appears to be both a reflection of Kelly's complex and sympathetic view of man's fallibility, as well as a direct acknowledgment of his own firsthand awareness of how difficult it is to rein in human appetites, infatuations, and ungenerous impulses.

Kelly in the 1960s

Despite the fatigue, health problems, and subsurface depression, Kelly kept up a whirlwind schedule into the early 1960s. His bad heart did cause him to occasionally scale back some of the chalk-talks and publicity tours, but he still accepted offers to write political commentary, visit troops overseas, and tour the globe as an ambassador and pundit for several newspapers. This social gregariousness and service-minded engagement with newspapers and organizations beyond the sphere of art and comedy, stood in stark contrast to a new breed of cartoonist typified by Charles Schulz (*Peanuts*) and, later by Bill Watterson (*Calvin and Hobbes*) and Garry Trudeau (*Doonesbury*)—artists who were more introspective and socially reclusive. Despite the exhausting toll of Kelly's whirlwind social appearances, his high public profile probably served him well, prolonging his general popularity among comics readers at a time when his star was waning—and cementing his status as one of the most significant social critics of the day.

But even as Kelly's general reputation as an important cultural critic remained secure in the mid to late 1960s, the quality of the strip declined in several respects. For one thing, that creeping grouchiness or misanthropy in Kelly's personal life seemed to spill over into the strip from time to time. In some episodes, for example, Kelly asserted his political perspective with too much sober stridency, and the narratives lost some of their vaudeville innocence or trickster tale playfulness. During this later period, Pogo could sometimes come across as a superior scold rather than a wise fool, and Kelly's caricatures of political figures such as Fidel Castro, Richard Nixon, J. Edgar Hoover, and Lyndon B. Johnson were at times too literal, specific, and heavy-handed. Finally, the layered political references of the strip began to overshadow its more comedic and entertaining aspects. This may have driven away many casual readers, or those who felt their partisan beliefs were in obvious conflict with Kelly's worldview.

Interestingly, even as Kelly's politics began to play a more prominent role in the strip, he made concessions to sensitive editors that have troubled some critics. Most prominently, he accommodated readers and editors that found his editorializing to be "too strong" by providing alternate strips—"bunny rabbit" strips that papers could print in the place of some of his weekly installments that were especially topical or too sharp in their satire (Kelly, "The Bunny Rabbit Strips," 198) (see Figure 1.5). To Kelly's credit, he seemed to mock the pressures that forced him into this arrangement by making these bunny strips simplistically bland and cute. It was as if he were saying, "What do you want, *bunny rabbits? I'll* give you bunny rabbits. . ." Kelly also discontinued the practice in the final years of the strip, but one is still left with the general impression that the courteous, "professional" newspaperman edged out the principled satirist or iconoclastic social critic in this late episode of his career.

Figure 1.5: Walt Kelly, excerpt from "Trouble with Bunny Rabs," *Pogo*, 14 October 1964.

The spirit of the mid to late 1960s was also a poor match for Kelly's methods, politics, and persona. Although the strip had become more overtly and consistently political, Kelly's brand of "elaborate whimsy" and layered satiric methods felt out of synch with a youth culture that valued direct protest and sometimes placed a utopian faith in alternative lifestyles and religions (Crinklaw 1). As Boyd Barry, a scholar at Virginia Commonwealth University observed, "From the point of view of the reforming activist, the gentleness, the veiled humor of *Pogo* . . . [made] the strip not tolerably intolerable, but intolerably tolerable and tolerant" (Barry 196).

Kelly's cartooning aesthetic also began to feel out of touch with the times. For example, *MAD* magazine and its eclectic and zany cartooning styles—a complement to the juvenile and hyperbolic tone of the magazine's parodies—seemed to capture better the cacophony of irreverent and dissenting voices of the 1960s. In addition, a new brand of minimalism emerged on the comics page and in animated shorts that stood in stark contrast to Kelly's baroquely detailed swamp scenes, deft brushwork, and old-fashioned Disney cuteness and dynamism. Perhaps the best examples of that new aesthetic were Charles Schulz' *Peanuts* and Johnny Hart's *B.C.* on the comics page, and the modernistic and angular cartoons of UPA studio on the animated front.

In sum, although Kelly seemed perfectly positioned to act as a folksy guru for the emerging counterculture, his bourgeois persona, pragmatic business practices, and distaste for any brand of radicalism, prevented this from happening. In other words, Kelly appeared, perhaps only somewhat inaccurately, to belong to the "status quo" media crowd that the youth culture rejected. Interestingly, some of the underground cartoonists of the late 1960s—those who were actually more in touch with the spirit of the times such as Clay Geerdes—cited Kelly as a "pre-underground" radical who fought and confounded censors of all forms of aesthetic expression with "symbolism and complexity." (Geerdes 91). Kelly might have appreciated the tribute and agreed with this description of his own methods, but the radical label would not have sat well with him. Indeed, Kelly, who preferred the traditional vices of alcohol and winking indiscretions, would have been slow to condone or sympathize with the anti-bourgeois ideologies, drugs, and free-love practices of these cartoonists and the hippie generation to which they belonged. Their methods, too, of "outraging . . . [the establishment] by creating blatantly sexual and anti-intellectual comix" would have offended his more temperate worldview and thoughtful satiric sensibilities (Ibid., 93).

Kelly's Last Years

Kelly's final years were punctuated with a series of disappointments and dramatic incidents related to his ill health. One significant trial was nursing his wife Stephanie through a bout with cancer in the late 1960s that eventually led to her passing in 1970. While taking care of Stephanie, Kelly was also preoccupied with working on a half-hour film version of *Pogo*—a "last hurrah" of sorts for his declining strip. Having been both a storyboard man and an animator, Kelly was aware of the pitfalls in trying to shepherd an idea through Hollywood. As a result, he insisted on writing the script himself, perfecting every detail of the storyboards, and overseeing as much of the production as possible. But sadly, the final work, titled "The Pogo Special Birthday Special," was a disaster in Kelly's eyes because the producers had cut too many corners in an effort to save money—and because of the way the director of the film, Chuck Jones (of *Looney*

Tunes fame), attempted to place his own aesthetic stamp and comic sensibility on the work. Ward Kimball said that when Kelly went out to California to see the final product he was in a "towering rage" and wanted "to kill—if not sue—Chuck" because he had changed the story and short-circuited the satire of *Pogo* with "sweet, saccharine stuff" (Andrae and Blum 146).

While working on the animated film, Kelly was assigned Selby Daley as an assistant. Selby was an employee of the MGM animation studios and a former coworker at Disney. The two became fond of each other during this collaboration, and after Stephanie's death, Selby began to accompany Kelly everywhere. Their marriage took place under odd circumstances: in 1972 Kelly was suffering from the ill effects of diabetes (swollen and infected legs), and was thus admitted to a hospital in New York City. There, in the intensive care ward, Kelly and Selby were married a half hour before he went into surgery to have one of his legs amputated.

It should be noted that although Kelly faced some incredibly horrific, health-related traumas in these final years—swollen, gangrenous feet, pathetic falls on the city streets, strokes, and debilitating comas—he always seemed to face them with an impish good humor. For example, there are stories of him plotting practical jokes on the nurses at the hospital and telling friends that he would get back to his salooning habits once his stub of a leg grew back. He also philosophized cheerfully that "There is talk that growing up is tough. If so, then perhaps I have not grown up at all" ("Bard of the Okefenokee" 93). This sentiment is especially poignant not only for its stoicism in the face of crippling illnesses, but also because it reflects, perhaps unintentionally, the fun-loving but sometimes devastatingly irresponsible boy that Kelly remained to the end of his life.

During Kelly's final year, he and Selby worked on a new television special together—a work entitled, appropriately, "We Have Met the Enemy and He Is Us." The film, which Kelly hoped would more accurately reflect his satiric vision and aesthetic sensibility, was never aired because he passed away in 1973 while visiting Hollywood to work on the project. Selby related that Kelly may have speeded his decline during these final days by indulging in alcohol against doctors' strict orders (Crouch, "Interview With Selby Kelly" 220). After being in California for only a week, Kelly lapsed into a coma in his hotel room one morning, and died several days later, on 18 October 1973.

As early as 1972 a number of newspapers had begun to cancel the strip because of a general drop in quality and a displeasure at having to print reruns during the artist's health struggles. Even after suffering a stroke, Kelly continued to draw the strip while propped up to the drawing board. Poignantly, during this final year, Kelly's diminished state was reflected directly in the look of the strip: the characters shrunk in size and interacted with minimal movement in a featureless landscape; it was as if the once vibrant and busy world of *Pogo* was gradually fading into a newsprint void (Figure 1.6).

Attempts were made to keep the strip going after Kelly's death, and in the early 1990s the strip was revived for a short time. Given the complexity of Kelly's art and satire, it comes as no surprise that these efforts generally failed after a short time. Over the years other, more generic stand-by strips have been run in perpetuity by rotating stables of artists, but *Pogo* was too much of a direct

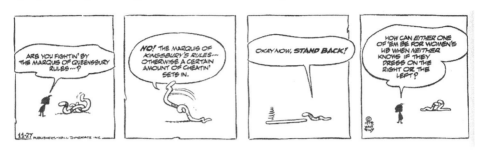

Figure 1.6: "Okay now, stand back!" *Pogo*, 27 November 1972.

extension of Kelly's sensibility and worldview to mimic that easily. In fact, it was such an intricate construction of voices, genres, and influences—drawn from so many different sources and traditions, over so many years of Kelly's life—that one has to study his career with both depth and breadth. The following chapters attempt this task, exploring the quirky genius of Kelly and the nuanced brilliance of his work through the help of a variety of sources including archival materials, personal letters, newspaper articles, colleague memoirs, the strip itself, and the ever jokey and "unreliable" voice of the artist himself.

CHAPTER 2

Comedy and Satire in *Pogo*

Kelly's comic strip is often celebrated as exceptional because of its topical sat-ire—the lampooning of the significant political figures and the cultural events of its day. In the minds of some critics, it is this satiric "seriousness" that saves *Pogo* from its surrounding medium (the overly commercialized and lowbrow comics page) and occasionally from itself (the perceived weaknesses of the strip: silly wordplay, slapstick, and overly cute aesthetics). The problem with fixating on the virtues of topical satire alone, however, is that it sanctions an elitist con-tempt for broad comedy and mainstream popular culture. It also compels one to discuss Kelly's work within the borrowed frames of literary satire or journalistic commentary. It ignores, in other words, the myriad ways Kelly's powerful satire is intertwined in the apparent silliness of his verbal and visual comedy, the aes-thetic tools of the cartoonist, and the democratically low cultural status of his chosen medium.

This study attempts to do justice to each aspect of his work, analyzing Kelly according to the peculiar factors that shape how readers enjoy popular comedic-satire on the funnies page. This chapter begins the discussion by exploring the interconnections between the comedy and satire in *Pogo*. First, one can identify the various visual and verbal tools at work in its comedy, tracing the roots of Kelly's narrative conventions and character types—and then speculating on the satiric meanings and uses that emerge from those methods.

To begin, it is useful to establish Kelly's own views on the supposed divide between serious satire and lowbrow comedy. At first glance, he seems to make a sharp distinction between his social commentary and slapstick humor. For ex-ample, although Kelly often referred to himself as a mere entertainer—a "Key-stone Cop and throwin'-pie humor man"—he also argued on other occasions that "good cartoonists are subversive—they are against things" (O'Sullivan 93; and Kercher 63). He elaborated, saying "'True humor or satire' . . . is a mode of expression ideally suited for 'social comment.' How 'are you going to have humor without it?' he asked. 'The only thing left is slapstick, and that gets tiresome quickly'" (Kercher 59).

Kelly does indeed make an important point here: it was his pointed social criticism that gave *Pogo* its conscience, direction, and force. What his statement does not flesh out adequately, however, is the way that the comedy in *Pogo* was a critical part (or even sometimes the whole) of his "social comment." The sillier aspects of *Pogo*, in other words, both amplified Kelly's topical satire and sometimes served as a type of satiric discourse in themselves. One can recognize those satiric qualities in Kelly's broad comedy by discussing his work within the frames of three lesser-known genres of satire: carnivalesque, cosmic, and deconstructive. A brief definition and discussion of each of these genres will lay a foundation for seeing the connections between the comedy and satire in Kelly's work.

The notion of carnivalesque satire is drawn from Mikhail Bakhtin's study of medieval carnival culture—the festive times of year in which people could enjoy unrestrained levity, mask-wearing, bodily function-oriented humor, and irreverent performances in which the fool traded places with the king. This form of earthy humor inverted class hierarchies, employed the grotesque as a challenge to societal norms, and challenged repressive social customs that denied corporeal pleasure and psychological release. It was also dialogical, allowing the "low" to speak out of turn or to openly criticize the high and powerful.

There was an ideological "ambivalence" to this folk humor in its original contexts, however, in that it simultaneously denied and revived that which it ridiculed, and acted as a release valve, reinforcing social norms once the festival had ended (Bakhtin, *Rabelais* 13). Nevertheless, Bakhtin recognized within this brand of folk humor (that continued to thrive in other forms of entertainment over the centuries) a persistent libratory power. In his words, the laughter that the carnival provokes

> purifies from dogmatism, from the intolerant and the petrified; it liberates from fanaticism and pedantry, from fear and intimidation, from didacticism, naïveté and illusion, from the single meaning, the single level, from sentimentality. (Bakhtin, *Rabelais* 123)

If one moves ahead to early to mid-twentieth-century American society—the context within which Kelly operated—it is also possible that these liberating powers far outweighed carnivalesque comedy's conservative tendencies; specifically, the flexibility of class strata, identity construction, and social debate within American society allowed for the effects of the carnival to linger beyond the irreverent moment or text.

It may seem like a stretch to identify this brand of medieval humor with *Pogo*—a twentieth-century comic strip—but as I will illustrate in this chapter, the dialogical spirit, irreverent slapstick, and subversive treatment of ideological dogmatism are all present in Kelly's work. Moreover, Kelly's medium was in many ways a mid-century carrier of vestiges of that carnival culture. To explain, as Bakhtin traced the cultural discourse of the carnivalesque into the modern world, he suggested that physical carnival sites gave way to imaginary worlds like those found in the sprawling, rowdy, dialogical novels created by politically independent writers. By engaging with these fictional, irreverent worlds, readers vicariously participated in imagined societal inversions and ritualistic mockery of all that was dogmatic and pious (Bakhtin, "Carnival and the Carnivalesque" 250). This description of irreverent, multi-voiced novels sounds similar to the early twentieth-century comics page with its multiethnic cast of characters, its sprawling narratives, its vivid caricatures of ridiculous social types, and its ambivalent inversions of the social order. Comic strips may have been even more purely carnivalesque than novels, in fact, because they were truly popular (an art of the people); they were lowbrow (the modern equivalent, arguably, of the folk status of real carnivals); and they were, at least in the medium's earliest years, before national syndication—or in rowdy holdouts like *Pogo*—a site where the democratic, dialogical mingling of voices, classes, and races was allowed.

Another type of satire used by Kelly is *Cosmic* satire. It differs from topical satire in its scope: topical satirists target specific historical figures, while cosmic satirists expose the universal, cyclical failings in society and human nature. If a comparison is made, the topical satirist is often seen as the superior social critic because of his or her courage in labeling evil and challenging the political leaders of the day. A philosophical maturity present in some cosmic satire, however, confers a weight and poignancy missing from social commentary that merely reacts to the news of the day. The cosmic satirist might acknowledge, for example, that individuals and groups cannot be the scapegoat for societal ills because the causes of those problems run too deep into intransigent human nature. As a result, the best cosmic work, according to the scholar John Tilton, is a

> larger, darker, more compassionate satire that transcends even the functions of the satire of attack or exposure: it creates a profound satiric vision, a vision ultimately tragic in its implications of man desperately—and unsuccessfully—trying to become what he thinks he ought to be. It probes the gap between the real and the ideal, reality and illusion. (Tilton 18)

While Kelly was always eager to take on truly deserving topical targets (most famously, Senator Joseph McCarthy), the bulk of his day-to-day satire tended to be broadly cosmic, highlighting the foibles in common social types, tracing cyclical patterns in society, and implicating readers in larger cultural ills. His most famous maxim, "We have met the enemy, and he is us," for example, seems to assert that a cosmic, self-reflective view is ultimately the best way to cope with (if not to solve) the chronic problems plaguing society. At other times Kelly reinforced his cosmic credentials, highlighting his realistic view of the incorrigibility of human nature ("very little we do will actually change the kind of people we are") and the cyclical nature of social ills. He stated, for example, that "a lot of people are extremely worried about the shape of the world, but I don't feel things are any worse now than they have been all through history. All *Pogo* tries to do is to satirize those elements in our society who seem to be overly worried about themselves" (Brandon 94; see also Kelly, "Pogo and Creator Walt Kelly Are Both for the People" 1). Kelly did not necessarily even make a distinction between the topical and the cosmic; in his mind the news of the day was simply a manifestation of the larger patterns he perceived:

> I finally came to understand that if I were looking for comic material, I would not ever have to look long. We people manufacture it every day in a hundred ways. The news of the day would be good enough . . . After all, it is pretty hard to walk past an unguarded gold mine and remain empty-handed." (Kelly, "Ten Ever-Lovin'" 41)

Finally, Kelly also embraced some of the darker, more bracing implications of a cosmic view of human behavior and society. He believed, for example, that "tragedy and humor are one and the same thing," and he had the skepticism of an existentialist when it came to "solving" problems or discerning "truth" (Kelly, "Unpublished Autobiographical Sketch 26). As a mid-century liberal-intellectual, he had a "preference for asking questions instead of inventing answers," and he was wary of dogmatic, overly confident formulas for correcting societal ills (Pells x).

These skeptical philosophical leanings point to the final category of satire featured in Kelly's work: deconstructive. An academic explanation of this brand of comedic satire is that it uses elaborate wordplay and metafictive self-reflexivity to "subvert hierarchies of value and to reflect suspiciously on all ways of making meaning, including its own" (Weisenberger 3). A more straightforward explanation is that it is a comedic-satiric mode that exhibits a healthy skepticism toward the stability of language, eschews efforts to identify truth with a capital T, and emphasizes the subjective nature of human perception. *Pogo* is deconstructive on two levels. First, its aggressive use of verbal slapstick—malapropisms, neologisms, dialect games, and miscommunications—emphasizes the unreliability of words as carriers of stable meaning. On a broader philosophical level, those verbal high jinks also point to the varied ways individuals perceive the world and emphasize the general need to tolerate ideological heterogeneity. Second, Kelly is consistently self-reflexive in the construction of his work, always acknowledging his own hand in the creation of the text and its meanings through playful metafictive devices. These acknowledgments include the characters talking about their construction as figures in a fictional setting (figures 2.1 and 2.2), as well as visual games that point to the artificial conventions of cartooning and comic strips. That self-reflexivity could be described as self-deconstruction— the self-awareness that should be a precondition for any satirist wanting to legitimately deconstruct or satirize other texts and discourses circulating in the culture at large (one must be willing to reflect in critical ways on one's own intentions and methods it seems, before applying the same critical lens to other creators and their texts or discourses).

Figure 2.1: Walt Kelly, "Sh!" *Pogo*, 7 February 1952.

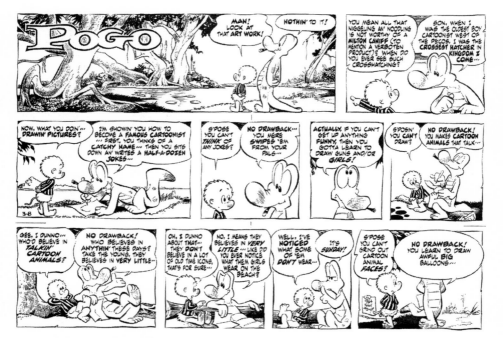

Figure 2.2: Walt Kelly, "Man! Look at that art work!" *Pogo*, 8 March 1964.

One might assume that such a thorough distrust of all claims to stable truth and perception would result in a brand of satire with a relativistic nihilism. In the hands of a social critic with a deeply humanistic streak such as Kelly, nevertheless, it retained a strong moral orientation. For example, his work still quietly championed the golden rule, eschewed any form of hypocrisy, and deplored scapegoating, racism, and misuses of power and authority. So although Kelly's desconstructive strategy prohibited elaborate alternative rules and verities, it did hold on to a stable center in terms of human behavior—and performed the arguably moral work of deconstructing some of the false moralities of mid-century American society. There is a cosmic timelessness to this strategy as well;

Kelly models for readers and satirists of any historical moment how one can use the tools of comedy to raze to the ground flawed moral structures, preparing the foundation, perhaps, for more stable ideologies to replace them.

The Comedy of *Pogo*

In light of this expanded view of the brands of satire at work in *Pogo*, one can examine the comedy in his text more accurately and appreciatively, seeing the interconnectedness of various comedic and satiric tools. To begin, there is no denying that Kelly did have some weaknesses as a comedian; like any cartoonist delivering strips on a daily basis, year after year, he could misfire occasionally with an especially lame pun, a contrived punch line, or a passage of cloying sweetness. Nevertheless, in contrast to other comic strips, *Pogo* consistently delivered satisfying verbal and visual entertainment. In addition, the strip was practically as baroque as a Rubens painting in its comedic complexity if one compares it to the typical, minimalist, gag-driven comic strip of today. Consider, for example, a sampling of what Kelly offered to his readers on a daily basis: an evocative Southern swamp setting charged with resonant narrative codings drawn from trickster tales and pastoral comedies; a sprawling cast of characters based on both classic comedic character templates and contemporary social types; vaudeville-style visual slapstick; multivocal wordplay featuring puns, malapropisms, dialect, Freudian slips, and deconstructive miscommunications; and humor that not only delivered consistently funny punch lines, but also featured situational comedy, character-driven gags, and folk-wise, philosophical ruminations.

The Setting of *Pogo*

To get a handle on this complexity, one can first take a panoramic view of the strip's setting. Exploring the narrative and symbolic functions of Kelly's swamp, in fact, helps to establish a foundation for understanding other aspects of Kelly's work such as character construction, story patterns, and satiric methods. In typical self-effacing fashion, Kelly often downplayed the significance of his strip's stories taking place in the rural South in the 1890s. For example, he asserted that he chose an earlier era "for humorous rather than nostalgic reasons . . . [and simply because he] always thought those guys with starched collars, cheroots and big hats were naturally funny, and even as relics they deserve a little notice" (Crinklaw 5). He also readily admitted that he had never actually been to a swamp in the South before creating the strip (other than seeing one on a train ride through Georgia), and he would talk about the regional setting as if it were purely arbitrary: "The only thing that inspired me toward an involvement with the Southern swampland, was my sincere conviction that people are universally frail. It struck me perhaps that Southerners as a much-maligned people would not mind being a little more downtrodden . . ." (Kelly, "Aesop Takes to the Swamp" 114). In sum, he was unhelpfully flippant about his level of thought or effort in constructing the site's Southern codings; his jokey comments in a letter to *Life* magazine in 1952 typify this attitude: "I've just sort of air-conditioned the place and taken out the mosquitoes" (Kelly, "Letter to the Editor").

Still, in a fashion similar to Mark Twain, Kelly's coy denials of deeper layers of meaning often belie an unusual level of thoughtful intention. He let slip once, for example, that he thought a swamp setting was symbolically useful because it is "a last frontier, a proper setting for American fairy tales" (Kelly, "Aesop Takes to the Swamp" 114). Were he completely forthcoming, he might have added that this swamp was part of a fictionally constructed Southern landscape that had already accrued layers of resonant meaning from earlier literary treatments of the region's dynamics relating to class, race, and politics. Indeed, it was a "proper" setting and time period for his purposes because within the cultural imagination at mid-twentieth century, the South of the late nineteenth century had taken on mythic, resonant qualities that allowed readers to test their values and ideologies with some allegorical distance. As a fairy-tale frontier beyond the reach of suburban America, it could have operated for readers as a place separated by time and space, a backwoods microcosm where modern ideologies could be tested against the pastoral ideals of community, folk wisdom, and organic tolerance and equality.

In unpacking these meanings, one must first acknowledge that Kelly was venturing into semiotically rich, but problematic territory when he chose to set his comedy in a mythic Southern landscape. He may have referred to a Southern swamp as a "frontier," but the term is not entirely useful or accurate if one considers the role frontiers played in the American cultural imagination during the mid-twentieth century. In the entertainment industries, notions of frontier evoked Western landscapes that were supposedly "innocent" and raw, waiting to accrue history and meaning, serving as fresh sites where American Adams and Eves could prove themselves exceptional. Those mythic qualities did not match the reality of the land, of course—real sites where tragic and epic histories had unfolded, and where violent conflicts over race and class had occurred; but for narrative purposes in genre entertainment, such as popular Western films, nevertheless, those notions of innocence and openness remained useful. In contrast, Southern settings often took on fatigued, nostalgic, and even Gothic meanings. History had already happened there; purportedly idyllic ways of rural and genteel life had come and gone in this region; and serious, cyclical mistakes had been made in Southern societies.

Given those foundational codings, rural settings in the South served two primary symbolic functions in the national imagination from the late nineteenth century onwards. First, to signify a Gothic backwater in the American body: a vestige of a corrupt antebellum South; a land that the modern world forgot; a place where poor white families wallowed in dysfunction and resisted progressive movement on issues of race and gender. The second coding was seemingly more positive, but perhaps equally reductive: as a site for nostalgic and romanticized views of a lost and authentic rural life. In the most racist iterations of this second use (such as in sentimental literature or the most two-dimensional forms of blackface entertainment), the audience could revel in a lost preindustrial paradise where "the sun shines bright" and "the darkies are gay" and "de time is neber dreary" (Strausbaugh 118). In more positive versions, such as those found in country music and the blues, the site could simply evoke notions of family or community that had been lost as the mechanisms of the modern world forced a rural-to-urban migration, displacing folk cultures with consumer culture and mass entertainment.

While elements of all of these ideologically loaded uses of a Southern setting are at work in Kelly's comic strip, his setting ultimately aligned with more progressive possibilities. First, the fact that Kelly set his strip in the 1890s rather than the antebellum South helped to make the stories less regressively nostalgic and racially problematic. I say *less* rather than *completely*, because despite Kelly's assertion otherwise, there is still some nostalgia at work in the strip. For example, his treatment of the Reconstruction era does provide an imaginative escape into an idyllic, pre-modern society even though the real South in the 1890s was plagued with disenfranchisement, lynchings, and social disruptions caused by the mass exodus of poor rural families migrating to Northern industrial centers. Kelly's nostalgia for this period and place, however, was less about the denial of those real troubles, than it was about an imaginative, pastoral alternative to the overly mechanized, harried, and categorized life of mid-century corporate America. The slightly removed time and setting of the strip also functioned nicely as an allegorical distancing device. For example, just as Billy Wilder's choice to place his cross-dressing comedy *Some Like It Hot* in the 1920's Jazz Age allowed 1950s audiences to question rigid gender identities of their own time with some comfortable distance, Kelly's use of the 1890s allowed him to satirize contemporary politics and social life with similarly layered boldness.

Kelly also transcended the most simplistic codings attached to his Southern setting by combining the progressive characteristics from a number of literary/comedic traditions including the worlds of Aesopian fables, trickster tales, blackface minstrelsy, Freudian allegories, and pastoral comedies. One can first look to some of the deepest fairy tale-like qualities present in Kelly's comic world; these motifs are drawn from the long tradition of using animals in fables and fairy tales to represent "abstractions" of "human virtues and vices" in order to teach a "maxim, proverb, or moral lesson" (Wadsworth 1126). An animal allegory could serve several purposes in this Aesopian tradition. First, it could be a narrative sweetener. Listeners or readers might be captivated by the antics of the vivid animals, thus exposing themselves to a cautionary tale that they might otherwise ignore. Second, the allegorical layering allows the teller of the story to soften harsh depictions of human vice and folly that might be "unpleasant, even frightening if expressed directly" to young listeners or readers (Ritvo 90). These first two purposes have Jungian dimensions: the general strategy of addressing collective societal sicknesses by communicating dark lessons about human nature through resonant animal archetypes in a distilled, fairy tale-like structure (Jung 516). Finally, the traditional audience orientation of animal tales (playful stories for children), and the allegorical layering of fables, allowed some creators to fly beneath the cultural radar, using these stories as vehicles for social critique. In other words, "if open challenge is not permitted" in a society—as was the case for many writers and filmmakers of the early 1950s—then storytellers "will turn to irony, indirection, innuendo, allegory, fable—to the fictions of satire" (Griffin, p. 139).

There are elements of all of these purposes at work in Kelly's allegorical world. First, the lowly status of comic strips and the allegorically layered quality of *Pogo*'s human-animal community allowed Kelly to engage in pointed satire that editors and cultural guardians of the early 1950s (a particularly reactionary time in American culture and politics), might not have tolerated in a more direct form. And second, the comedic antics of the appealing animal characters acted as sweeteners for readers of all ages, giving Kelly opportunities to use his strip as a platform from which to moralize about some of the collective societal sicknesses of his time: xenophobia, scapegoating, and ideological dogmatism among other things.

Beyond this inheritance of the general functions of animal fables, Kelly's work was also a product of a particular intersection of cultural and economic forces in the late nineteenth century and early twentieth century that affected the contours of popularly produced animal allegories. First, Kelly explicitly tapped into the resonant meanings of African American trickster tales dating back to antebellum times that featured Southern rural settings in which anthropomorphized animals engaged in physical contests and wordplay. In their original iterations, these trickster worlds were largely naturalistic, featuring struggles between predator and prey, and stark themes about both the human capacity for evil and the resilience of oppressed peoples. The setting of trickster tales, in fact, were often incredibly harrowing—sites filled with "unrelieved hostility and danger, violence and cruelty, terror and revenge" (Bickley 137–38).

According to Lawrence Levine, these stories could be read as allegorical reflections of the strained dynamics between black and white cultures, with trickster figures (representing oppressed blacks) using folk wit and guile to fool larger predators (who stood in as symbols of a corrupt and hypocritical white culture). The hypocrisies of that dominant culture were often underscored when the trickster used the inherent foibles and vanities of their targets to bring them down—a comedic jujitsu of sorts. These stories had explicit political and cultural uses as well. Levine speculated they were part of a covert, layered counterdiscourse that resonated with African American slaves: they "encouraged trickery and guile; they stimulated the search for ways out of the system; they inbred a contempt for the powerful and an admiration for the perseverance and even the wisdom of the underman" (Levine 132).

But the rough edges and pointed political meanings of these tales were largely excised as the genre was appropriated and commodified in the late nineteenth and early twentieth centuries. First, during the Victorian or Gilded Age there was a general trend of softening animal fables drawn from Aesop, fairy tales, and folklore. This shift represented an upper middle class white preoccupation with glossing over the grittier aspects of life and looking away from difficult social issues, but it also may have been a reaction to the growing body of scientific knowledge about the harsh realities of a Darwinian natural world. One scholar explains that "as zoology brought animals and people closer together, real animals became inappropriate carriers of moral lessons. Only animals that had been humanized and sentimentalized could be admitted into Victorian nurseries as teachers" (Ritvo 90).

The most significant participant in that general process of gentrifying trickster tales in the United States during the Gilded Age was Joel Chandler Harris. Harris, a newspaperman working in Atlanta in the 1890s, appropriated and commodified these folktales, marketing them successfully as nursery readers for Anglo American homes across the country. The contents of the stories were gentrified too, creating a sentimental and patronizing view of African American culture and muting the stories' originally subversive meanings and uses. The most significant alteration to these stories was their orientation; Harris created a narrator, Uncle Remus, a passive, kind-hearted, former slave who remained devoted to his master after emancipation and spent his time sharing his storehouse of trickster tale wisdom with the privileged white children in the neighborhood. In sum, the original codings of the trickster's world—a primal struggle between dominant and slave cultures—were replaced in the Harris versions with nostalgic reflections on a quaint, decontextualized, Southern folk wisdom (Blair and Hill 271).

In the early twentieth century, syndicates and animation studios picked up the baton of commodifying and softening animal allegories and trickster tales. These entertainment companies were attracted to allegorical animal characters and settings because of the flexible, polysemic qualities of these texts: the anthropomorphic appeal of the characters and open-ended ability of the settings to symbolize human comedies and dramas in a slightly softened, allegorical fashion made them highly merchandisable and immensely profitable cultural products (Gordon 62, 75). The Disney writers and animators, of course, became the masters at this process. Starting in the 1930s, they capitalized on the broad appeal of anthropomorphized animal cartoons and pushed the settings of their stories even further from the stark naturalism of Aesopian or trickster tales and the dark, Jungian themes of traditional myths and fairy tales. Instead, the animals took on a rubbery, bourgeois cuteness, and the stories and settings were softened to the point that they rarely disturbed a child's imagination (unless one counts the death of Bambi's mother or the dancing Hippos' scene in *Fantasia*). As Richard Schickel, a Disney scholar explains, "wild things and wild behaviour were often made comprehensible [at Disney] by converting them into cuteness, mystery was explained with a joke, and terror was resolved by a musical cue or a discreet averting of the camera's eye from the natural processes" (Schickel 51–52). Those aesthetic, narrative, and musical choices resulted in entertainment that often robbed the adapted myths and folklore within the Disney canon of their potential to be complex and cautionary tales or ideologically subversive allegories.

As a result of Kelly's training at Disney, *Pogo*'s world bore traces of the studio's cutely contained aesthetic. Visually, for example, many of his characters had that dynamic, rubbery quality distinctive to Disney animation at mid-century, and the joke-driven arc of each day's installment sometimes conspired against the strip developing more poignant layers of meaning. Nevertheless, because Kelly was determined to harness his animal allegory to different purposes than those of his former employer—to creating unflinching satire on collective societal ills, rather than a sweetly packaged and bowdlerized adaptation of a classic fairy tale—the resemblance was only skin deep. It took Kelly several years, however, during his comic book phase, to figure out the best way to modify both his Disney aesthetic and his trickster tale borrowings to fit those ambitious, satiric objectives. For example, Kelly initially replicated Harris's softened trickster world in his *Animal Comics* series in unimaginative ways; Pogo and Albert spoke in a hammy version of an African American dialect, they were two-dimensionally cute and predictable in their trickster-oriented shenanigans, and the storylines did not generally venture beyond battles over cakes and hidden treasures.

In 1949, however, as Kelly entered into the medium of comic strips, his construction of meanings in his Southern swamp drew from templates and influences of a higher caliber such as regionalist humor, Freudian theory, vaudeville, late-period blackface, and pastoral comedies. Moving the swamp from comic books to comic strips, in fact, was critical to the expansion of the setting's semiotic possibilities. Because the newspaper comics page could be targeted to adults as well as children, and because it existed within the orbit of other journalistic crafts such as punditry, investigative reporting, and political cartooning, Kelly could infuse his setting with more complex literary and journalistic codings. For example, in the newspaper version of the strip, Kelly's use of Southern dialect became more deconstructively sophisticated, he addressed more complex and topical issues in the strip's comedy and satire, and his characters took on adult foibles and hypocrisies.

Some of these new methods and ingredients placed him within the heritage of regionalist humorists featured in late nineteenth-century newspapers who used rural voices and settings to comment on the practices and ideas of "modern" urban life and politics. They also aligned him with literary satirists such as Mark Twain (*The Adventures of Huckleberry Finn*) and Charles Chesnutt (the Uncle Julius "conjure tales"), who used rural dialects and mythic Southern sites in satiric ways. Twain and Chesnutt, in fact, had preceded Kelly in their use of trickster tale conventions for the construction of settings and storylines, but one can set them above mere appropriators such as Harris because of their higher level of satiric, political engagement with race and class issues in the South (and by allegorical extension, in the country at large). In addition to being more politically engaged than Harris, they were also more syncretic (creating wholly original works) and narratively ambitious (coding those trickster conventions into more naturalistic human comedies).

Returning to Kelly, one can see how his setting achieved, as it moved from one medium to another—and borrowed from these varied traditions—a composite and syncretized quality: the aesthetic shell of a Disneyesque, gentrified trickster's world, but the layered and serious codings of politically engaged literary satire. The adult orientation of Kelly's comic strip also allowed him to incorporate the comedic and satiric codings of the early nineteenth-century blackface world into his setting. For example, as the different social types in the community went about their daily business, Pogo, like a banjo-playing, leisure-loving minstrel character on the margins of the action, was able to deliver wry commentary on the foibles of human nature and society. Because the swamp featured anthropomorphized animals rather than real people, however, the overt racial codings of the blackface world were muted. But the dynamics of the genre remained intact, allowing the setting to feature both the comic themes of blackface (the fixations on food and love and humor derived from malapropisms, wordplay, and slapstick shenanigans) as well as the satiric layering of the most sophisticated versions of the form (the critiques of mainstream values from a wise fool's perspective). Finally, it could also evoke the deeper cultural resonance of the blackface setting: an imaginative escape from a suburbanized/corporatized 1950s culture into a simpler world with more "authentic" activities and pleasures.

The mature setting of the strip also added elements of the deep literary tradition of pastoralism (Mendelson 17). From Roman times, the themes and conventions of pastoral poetry and literature have allowed readers to escape into a "golden" rural age that was both a nostalgic escape from modern stresses as well as an allegorical site for testing out contemporary values and ideas. Shakespeare's comedy *As You Like It* is a classic example of those conventions at work. Within the story, political intrigues at court have forced educated members of the upper classes to retreat into the Forest of Arden where they live for a time as

Robin Hood's merry men or as the shepherds did in a lost golden age—making romance, enjoying music, and engaging in philosophical banter. Living within this rural idyll allows the main characters, Orlando and Rosalind, to enjoy the liberating power of carnivalesque comedy—false identities, cross-dressing, social inversions, and so forth—in the name of testing out both "old order" and "new order" notions about romance, gender relations, and family/class hierarchies. The resulting ideological orientation of the play is cautiously progressive, one that melds elements of the past and the present, rejecting the worst ideas from both worlds and fusing the best (Snyder 232, 237, 241).

Those pastoral themes and tones gradually supplanted many of the grittier, more desperate trickster tale dynamics of Kelly's setting as the strip began to address more explicitly the psychological needs of its core audience—college students and liberal intellectuals in the 1950s. In the earliest versions of the comic, Pogo had to evade the real danger of being eaten by predators; as the strip matured, his challenges became less physically dire (no animalistic struggles for literal survival), but more philosophically complex (how to live a peaceful life in the face of consumer and political cultures that encroach on a community). As a result, playful, open-ended debates involving elaborate wordplay became the focus of the strip's action, and Pogo started behaving more like a laid-back, lute-playing, wise fool from a pastoral comedy than a desperate trickster trying to figure out how to save his own skin. Indeed, with rarely any real danger present or serious consequences at stake, Pogo was content to ask playful ques-

Figure 2.3: "After all that ex-citements . . . ," *Pogo*, 30 July 1952.

tions and offer wry commentary, never getting riled up about discovering the Truth (in a definitive, universal sense) or deciding on an ambitious plan of action. The extended community, too, liberated from the life and death battles of a naturalistic world, were free to spend their time the way pastoral characters would—enjoying an abundance of food, lazing about, singing, dancing, engaging in carnivalesque comedy, and speculating about the meanings of love (Figure 2.3).

The literary artificiality of the peace and nostalgia within the pastoral world also allowed Kelly to distance himself from a less-admirable type of nostalgia—one that might forward an image of the Reconstruction South free of lynchings, racial strife, and other festering animosities (Dennison 439). Indeed, Kelly was somehow able to avoid depicting those gritty realities within his pastoral frame, while still obliquely addressing their chronic existence through his satiric attacks on McCarthyism and other divisive ideologies. In sum, the pastoral motifs in the strip matched the psychological needs of a liberal readership "wary of messianic dogmas, apocalyptic thinking," and that had a "preference for asking questions instead of inventing answers" (Pells x). Indeed, the imaginative escape into a pastoral world where old order and new order ideas could be explored without an overlay of partisan rancor must have been a welcome escape for newspaper readers overwhelmed by the shrill debates of the McCarthy era.

Finally, Kelly also addressed the needs of his core audience by replacing the trickster world codings with the more culturally current dynamics of Freudian theory and existential questioning. For example, as Albert and Pogo began to behave more like adult characters in a pastoral comedy (rather than opponents in a trickster tale struggle), they stepped back from their animalistic impulses in order to speculate about the psychological impulses that drive appetites and obsessions. Albert thus became a neurotic brand of predator, forever engaging in unconscious slips of word and behavior, or sublimating his old appetites into cigar-chomping and various manic hobbies. Furthermore, darker, existentialist tones emerged in Pogo's interactions with Porky Pine, the resident malcontent in the swamp. As the other characters went about their carnivalesque craziness, Porky Pine reflected on the futility of human endeavor or the meaninglessness of any isolated debate. Pogo rarely had a positivistic rebuttal to this dour commentary—a sign that he was skeptical of overly confident ideologies himself—but he did prove, in existentialist fashion through his actions, that a life of purposeful integrity could fill much of the void left by the false moralities of society.

In closing this discussion of the setting's meanings, it is interesting to note that Kelly ultimately visited the Okefenokee Swamp in person in 1955, drawing a significant amount of media attention to the excursion. While he did spend time with the locals and studied some of the flora and fauna up close, his impressions of the experience seemed to be filtered through his own romantic expectations. For example, he stated that,

The real Okefenokee is every bit as unreal as the unreal Okefenokee whose headwaters rise in my skull . . . These sounds seemed to make the peace of the deep woods all the more serene . . . The dark-tunneled corridors of trees, reflecting their grace in the winding waterways, gave promise of hidden mysterious wonders. Waiting there, somewhere, everywhere, were all the delights usually known only to small boys and old men. There was peace, and with it, excitement. It was as much fun as lying on your stomach on a summer hillside and watching ants among the grasses . . . What this world [modern society] needs is more natural swamps and fewer man-made ones disguised as civilization. (Lockwood A2)

Kelly also recalled meeting some of the locals and finding there had been battles between developers and conservationists over construction projects that would have robbed the area of its wild qualities. Kelly was relieved to hear about the literal preservation of the animals and environment, but he also could not resist incorporating that drama into his own fantasy of an enchanted island hidden somewhere in the depths of the swamp—a place once inhabited by Indians, and now in need of protection from the ravages of progress: "Naturally I treasured this opinion [that conservation should trump development] for it meant that the swamp might continue as a wild game refuge forever and that a certain island in there wouldn't be covered with oil derricks. I went to sleep that night in the Hotel Ware in Waycross thinking of the Enchanted Island, which was still my secret . . ." (Kelly, "Okefenokee" 32).

There is nostalgia in these passages, though of a generalized and innocent variety about lost wilderness, rather than the racially loaded recollections of an idealized antebellum South (the kind that Harris favored). Pastoral notions are also on display, emphasizing the softening effect of the untainted natural world on the human psyche. The island motif, in particular, recalls classical pastoral themes of enchanted islands like Cythera where the golden age of peaceful shepherds lives on while the rest of the world marches into a rancorous and over-populated modern era. And finally, Kelly affirms that his core intentions in using this Southern hinterland is to create an allegorical site and imaginative escape from, or antidote for, the ills of a frenetic mid-century society.

Storylines

Comics readers today are accustomed to seeing only a handful of genres on the funnies page. First, there are the gag strips, which feature three or four spare frames, minimally constructed characters, and a one-two-three-punch line construction. This type of strip, typified by *Garfield*, dominates the funnies page because the diminished size of strips today allows only for the type of comedy that can take place in postage stamp-sized boxes. One can also find creaky, old, earnest continuity strips (like *Mary Worth*) on the current comics page, but they are a dying breed, given the difficulty of delivering a daily dose of soap opera in so few words and images. Finally, there are the few truly ambitious strips such as *Doonesbury*, *The Boondocks*, or *Get Fuzzy* that feature an ongoing narrative, a complex cast of characters, and comedy or satire that is verbally rich and sometimes challenging. The diminished conditions of the comic strip page conspires against the health of these strips too; in order to make their generous dialogue legible, the creators are often forced to draw only talking heads crammed beneath large speech balloons.

Given the low expectations today's readers have thus developed for the typical comic strip, what a pleasurable discovery it must be to find a work like *Pogo* that features such riches: generous verbal slapstick; a huge cast of engaging characters; an ongoing narrative that reads like a sprawling comic novel; topical satire; and an engaging aesthetic world, replete with fully constructed backdrops, and the complete figures of dynamically drawn characters. That comics in the 1950s were printed at more than twice the size they are today, helps to explain, in part, how Kelly was able to achieve this complexity. But even with the advantage of additional space, not all comics creators during Kelly's time were that ambitious—especially in terms of elaborate storylines. There are only a few comedic strips in the history of the medium, in fact, that can compare in terms of narrative richness; these might include *Bringing Up Father*, *Popeye*, *Gasoline Alley*, *Little Orphan Annie*, *Li'l Abner*, *Bloom County*, *Doonesbury*, and *For Better or Worse*.

Kelly's ambitious storylines deliver comedy on two levels: first, as daily vignettes, and second, as sprawling narrative arcs made up of several weeks worth of strips. The comedy in Kelly's daily episodes differs from the gag strips of today in that he infuses them with humorous payoffs throughout, rather than the single punch line at the end. Because Kelly's characters—all of them rich with neuroses and distinctive ways of speaking and talking—continually misunderstand or speak past each other, almost every frame in Kelly's daily installments contains a pun, malapropism, or funny misunderstanding (see example in Figure 2.4). The final frame often delivers the biggest punch line, of course, but

Figure 2.4: Walt Kelly, "Where is the candidate?" *Pogo*, 8 July 1952.

the reader is more likely to smile throughout the four frames than simply to guffaw at the end. In fact, because so much of the humor is character-driven and situationally constructed, it almost appears as if there were no author behind the strip's shenanigans. The strip seems to write itself, in other words, as these three-dimensionally vivid characters intersect, erupting in inevitable verbal and physical slapstick.

Bill Watterson described *Pogo* as "the last of the Enjoy the Ride strips," because each installment is embedded within a flowing, unpredictable narrative featuring a comedic richness uncommon to most comics (Dusser 136). While the *Pogo* characters do not age or change dramatically over the course of the strip's long run (the strip is like a classic television sitcom in this respect), they do engage in a variety of elaborate traditions and activities that suggest the flow of seasons and life in a small community. Within that seasonal structure, Kelly introduces weeks-long comic stories that have the rough arc of a comic play or sitcom: first, a crisis to start things off (usually something trivial that is treated in the classic burlesque mode as a dilemma of monumental proportions); second, farcical developments involving elaborate verbal and physical slapstick that heighten the stakes; next, chaotic efforts to resolve the crisis, which include carnivalesque zaniness such as gratuitous pratfalls, mistaken identities, or bungled plans; and finally, a vague resolution or denouement before the next plot begins.

Because Kelly was not tied to constructing stories that had to hold together as a tight, stand-alone text, there is an open-ended, meandering quality to these episodes. As Kelly described it, the stories flow along the "line of least resistance, just like water trickling downhill and following the easiest path" (Gerson 2). Watterson admired that sense of fluidity and tried to emulate Kelly's convoluted narratives in which "the stories wandered down back roads, got lost, and forgot their destinations" (*C & H 10th Anniversary* 17–18).

One reason that Kelly may have written stories in this loose, flowing fashion is that it made his job easy: the characters' personalities dictate the ebb and flow of the action, and there is no need to engage in elaborate plotting. There are also comedy-writing advantages to that lack of structure; stories, for example, can unravel with an improvisational freshness, and there is room for inspired free association or comedic serendipity. Finally, philosophical justifications are also at work in this style of storytelling. Kelly's worldview—one that tolerates ideological heterogeneity, existential uncertainty, and the vagaries of random fortune—can be expressed much more accurately through a messy narrative structure than through a tightly scripted plot. In this respect, his stories stand in contrast to the pat, sentimental arcs of Disney stories. Kelly disliked the neat, happy conclusions of Hollywood stories, in fact: he refused to put them in his own fictional world because "there are no payoffs in life" (Gerson 2).

On a theoretical level, the construction of a chaotic, multi-voiced narrative that resists reductive conclusions also places Kelly's work within postmodernist paradigms and Bakhtinian notions of heteroglossic literature—theoretical frames that further aid in showing the interconnections between his comedic methods and satiric intentions. Kelly's storytelling could be described as postmodern for several reasons: first, the narrative is propelled by multiple voices and perspectives, reflecting the emerging complexity of cultural debates at the dawn of the postmodern cultural era; second, the stories were open-ended and entropic, continually spiraling away from the tight structure that marked traditional melodramas—or modernist literature that flowed from a single voice and was designed to carry a core of stable truth or profundity; and finally, they favored ambiguity and terminal questioning over formulaic conclusions and answers. In a Bakhtinian frame, this multivocal complexity places Kelly within a deeper cultural tradition of sprawling, carnivalesque literature or comedy such as the writings of Rabelais or the rowdy performances featured at traditional folk festivals or carnivals. Like carnivalesque comedy, Kelly's stories feature social inversions, mask wearing, earthy physical humor, and a general irreverence toward all that is serious and earnest in mainstream culture. Furthermore, Kelly's emphasis on so many competing voices and perspectives in his storytelling (even assigning each character an individualized typeface) also connects his work to those sprawling nineteenth- and early twentieth-century novels that Bakhtin conjectured were the new carriers of the carnival tradition. Kelly's work, like those dialogical texts, meshes primary "narration, secondary voices, different genres, oral everyday speech . . . [and] stylistic, individualized speeches of characters" (Bakhtin 263). In sum, the only other mid-century texts that compare favorably to Kelly's in terms of this dialogical complexity are novels such as Heller's *Catch-22* or Kerouac's *On the Road*. The fact that Kelly achieved this on the highly mediated and narratively restricted funnies page is astounding.

Verbal Slapstick in *Pogo*

Looking more closely at the verbal humor in *Pogo*, one can recognize a number of literary influences that shape the playful, dialogical flavor of Kelly's comedy; by his own acknowledgment, these figures include Samuel Clemens, Stephen Leacock, Lewis Carroll, James Joyce, James Thurber, and A. A. Milne (Kelly, "Unpublished Autobiographical Sketch" 26). Kelly borrows devices from each: vernacular dialect from Clemens; distinctive small-town archetypes with funny worldviews and speech patterns from Leacock; meandering, absurdist allegory from Carroll; an inventive, heteroglossic complexity from Joyce; an inspired parodic silliness from Thurber; and a wryly gentle, character-driven humor from Milne. Kelly fuses these influences in highly original ways, of course—adding Freudian word games, neologisms, and malapropisms to the mix. The resulting, syncretic mélange helps establish Kelly as perhaps the best verbal comedian to ever thrive on the comics page. The comics historian R. C. Harvey asserts that

> Among the most individual comic strip creations are the achievements of George
> Herriman and Walt Kelly. These cartoonists are the lyrical clowns of the medium.
> Their creations were bursts of poetry. Poetry in the literary tradition is a kind of
> word game: its great appeal lies in the sound and rhythm of the language and in
> the nuance and interplay of metaphor and meaning. Poetry is a game for the mind,
> an intellectual sport. And the creations of Herriman and Kelly—*Krazy Kat* and
> *Pogo*—are likewise divertissements for the mind. Their humor is intellectual rather
> than intestinal: we laugh in our heads not in our bellies. (Harvey 171)

While agreeing with the core point of Harvey's judgment—that Kelly is one the
great lyrical clowns of the medium—one can quibble with his view of poetry
(and, by extension, with Kelly's verbal gymnastics) as purely intellectual modes
of communication. The best poetry often appeals to readers precisely because
the sound and rhythm is tied so directly to physical sensations; it often bypasses
the logic of dry, essayistic thinking, and hits us with a physical and emotional
punch. To be more accurate, Kelly's *ideological vision* speaks to the mind powerfully because it was often delivered in a poetic shell that appealed to the ear,
heart, and intuition. One can also classify Kelly's verbal tools more specifically,
pointing out that the brands of poetry that Kelly employs are much earthier
than the conventional verse one would encounter in a traditional literature
course. These irreverent brands of poetry include inventive punning, doggerel,
malapropisms, carnivalesque free association, slips, and dialect humor.

The seeming lowbrow silliness of this kind of language play makes it an easy
target for readers or critics who favor, in Cicero's delineation, the "wit of matter"
(joking based on clever stories and sophisticated insights), over the "wit of form"
(the mere playing with words and puns) (Bremmere and Roodenburg 4). For example, Walter Ong, one of the earliest writers in the 1950s to consider Kelly's
work as a serious art form, concedes that Kelly's comedy represents a "popular-
ization of the high modernism of James Joyce and Gertrude Stein," and allows
that it could qualify as a type of "automatic writing for the common man." But he
also complains about the "infantilism" in Kelly's language play—the continual
chuckling over linguistic blunders like "nature's screetures" that children often

Figure 2.5: "Uncle Porky, was Venus the Goddess of Love?" *Pogo*, 11 November 1966.

commit to the secret delight of their parents (Ong 87, 100). A bit of detached dabbling in *Pogo* might reinforce Ong's views, giving one the impression that the strip often lacks serious substance or purpose—that Kelly is merely a clever punster, engaging in gratuitous verbal fireworks. A more sustained reading of the strip, however, suggests that Kelly's "wit of form"—his word games—are, despite their surface silliness, an integral part of the serious "matter" in *Pogo* (see Figure 2.5). In other words, Kelly's devotion to relentless verbal jokiness is not only critical to the effectiveness of his satire, it often *is* the satire.

A brief definition and additional examples of some of these verbal tools at work in *Pogo* will lay a foundation for discussing their philosophical meanings and satiric uses. To begin, much of the verbal humor in *Pogo* is based on punning, the exploitation of words with similar spellings or sounds, but which have different meanings, for comic—and often satiric—effect. Puns have a bad reputation in our comic culture because of their association with elaborate story jokes that culminate in a contrived, one-note punch line; but in the hands of Kelly, or other early to mid twentieth-century masters of the craft such as the Marx Brothers, the sheer number, variety, and creativity of the puns in their work creates a cascading, comic effect. One could define this strategy as saturation comedy: some of the jokes hit the mark, others miss, but the cumulative effect is one of irreverent hilarity. Moreover, the relentlessness of the wordplay in the best saturation comedy takes on philosophical dimensions, suggesting the foundational instability of language.

The raw material of wordplay in *Pogo* also includes neologisms, doggerel, malapropisms, and Freudian slips. Neologisms are simply made-up words that Kelly employed for two reasons: their honesty, and their capacity to surprise, providing a release of pent-up psychological energy. One of Kelly's operating rules in this practice was the avoidance of sweetly artificial made-up words that were "just a little wet" such as "Putty-tat." Instead, he believed the word should be based on child-like efficiency (more direct than pretentious adult jargon), visceral appeal (it is fun to say), and humorous proximity to a real word ("catterpiggle" instead of caterpillar) (Kelly, "Ka-Platz" 8–10). That last requirement is associated with the freedom and naïveté with which children use words. Adults can laugh at mishearings and misspeakings of children, but they might also envy a child's detachment from the rules of proper speech. In a Freudian sense, there is a pleasurable sense of relief and surprise in defying the small rules of accurate grammar or precise word choice. That sense of release is even more acute when the neologism is a made-up swear word—a common device in *Pogo*. For example, in seeing/hearing a word such as "Rowrbazzle!" the reader enjoys the mild jolt of carnivalesque irreverence associated with funny profanity and the honesty and accuracy of a new word suited for a specific moment.

A word such as *rowrbazzle* also points to Kelly's clever use of onomatopoeia. While early comic strip artists in general are credited with making onomato-

Figure 2.6: Walt Kelly, illustration accompanying the article "Ka-Platz: The Delight in the Unexpected" (reprinted in Pluperfect *Pogo*, pp. 7–11).

poeia into a high (or rather, appropriately "low"?) art form—even contributing new words to the cultural lexicon—Kelly took it to even greater heights, adding a layer of deconstructive absurdity to the practice. For example, the first part of *rowrbazzle* sounds like a roar of anger, but the second half is so silly and surprising that it draws attention to the constructedness of onomatopoeiac effects. Other examples of this metafictive use of neologisms include a trumpet blaring the sound "Waukeeegan!" or a shotgun registering the crack of "Terre Haute!" (Figure 2.6).

Doggerel, another verbal device employed by Kelly, is light verse of a humorous and sometimes bawdy nature. In Kelly's case, that bawdiness is replaced with the inventive neologisms and blanket irreverence one finds in song parodies created by rowdy school children. The lyrics in these songs also resemble a type of vaudevillian scat—free-flowing, jazz-like lyrics with hammy, old-time

Figure 2.7: Walt Kelly, "Oh, deck us all . . . ," illustration accompanying the article "Ka-Platz: the Delight in the Unexpected" (reprinted in Pluperfect *Pogo*, pp. 7–11).

comedy connotations. Kelly enjoyed performing the lyrics himself, using his own "boozy Irish baritone" on a recording of his compositions, "The Songs of Pogo" ("Walt Kelly," *Wikipedia* entry). The general carnivalesque irreverence of Kelly's songs also carry a pointed satiric punch at times. For example, Kelly's famous parody of the holiday song, "Deck the Halls" (see Figure 2.7) is meant to mock the over-saturation and commercialization of Christmas songs and sentiments in mid-century culture. Kelly describes his motivation for writing the lyrics, saying, "The radio-TV sandblast of carols for commercial purposes grated not only the ear but the sensitivities. So about 1949 I had the characters parody a carol. The attempt was to parody the use of carols [rather than the content of traditional carols]" (Kelly, "Ka-Platz" 11).

Whereas doggerel is an intentionally playful distortion of language, malapropisms are unintentional misuses of words—instances where one accidentally substitutes one word for another with a similar sound. Traditional comic types who employ malapropisms, like Archie Bunker in *All in the Family*, *Zip Coon* in blackface comedies, or Albert in *Pogo*, are often uneducated buffoons (Figure 2.8). Their desire to appear educated, combined with their assertively ignorant opinions, trip them up, causing them to commit these verbal blunders. The resulting humor is usually meant to be at their expense, but malapropisms can

Figure 2.8: Walt Kelly, "Hard for me to figger . . . ," *Pogo*, 11 August 1953.

also be a device used by tricksters and fools; they pretend to be ignorant so that they can use words creatively, making a satiric point that appears like a slip, but which is subversively intentional. Freud calls these jokes tendentious (they have a sly "purpose" as opposed to "innocent" verbal jokes); he believes they bring pleasure by enabling us to evade obstacles to our expression of repressed hostility—and thus the comedy becomes a type of shared aggression toward the satiric target.

In *Pogo*, malapropisms sometimes indicate two or more characters are not communicating effectively. The reader of the comic strip can see that one character is talking and thinking about one thing, while the other is on a wholly different page. There is dramatic irony to be enjoyed in seeing this confusion unfold, and Kelly communicates the essential instability of language through such comic misunderstandings (Figure 2.9).

Figure 2.9: Walt Kelly, "The pony died!" *Pogo*, 20 October 1950.

Closely related to malapropisms are Freudian slips (or parapraxis)—errors in speech that reveal repressed feelings or ideas. In *Pogo* some of the malapropisms qualify as psychological slips or burps. For example, when Albert misunderstands other characters and replaces their words with his own words and meanings, he is often revealing his hidden desires or prejudices. He continually, unintentionally (but revealingly) warps the language so that situations conform to his wishes and appetites. Deacon Mushrat also commits verbal slips at times, revealing the hypocritical or dogmatic thinking of his judgmental and rigid social type. Occasionally these comic errors of speech in *Pogo* take on a societal or cosmic quality, as if the character is not just giving voice to his or her own peculiar repressions, but also revealing a systemic flaw or blind spot within a sort of collective cultural unconscious. The individual committing the slip can thus engage in a type of truth-telling, using the pose of the unconscious fool to deliver the uncomfortable barb.

Looking at the deeper cultural meanings and uses of carnivalesque word games in *Pogo*, one can recognize their venerable tradition in European folk culture. Although verbal slapstick was long considered lowbrow by representatives of the official culture, it thrived in folk traditions in the form of limericks, doggerel, and the jokes of jesters and fools. It also took center stage during times of carnival, when irreverence, irrationality, and earthy humor trumped the earnest discourses of the official culture. Shakespearean comedies illustrate nicely how the principal master of those verbal games, the fool, speaks a type of "nonsense" that is often more truthful and sane than the composed, but hypocritical or self-delusional speech of the main characters. Moreover, the Shakespearean jester is often charged with the task of using word games to test the validity of others' speech, or the substance of their character; they are "Touchstones" (like the character of that name in *As You Like It*) that determine the purity of the matter they encounter. Some of Shakespeare's fools even take this critical use of nonsense language into deconstructive territory. Feste, in *Twelfth Night*, for example, speculates about the "wanton nature" of sentences and the instability of "rascal" words. He also acts as a "corrupter of words" in order to highlight how a delusional self-seriousness or devotion to rigid literalness prevents characters such as Malvolio from accurately reading traditional texts (such as "love" letters). In sum, Feste's "wit of form" turns out to be more critical and incisive than the "wit of matter" favored by characters less foolish; as he says, "Better a witty fool, than a foolish wit."

All the characters in *Pogo* contribute to the dialogical mayhem in the strip, and their malapropisms, neologisms, and misunderstandings help illustrate the instability of language. The core ideological point drawn from this relentless verbal silliness is that the univocal dogmatism of political parties and some religious traditions is too simplistic (and sometimes coercive) given the way individuals see and experience the world differently—and the way that people inevitably fail to communicate the truth they experience in a stable way. Kelly is satirizing through his verbal slapstick, in other words, the official voices of 1950s culture and politics that used language in authoritative and punishing ways: creating rigid categories, denouncing departures from an enforced consensus, or forcing individuals to engage in testimony against allegedly subversive peers.

Kelly's well known McCarthy-targeted episodes from the early 1950s are good examples of this satiric point at work. These strips highlight the contrasting ways that Malarkey (McCarthy) and most of the other citizens of the swamp use language. Whereas the longtime residents of the swamp engage in relatively playful and harmless misunderstandings in a democratically dialogical culture, Malarkey enters the swamp and tries to use language as a weapon, insisting on literal meanings, twisting others' words to incriminate them, and forcing the citizens to take binding, restrictive oaths. The strip in Figure 2.10 illustrates nicely his self-serving manipulation of definitions, labels, free speech, oaths, and legal documents.

Joseph Heller's novel *Catch-22*, another mid-century work of resonant satire that exhibited the foundational caution and skepticism of existentialist thinking, makes a similar satiric point about the misuses of language through its contrast between relentless punning and irreverent joking on one side, and bureau-

Figure 2.10: Walt Kelly, *Pogo*, "How can I be insubordinate?" 7 May 1953.

cratically abusive uses of words and texts on the other. Specifically, Yossarian's wise-fool word games (the twisting of other's words to test their substance, or his irreverent treatment of official letters and texts) stands in stark contrast to the manipulative and essentially corrupt ways military leaders, such as Col. Cathcart, and entrepreneurs, such as Milo Minderbinder, use language. Yossarian's insane joking, in effect, is ultimately more truthful and humane than their "sane" and civilized uses of words and texts.

Heller's work, too, like Kelly's, was occasionally criticized for its seeming lack of seriousness. The argument was that Heller could have been a great writer if he had simply shown some restraint with the "omnivorous nonsense" of his incessant wordplay, joke-telling, and silly, metafictive character names (Major Major Major Major). But the point lost on these critics is that it is precisely that silly word-gaming that gives his work its satiric potency—that allows it to engage in the serious work of deconstructing the seemingly more stable but corrupt language of the surrounding culture (Green 187). To elaborate, Heller's relentlessly jokey prose is a sustained dissection of the platitudes, civilized lies, and bureaucratic double-speak of official cultural institutions. Their top-down manipulation of words to create dogmas, classifications, and coercive rules is disrupted from below with democratic and deconstructive comedy.

Slapstick in *Pogo*

From a distance it may seem that the project of tracing the roots of Kelly's comedic conventions and character types into deep historical and literary traditions is over-intellectualizing what is meant to be enjoyed on a visceral, immediate level. While one always runs the risk of semiotic aggrandizement when treating supposedly ephemeral popular texts with seriousness, the end goal of this study is to be true to both the lowbrow *and* satiric "seriousness" of Kelly's work, thereby illustrating the essential interconnections between the two modes. Moreover, the deep roots discussed here may occasionally include a genre such as pastoralism, which has a vaguely genteel pedigree, but for the most part they consist of folkloric and carnivalesque genres of comedy—traditions that are unapologetically broad and irreverent. Kelly emphasizes his own devotion to these lowbrow traditions when discussing his character-driven comedy:

> There is really nothing subtle about any of the characters, or so Kelly believes and he is amazed every once in a while to find *Pogo* being called an intellectual strip. He thinks it is full of mental pratfalls and pitfalls to be sure, but he feels it still has a little pie in it. It gave him pause when *Time* magazine recently slugged a review of his book, a very nice one, with "Possum with Snob Appeal." Then he figured it out, "They mean we get the snobs, TOO." [sic] He explained to a worried reader." (Kelly, Unpublished Autobiographical Sketch" 28)

The "pie" that Kelly mentions could represent the nearest and most obvious influence on Kelly's construction of funny characters: the slapstick comedy and stock characters of vaudeville Kelly had loved so dearly from childhood. Indeed, the histrionic tone and exaggerated physical contortions of many of Kelly's core characters—as if they are emoting and gesturing to the back seats in a large auditorium—seem to be part of that hammy stage tradition.

Before discussing some of the particular tools of broad comedy in *Pogo*, a bit of background philosophy on the functions and status of slapstick in the Western cultural tradition is in order. Long before thriving on the vaudeville stage, broad physical comedy was a significant ingredient in many classical genres. Earlier comedy creators such as the great Greek playwright Aristophanes or Shakespeare and Moliere, for example, did not separate the high and low, the physical and the intellectual, in a work of comedy; satire and slapstick went hand in hand. Alan Dale does a fine job arguing this point in his book *Comedy Is a Man in Trouble*, showing that the lowbrow stigma that comes with the genre is largely a product of the transition from silent to sound film in early twentieth century society. Because silent film was limited almost wholly to physical slapstick, the introduction of sound and verbal comedy was seen as an evolution toward more sophisticated, cerebral humor. Dale points out, however, that low, earthy and physical comedy makes a strong showing in both classical Greek and Roman theatre and in Shakespeare's comedies. Furthermore, the slapstick in those works supports, or is even an integral part, of the "matter" of these plays—thus resonating with audiences for philosophical as well as intuitive reasons. His core point is that slapstick comedy humbles and comforts us, reminding viewers that we are all subject to the treacheries of the physical world and our imperfect bodies, and that it is better to laugh at our earth-bound foibles than it is to feel perpetually anxious about how far we fall short of the ideal. It allows us to be reborn "as one of the happy, comfortable crowd not expected to uphold any impossible, vaguely aristocratic standards" (Dale 16).

Kelly had a similarly democratic and tolerant view of human nature: "[I] like to state over and over again that we shouldn't ever expect too much of ourselves because we're frail and we're inclined to break very easily" (Kelly, "London Calling" 94). It makes sense, then, that broad character types engaged in the constant self-deprecating humor of perpetual slapstick (of both the verbal and physical variety) would be foundational to both the topical and cosmic sides of Kelly's satire. Some of the broad comedic tools in *Pogo* include burlesques, mugging, physical contortions, parodies, cross-dressing, mistaken identities, figurative mask wearing, and cartoonish violence. Some definitions and examples from the strip will help illustrate how integral these devices were to Kelly's larger satiric intentions.

Like popular turn-of-the-century stage comedy, *Pogo* often features traditional burlesques—skits or short plays in which the material at hand is treated in one of two ways. If the subject is of high import, it is treated with irreverence or playful disrespect; if it is of low import, it is treated with unwarranted seriousness. Kelly and his peers had a more direct term for this strategy; they called it the "inverted approach" (Kelly, "Unpublished Autobiographical Sketch" 8). The concept of inversion helps to connect this burlesque mode to traditional carnival comedy in which social inversions abound: the high and low trade places, gender roles are reversed, and all kinds of chaotic but temporarily liberating mayhem ensues.

In *Pogo*, the burlesque inversion is often the catalyst for inciting comedic chaos. A small problem in the community, for example, such as the disappearance of a baby worm, is treated as if it were a national crisis. As a result, the entire flow of life is disrupted, speeches are given, plots are hatched, elaborate misunderstandings complicate matters, costumes and false identities are worn, and so on. Beyond being a handy device for triggering funny mayhem, the inversion acts as a satiric device, creating allegories of how society deals with crises in hysterical ways or allows its values and priorities to become distorted or corrupted.

The broadness of the facial expressions and physical contortions of the characters in *Pogo* can also be traced to the popular stage. In vaudeville, as with earlier brands of classical stage comedy, the simplification of facial expressions and body language into exaggerated expressions of emotion was critical to communicating effectively with a large audience. Because comic strips are printed in relatively small frames and consumed as light entertainment, the comedy has to spell out the emotions and thoughts of the characters in broad strokes (the equivalent to playing to the back of the gallery in theater). But that breadth and simplification does not necessarily mean that stage comedy or comic strips are simplistic. Scholars have effectively argued that the distorted masks and slapstick-laden vignettes in Greek comedy could feature "high degrees of subtlety and psychological insight" in their "portrayal of characters and their interactions" (Vervain 250). Scott McCloud has echoed this argument in his treatise on comics, arguing that the simplified, iconic faces of comic strip characters can both amplify ideas and emotions, and act as portals that invite imaginative engagement and identification with cartoon characters (McCloud 30).

As with other brands of carnivalesque comedy, the inversions in *Pogo* often include farcical plots, cross-dressing, and mistaken identities. Because the strip features animals, these identity switches do not have the same irreverent frisson one feels in a Shakespearean comedy that features cross-dressing (it is hard to feel surprised or vaguely scandalized when you're already dealing with talking animals); and thus the reversals in an allegorical comic strip do not carry the same ideological weight as those in live theater. It is still funny, nevertheless, to see Albert mistaken for a housewife and Churchy falling instantly in love; and the general instability of identities in the swamp reinforces the notion that anything entering into Kelly's comedic territory is open for questioning, inversion, and satiric dissection (Figure 2.11).

Figure 2.11: Walt Kelly, "Good morrow, madam . . . ," *Pogo*, 5 February 1953.

Mask wearing was also integral to vaudeville's ethnic comedy and blackface traditions that were a part of *Pogo's* heritage. In the most complex iterations of that racial comedy (say, for example, when Bert Williams, who was black, wore blackface), the mask could act as a tool of the trickster comedian. Wearing the reductive identity assigned by a racist society, he could draw the audience in with the expectation that the lighthearted joking would be at his expense; and then he could infuse his performance with emotional complexity and satiric layers. As discussed in greater length in chapter four, *Pogo* had shed any outward use of racial caricatures by the time it reached maturity, but there were vestiges of the layered uses of comedic "masks" that remained in the strip's comedy and satire until the end. The animal characters in the strip play the roles of reductive social types, for example, and the audience is generally attracted to the comedy because of the promise of broad laughs that accompany amplified comedic types and their seemingly simplistic comic masks. But behind that reductive facade is a world of emotional complexity and satiric intention that could challenge or target readers.

There was a shelf life, nevertheless, to the exaggerated facial expressions and bodily contortions in *Pogo*. While they may have acted as comedic sweeteners for Kelly's pointed satire in the 1950s—a time when mainstream cultural industries preferred to feature texts that delivered broad laughs and diverting spectacle—they were out of sync with the cultural sensibility of the late 1960s and early 1970s. A new comedic style was emerging during that time—one that favored affectless, deadpan and sharply honed irony (think of the Smothers Brothers or Trudeau's *Doonesbury*) instead of overwrought vaudevillian gags.

Pogo also features a great deal of parody, another comedic mode common to the popular stage. Throughout the twenty-year run of *Pogo*, Kelly lampooned other comic strips (such as *Little Orphan Annie*, *Dick Tracy*, and *Li'l Abner*), literary texts (sentimental romances, social realism, and the writings of Raymond

Chandler), and the conventions of Hollywood genre films. These parodies were entertaining for fans, obviously, because they capitalized on the readers' built-in familiarity with those popular texts, but they also gave Kelly the opportunity to flex some satiric muscles. In the broadest sense, they gave Kelly the chance to be critical in a deconstructive, metafictive sense (an inherent quality of much parody)—drawing attention to the artificial conventions of storytelling generally and the mechanisms of his own craft and industry in pointed ways. More specifically, he could mock particular texts and creators that he disliked in mainstream entertainment or on the comics page, such as Harold Gray and his earnest and contrived melodramas in *Annie* (recast as "Li'l Arf an' Nonny" in Kelly's work). Notice in Figure 2.12 the "[sic]" after "funny"—a seemingly throwaway detail that works as an additional jab at the corny or overwrought strips that populated the page in Kelly's day.

Figure 2.12: Walt Kelly, "That Cleopatra lure . . . ," *Pogo*, 15 May 1953.

Nevertheless, parodies are not the most reliable carriers of an ideological message. By nature they are inherently ambivalent, both denigrating and celebrating their targets. Kelly thus ran the risk of amplifying the popularity or power of the texts he targeted. Moreover, as Brian Connery has observed, parodies can sometimes dilute the critical punch of a work of satire—especially one that is meant to tweak the conscience of a reader—because "the pleasure of parody is capable of overwhelming any irony which might support a satirical attack against the reader." He continues, however, suggesting that "[i]n the hands of a master-satirist . . . the promise of the pleasure of decoding parody can lure readers into satiric ambushes which they might otherwise have avoided" (Connery 126). Kelly displayed, in most cases, that master's confidence with parodic tools, and he certainly capitalized on the appeal of the device in a number of cases—most notably, perhaps, in his retelling of *Alice in Wonderland* as an allegory of McCarthy-era Senate hearings to root out alleged subversives in American society.

Finally, *Pogo* features the most quintessential ingredients of physical slapstick stage comedy: random blows, falls, and other acts of "pie-in-the-face" violence. Dale suggests that these falls and blows serve numerous purposes in slapstick, depending on whether the character is the perpetrator or the receiver of the comic abuse. If the protagonist falls or receives a blow—which often happens to Pogo in the early years of the strip—the viewer experiences a mingling of the emotions of schadenfreude and empathetic identification. Observing the hero's loss of dignity also reminds the reader of his or her own foibles and shortfalls. If the receiver of the abuse is a pompous or otherwise deserving authority figure, the viewer enjoys the shared aggression of seeing someone high brought low. The protagonist cannot give blows maliciously and gratuitously, however—even if the receiver of the abuse is an unlikable character; uncalled-for violence, even of a comic nature, would undermine the viewer's ability to identify and sympathize with the hero of the text (see Figure 2.13) (Dale 3, 11–15). This last rule plays out in characters like Charlie Chaplin's The Little Tramp, Stan Laurel, and Mr. Magoo—wise fools who unintentionally cause a great deal of slapstick chaos. In *Pogo* a similar dynamic unfolds as Pogo is perhaps the least intentionally violent of all the denizens of the swamp, and most of the mishaps in the strip are usually accidents rather than malicious attacks.

Interestingly, the only time that real, unfunny violence seems imminent is when Malarkey and his gang invade the swamp. In tandem with their coercive (rather than comic) word games, they wield shotguns and axes that threaten to do more than damage a character's dignity. Bill Watterson recalled that one of

Figure 2.13: Walt Kelly, "So help me, Albert . . . ," *Pogo*, 3 February 1953.

Figure 2.14: Walt Kelly, "You realize, pally . . . ," *Pogo*, 9 June 1953.

the few times that he was truly scared when reading the comics page as a kid was when he witnessed these passages—particularly a scene in which Mole Mac-Carony and Malarkey pursue one another through an ominously dark bayou, brandishing above the soupy waters a decidedly uncartoony ax and pistol (Figure 2.14) (Watterson 13).

Character Types in *Pogo*

Kelly's character types can also be traced to classical comedy traditions. The strip, for example, behaves as a satiric allegory in which the characters represent distinct social types: a business huckster, a pious religious spokesman, a depressive malcontent, and so on. That fable-like quality gives the characters a static and sometimes two-dimensional quality because they all behave fairly predictably according to their assigned traits. There are varying degrees of complexity within the cast, nevertheless: characters closest to the center of the strip (Albert and Pogo) are the most nuanced, playing several shifting comedic roles; secondary characters in the main cast (about ten figures) remain fairly true to their two-dimensional, but largely sympathetic profiles (Figure 2.15); and then a huge cast of tertiary critters that come and go over the years serve as comic props, representing either a singular comic obsession or some truly reprehensible fringe of the human psyche.

One of the core satiric points that can be made in comedic allegories that freeze characters into particular personality patterns is that human behavior and thinking have a timeless, cyclical quality. Habits of hypocrisy, vanity, and self-delusion are chronic human failings, and the sooner one can reconcile with that reality, the better one can navigate treacherous social shoals, unhindered by naïveté or unrealistic expectations. This does not mean that satiric fables cannot have a reformative effect on readers; the comedic character may be trapped in his or her chronic foibles, but the reader, in theory, can learn to behave different-

Figure 2.15: Walt Kelly, cast of characters in an installment used to introduce the strip to new subscribing papers, *Pogo*, 1962.

ly after seeing this "dramatic picture of the ridiculous" (Aristotle 69). Most of the great satirists, nevertheless, such as Swift and Twain, are not terribly sanguine about readers' ability to reform themselves through the reading of satire. Swift suggested that satire is a warped mirror in which we see everyone's reflection but our own, and Twain became thoroughly misanthropic and pessimistic about the promise of the human race by the end of his career.

In some respects, Kelly seemed to share Twain's sense of discouragement. He stated in an interview that

> No matter what we do to enhance our position or to make it worse, why, we remain just about where the good Lord intended us to be at the moment . . . This is not a philosophy of weariness so much as it is one of knowing that we are what we are, and we can always try to be better. But very little we do will actually change the kind of people we are. We can always expect the "boob," as we call the fool in America to show up . . . Not that I'm weary, not that I think people should be weary, but I don't think we should be too upset if something comes along to upset an apple-cart, or our children. We can expect a lot of this. (Brandon 94)

This worldview may sound fatalistic, but if seen within the larger frame of Kelly's strategies of character construction and his overarching satiric intentions, it can harbor some hopefulness. Kelly, for example, believed that "*Pogo* [the strip] was not . . . a 'panorama of popular human types' but the 'projection of all the characteristics' that can be found within one person" (Kercher 65). If one adopts this idea—that every individual is prone to the array of failings on display in the character types populating the strip (even in those capable of genuine acts of evil)—then it is impossible to read Kelly's satire while harboring an attitude of condescending misanthropy or engaging in the self-righteous scapegoating of others. This is another way the strip teaches implicitly that if one wants to find the enemy, the first place to look is within one's self.

While admitting one's imperfections and complicity in larger societal ills may not sound like an especially hopeful or reformative satiric vision, it does have a bracing brand of morality at its core. Perpetual self-inspection, prodded by the reading of satiric allegories that implicate the self in the quirks or failings of human nature, can at least protect society against the type of divisive rancor and fascistic abuses that can sometimes creep into a culture rife with ideologies that nurture high self-regard and contempt for other groups or individuals. A foundational code of moral behavior thus emerges from the rubble created by the carnivalesque mockery of the chronic failings we all share.

While we may have a bit of each character in *Pogo* within our own personalities, it is with the eponymous protagonist that we most likely identify. He is the placid Everyman figure holding the strip together, the sometimes unremarkable "nothing" at the center of the social chaos in the swamp (Kelly, "Unpublished

Autobiographical Sketch 27; and Crinklaw 1). He did not start out this way, however. As chapter four discusses, Pogo was originally a sassy and opportunistic trickster figure, forever trying to save his own skin from larger predators through guile and elaborate pranks. But as the strip shed its naturalistic trickster tale setting, Pogo added to his trickster role an array of more complex comedic types including the wise fool, singing minstrel, social jester, and everyman hero. Figures 2.16 and 2.17 illustrate this progression—first showing the two-dimensional trickster figure orientation of the earliest version of Pogo, and then

Figure 2.16: Walt Kelly, "Albert Takes the Cake," *Animal Comics* #1, December 1942.

Figure 2.17: Walt Kelly, "*Pogo* kin be first up!" *Pogo*, 9 October 1960.

illustrating how the mature Pogo engaged in trickster shenanigans less fraught
with life and death outcomes, and combined with the more playful behaviors of
a lazy minstrel and pastoral fool.

In the mature strip Pogo's new status as laid-back wise fool in a pastoral setting does not translate into completely disinterested passivity, nevertheless. As
an embodiment of the tolerant and cautious brand of liberalism Kelly espoused,
Pogo is simply thoughtful and nonpartisan—listening and observing more than
acting (Figure 2.18). Like traditional fools in pastoral comedy, Pogo also acts as
a touchstone against which the opinions and behavior of the more manic, and
often more "civilized" or educated characters, can be tested. His expression of
that common-sense wisdom can be subtle: a silent reaction to expressions of
hysterical delusion, a raised brow of incredulity at another character's misguided
mania, or a sotto voce aside that points out a contradiction or irony in a companion's thinking or behavior (Figure 2.19). Those asides often qualify as wordplay,
but Pogo's verbal games and errors are usually an outgrowth of inventive playfulness, innocent ignorance, or a lack of formal education.

Figure 2.18: Walt Kelly, "It's complete over my head," *Pogo*, 9 February 1952.

igure 2.19: Walt Kelly, "Copy down my election speech . . . ," *Pogo*, 4 November 1950.

In contrast, other main characters, such as Albert, Howland, Churchy, and
Deacon, make verbal errors that are a result of self-delusion or the desire to
manipulate others to meet their selfish needs. In other words, if we use a Shakespearean text as a point of comparison, their word games are more similar to

those of Malvolio in *Twelfth Night* than they are to Feste's (from the same play). Like Malvolio, they cannot see themselves clearly, they hear what they want to hear, and they misuse language and misread texts (such as a mock love letter) to feed their vanities. Within this dynamic, then, Pogo effectively plays the part of the clear-eyed fool, commenting continually in ironic and truthful ways about the blind spots and inconsistencies in the other characters.

In addition to behaving like a Shakespearean fool in this respect, Pogo also takes on the pedigree of a satiric minstrel or griot. The truth-telling minstrel figure has deep roots in the European tradition; like the jester or fool, the minstrel in some cases had special license to criticize authority figures or parody the official voices and texts of the culture. West African culture had its own version of this privileged social critic—the griot, a feared, but protected community jester who "combined the talents of the musician with those of the innovative poet (weaving 'his own comments, moral judgments and isolated poetic images' into his songs) and the clever trickster-jester to accomplish his ends" (Watkins 64). That license to mock was revoked in the earliest, most racist iterations of American blackface minstrelsy—when white men put on burnt cork and made the minstrel the butt of condescending jokes. But in later versions of the genre— when black men and ethnic immigrants played the role of the minstrel—he could exercise a limited license to play a trickster figure and satirist, using his outsider status to question and mock the values of the dominant culture. The seemingly light verse and playful music of the blackface tradition provided a sugary coating and allegorical layering to those attacks.

An essential tool in the subversive blackface minstrel's arsenal was the inventive use of vernacular speech. Gavin Jones describes the "counterhegemonic" qualities of the African American dialect central to minstrel's satiric arsenal:

> The antagonistic power of black English is also rooted linguistically in its creative, improvisational disruption of accepted norms, its skill in masking subversion within a seemingly common tongue, its counterhegemonic capacity to "take the oppressor's language and turn it against itself." Black language does not simply stand for a wider cultural subversion. It demonstrates [that] . . . dialect can be an act of political resistance in itself. (Jones 213)

Christie Davies elaborates on how the malapropisms and neologisms in this type of ethnic dialect can be used for layered, comedic purposes:

> Jokers may deliberately and cleverly misuse language and exploit error so that we laugh at the cleverness of the pseudo-foolishness. A person who makes a statement with an ambiguous or contradictory meaning may be regarded by his or her listeners as a silly fool who has made a risible mistake or as a subtle wit who has produced a clever joke. Either way, the audience may laugh, but their estimation

of the speaker's abilities will differ greatly depending on how they interpret his or her intention or meaning. Also jokes, repartee, the pretense of error or stupidity can be used as a skillful means of manipulating other people, so as to evade responsibility, to avoid answering a question, to reduce anger to amusement, or simply secretly to mock the other party. To succeed in such a game requires a great deal of shrewd understanding and/or gift for language. Only the clever can play the fool. (Davies 147)

As a result of the trickster tale and blackface minstrel roots in *Pogo,* the strip's Southern vernacular takes advantage of the satiric layering inherent in minority dialects. The mature strip, of course, moves beyond black speech, adding Freudian, vaudevillian, and absurdist tones and devices, but the overall effect is still one of organic, dialect-driven satire.

Although Pogo can trace his comedic pedigree into these European and West African traditions, he is also a distinctly twentieth-century American wise fool in several ways. First, there is a casual equality among all of the denizens of the swamp. Pogo may play the roles that are traditionally low on the social strata, but no one seems especially aware of, or concerned with, harsh class distinctions. With the race dynamics muted in the strip as well, Pogo's outsider position does not create a sense of double consciousness or force him into playing the fool or trickster as a strategy of mere survival. Pogo also refers continually to being able to say or do things effectively because of his "natural born self"—as if no formal education is needed in achieving that kind of foundational morality and common sense. This quality aligns with the general American taste for popular texts that celebrate homegrown folk wisdom or humor over "old-world pedantry" (Blair 35, 68). That Pogo would qualify as an appealing mock-serious candidate for president—a populist hero of sorts—suggests that this organic wisdom is valued in American culture even beyond the artificial confines of traditional pastoral comedy.

In closing this discussion of Pogo, profitable comparisons can be made with the construction and social meanings of two similar cartoon protagonists: Krazy Kat and Mickey Mouse. Krazy, like Pogo, bears some muted racial codings and uses dialect and the word games of a fool to subvert the civilized hatreds and divisions of society. These satiric talents made Krazy popular with intellectuals too—e. e. cummings, for example, argued that "Krazy Kat—who, with every mangled word and murdered gesture, translates a mangling and murdering world into Peace and Goodwill—is the only original and authentic revolutionary protagonist" (cummings 8). Krazy differed from Pogo, however, in not achieving the breadth of popularity that comes with being a sane everyman hero as well. Because Herriman was less worried with creating a hugely popular strip (William Randolph Hearst vowed to protect it from cancellation despite low syndication numbers), he was content to make the character a true fool (Stewart 20).

Krazy, then, commits malapropisms that are more outrageous; his/her gender remains ambiguous; he/she is thoroughly delusional and detached from reality (though in sweetly innocent ways); and he/she is less visually and comedically "cute." The sum result is a character that is not as polysemically marketable as Pogo, but is more bracingly true to the fool's code of subversive conduct.

The early Mickey Mouse, like Pogo, had roots in blackface tropes and trickster tale dynamics (the early version of the character, a copy of blackface-inflected Felix the Cat, was "quite rowdy"), and he too gradually shed those racial codings as Disney began to capitalize on the flexible and marketable quality of his cute, generic animal persona (Solomon 45; and Gordon 62, 75). But while Pogo achieved the popular appeal of an everyman without losing entirely his ability to behave as subtle trickster, wise fool, and satiric commentator, Mickey lost those qualities because he was used in so many different story contexts, merchandized so aggressively, and required to behave essentially as a personality-free logo for an entire corporation. In his most mature phase he was an overly anthropomorphized, bland reflection of a suburban milquetoast, living in a picket fence house with Minnie, and taking care of a rascally dog, Pluto—a "true" animal who seemed to have absorbed all of his master's earlier energy and edginess.

Pogo's sustained viability as a complex comedic and satiric character was an outgrowth of Kelly's auteur-like clout and principles. In refusing to over-merchandise his characters, in keeping Pogo situated in one context, and in continually harnessing him to a coherent political philosophy, Kelly allowed his central character to be an everyman who retained some of the comedic potency of a traditional fool or satiric minstrel. Pogo may not have been as radically "true" as a revolutionary protagonist as Krazy, but he achieved greater iconic potency in the popular realm than did Herriman's creation. Moreover, Pogo kept his core comedic integrity, avoiding the bland impotence that often comes with the over-commodification of some cartoon characters.

The second most significant character in Kelly's strip is Albert the alligator. Like Pogo, Albert's roots can be traced to trickster tales; in that context he was originally Pogo's nemesis, the predator to Pogo's prey. As the strip evolved, however, Albert became Pogo's buddy and they behaved like a classic comedy duo,

Figure 2.20: Walt Kelly, "That riles me!" *Pogo*, 21 November 1958.

engaging in physical slapstick, pursuing outlandish projects, and talking past each other. Their contrasting physiques, in fact—one tall and angular, the other short and round—recall similar visual juxtapositions found in Laurel and Hardy or Abbott and Costello pairings (see Figure 2.20).

Because so little is at stake in the comedic dialogues between Albert and Pogo, the exchanges take on an abstract philosophical quality. Maurice Horn, a French comics scholar, catalogues some of the interpretations of that dynamic:

> Reuel Denney, in his work *The Astonished Muse*, compares Pogo to Socrates, in the presence of Albert, the Sophist. Psychologists, such as Franklin Fearing, see there a symbolic representation of the Freudian concepts of the Ego (Pogo) and the Id (Albert). For my part, I tend to believe that Pogo and Albert symbolize the two-fold aspect of art and the artist; Pogo the Apollonian showing us its bright face, Albert the Dionysian its dark side. (Horn 104)

Given the circular, inconsequential absurdity of some of Pogo and Albert's discussions, one could also compare them to the hapless fools that one would find in a Beckett play such as *Endgame* or *Waiting for Godot*. That interpretation aligns nicely with Kelly's brand of liberalism, which eschewed a faith in rigid metanarratives and preferred asking questions over asserting confident answers. Pogo and Albert illustrated those vaguely existentialist views in their playful miscommunications and organic deconstructions of conventional wisdom through absurd and meandering wordplay.

A Freudian interpretation is also useful for framing Pogo and Albert as resonant archetypes for the core audience of Kelly's work—intellectuals and college students in the 1950s. Although Albert gradually abandoned his carnivorous impulses as the strip matured, he occasionally slipped up, "accidentally" cannibalizing pollywogs or being tempted to bite Pogo. Lawrence Levine argued that traditional trickster tales resonated on an ideological level with antebellum slave communities because the life and death naturalism of their struggles matched the psychological needs of their listeners (Levine 132). Using that interpretation as a model, one could then argue that Kelly's Freudian-style trickster tales—

Figure 2.21: "People don't swallow other people . . . ," *Pogo*, 15 November 1948.

where the struggles are largely internal, with Albert wrestling with guilt, and trying to navigate between the pressures of societal rules and his own carnal and selfish appetites—reflected the preoccupations of Kelly's core readership (Figure 2.21).

Albert's ever-present cigar is also a nice Freudian detail. Kelly suggested that the cigar was a handy symbol of adulthood, a sign that one is "old enough to smoke it, big enough to hold it, and rich enough to buy it" ("Walt Kelly Insists" 1). There is also something vaguely infantile, however, about Albert using this accessory so obsessively and aggressively. Indeed, from a classical Freudian perspective, Albert could easily be diagnosed as an adult who never completely grew up in a sense—one who got hung up on a maladaptive oral fixation. The fact that he is a reformed predator with enormous jaws heightens the subtext of that arrested development. Within the frame of this animal allegory, however, there is probably little incentive among his companions to cure him of this minor vice; better that he sublimate his carnivorous impulses into this semi-acceptable adult activity than use his jaws for their intended purposes. Given that Kelly also chomped on a cigar as he went about his work day and, like Albert, dealt with Falstaffian appetites, it is tempting to imagine that the strip says more about its creator than he may have intended (Figure 2.22).

In charting Albert's character progression as Kelly's work transitioned from comic book to comic strip, one also notices some changes in the type of buffoon

Figure: 2.22: Walt Kelly, promotional drawing of Kelly and Albert, 1956.

Figure 2.23: Walt Kelly, "Albert Takes the Cake," *Animal Comics* #1, December 1942.

Figure 2.24: Walt Kelly, "Nothin to it!" *Pogo*, 22 December 1952.

he embodies. The trickster tale version of his character was arrogant and grasping—an echo of the predator in antebellum trickster tales who could symbolize a white culture that would often trip over its own greed and pride (Figure 2.23). The mature Albert, however, is a more nuanced buffoon, forever pretending to be magnanimous and civilized but frequently tripping over his own pride, selfishness, or competitive spirit (Figure 2.24). He is often funny because the gap between his grandiose self-perception and the mundane reality of his true intelligence and abilities is so immense. Braggarts in classical comedy such as Moliere's Tartuffe or Malvolio in *Twelfth Night* are meant to be comic but reprehensible characters—wholly delusional, self-righteous, and selfish. Albert's brand of arrogance and obliviousness is fairly benign, however. Like Michael Scott in *The Office*, he is an endearing buffoon—an everyman clown whose malapropisms and misperceptions lack maliciousness. Kelly confirmed these gentler codings by equating him with "the average American male." He stated that Albert "is anxious to prove he's a man, he boasts just a little more than is necessary, rushes in where fools fear to tread at times, but has courage when he finds he has to fight it out" (Kelly, "Unpublished Biographical Sketch" 27).

Figure 2.25: Walt Kelly, "Did you see the buttons
. . .," *Pogo*, 16 May 1952.

That softening of Albert's persona may seem, at first glance, like a dilution of satiric potency, as if Kelly is going easy on deserving targets. A closer consideration of Kelly's core satiric maxim, however—the need for readers to first target themselves before looking for flaws in others—suggests that making Albert sympathetically flawed is an effective device. If one can identify with Albert's brand of selfishness and myopic arrogance (rather than seeing them as such awful traits that they could only occur in a villainous caricature), then perhaps one is more likely to make efforts at reining in those foibles in one's self.

Beyond Albert and Pogo, there are a number of secondary characters that represent both classic comedic archetypes as well as identifiable social types. These figures include Deacon Mushrat, Howland Owl, "Churchy" LaFemme, Beauregard Bugleboy, Barnstable Bear, P. T. Bridgeport, Seminole Sam, Porky Pine, Miz Beaver, and Miz Mam'selle Hepzibah. Deacon, a pompous clergyman, is perhaps the best foil to Pogo's untutored goodness and wisdom—as well as the best superego to Albert's id (Figure 2.25). Kelly described him as the most reprehensible character in the strip—"about as far as I can go in showing what I think evil to be" (Kelly, *Ten Ever-Lovin'* 284). Echoing Twain, Kelly makes Deacon, representative of organized religion, a symbol of sophisticated hypocrisy, false moralities, and self-righteousness. Some of his specific failings include a Pharisaic obsession with outward appearances, an insistence on letter-of-the-law compliance to bureaucratic rules, a harshly judgmental streak, a fixation on hierarchies of purity, and a willingness to wed his religious ideals to abusively partisan crusades.

Kelly's biting, satiric use of this man of the cloth is in line with some of the general contempt among 1950s liberal intellectuals toward organized religion and what were perceived as regressively puritanical streaks in the American character. Arthur Miller's play *The Crucible*, for example, articulated some of those ideas, positing that a culture that embraces Christian ideologies that are too dogmatic and rigid (devoid of the core principles of love and forgiveness) inevitably becomes rife with hypocrisy and factional rancor. *The Crucible* too, like *Pogo*, effectively traced those free-ranging tendencies in American culture from religion into McCarthyism, a specific flare-up of that brand of Puritanical witch-hunting. Indeed, Deacon is one of the most avid followers of Malarkey when he begins to self-righteously bully the other denizens of the swamp (that is, until Deacon falls under suspicion from Malarkey as well).

Howland Owl is another type of laughable authority figure—an academic or expert in a variety of fields of arcane knowledge. In contrast to Pogo's organic wisdom, Howland is a pretentious pedant concerned with impressing others through the use of big words or through the introduction of elaborate but foundationally flawed programs. Howland's horned rim glasses and pontificating poses (eyes closed, balanced to one side, arm gesturing dramatically) advertise his social position. His partner in most of his failed projects is Churchy LaFemme, a highly gullible, passionate, and superstitious fellow. LaFemme's warped naïveté makes him susceptible to Owl's claims to knowledge and authority, and thus flawed ideas go from bad to worse when the two of them work together. Exaggerated strife, in fact, is the usual outcome when their plans go awry.

Porky Pine is the resident malcontent in the swamp (Figure 2.26). Forever melancholy, he effectively undercuts the manic optimism that often infects the other main characters. For readers too, his bracing pessimism acts as an effective antidote to the overdose of sweetness the strip sometimes delivered in terms of cute aesthetics and clever wordplay. In terms of narrative functions, Porky Pine

Figure 2.26: Walt Kelly, "That's a ballface lie!" *Pogo*, 20 December 1952.

is similar to Jacques in Shakespeare's pastoral comedy *As You Like It*. Both characters are unmoved by the liberating force of carnivalesque comedy; instead, they prefer to dwell on the realities of disappointment, loss, and inevitable death. One would not want to emulate that level of depressiveness, of course, but the presence of these walking memento moris within the midst of pastoral sweetness and festive inversions is an effective reminder that one cannot remain in a nostalgic or comedic free-zone indefinitely. A periodic, imaginative escape into a timeless, pastoral comedy is a nice break from reality—as well as an effective way to test one's values or to imagine more flexible ideologies—but one needs to be grounded in the temporal world as well, and Porky Pine effectively serves as the melancholic ambassador of that message.

Kelly's construction of female characters is perhaps a significant weakness in the strip. The small handful of regular females—Miz Beaver, Miss Sis Boombah, and Mam'selle Hepzibah—all seem drawn from contemporary cultural stereotypes rather than deeper, more complex comedic archetypes. Miz Beaver and Hepzibah, for example, represent the two most limited, polar notions of 1950s femininity: the unfeminine, brow-beating, battle ax of a wife, on the one hand, and the hyper-feminine object of male desire on the other (see figures 2.27 and 2.28). Miz Beaver, however, at least gets to be funny, continually worrying about her children, rampaging after a lazy husband, and chomping on a corncob pipe. And the third most prominent female, Miss Sis Boombah, is a large gym teacher and fitness maniac, who also gets to engage in a bit of physical slapstick (usually dominating the men in the community at some athletic endeavor), as well as play a part in some funny satiric runs (such as a parody of the Kinsey reports and various feminist crusades). In contrast, Mam'selle Hepzibah, a French female skunk, is truly a two-dimensional type. Within the traditional pastoral frame she might represent the idealized object of infatuation or unrequited love—her two-dimensionality a requisite part of the male characters' yearning fantasies. But in terms of updating comedic types and conventions to fit a mid-century American context, she is fairly uninteresting: a Marilyn Monroe–esque object of male attraction who stands outside the action, never able to engage in slapstick or hold her own in funny dialogues. She does occasionally get to commit a malapropism because English is her second language, but these speech errors are usually cute rather than funny or intentionally deconstructive (see Figure 2.29). Hepzibah is essentially placed on a pedestal, removed from the rollicking, satiric chaos of the community and given the cutesy dialogue of a coy, perpetually naïve secondary character.

The practice of placing the marriageable female protagonist beyond the influence of carnivalesque comedy is a common trope in American comedic texts. Slapstick comedy is fair game for the "she-moose" sidekicks, married women (Miz Beaver), females with manly or androgynous identities (Miss Sis Boombah—Figure 2.30), and females belonging to a racial underclass. But as Alan Dale

Figure 2.27: Walt Kelly, "Besides . . . ," *Pogo*, 26 August 1952.

Figure 2.28: Walt Kelly, "An' so brainy . . . ," *Pogo*, 30 April 1952.

Figure 2.29: Walt Kelly, "Ah! Zee conteenental touché," *Pogo*, 1 November 1950.

Figure 2.30: Walt Kelly, "You're cute," *Pogo*, 12 December 1953.

explains, the object of male desire within the comedy is protected from taint of physical falls and blows because those slapstick staples vaguely connote a loss of virtue or purity (Dale 162).

This protection and elevation of an essentialized notion of female goodness and beauty may seem sweet, but it actually contains an element of condescending misogyny. Hepzibah is defined by an exaggerated, exotic sex appeal and an aura of female purity, but she is both a boring character and a vaguely unlikable stereotype of femaleness: needy, narrowly domestic in her interests, and incapable of philosophical conversations. Pogo, like all the male denizens of the swamp, finds her beautiful, but exhibits a mild form of condescension and ambivalence about her supposedly "typical" female qualities. Though deeply smitten by Hepzibah and worshipful of her female charms, he ultimately prefers the company of men and is forever dubious about the prospect of becoming romantically entangled with, or domestically attached to any woman.

That resistance to the obligations and repercussions of love does have a legitimate comedic legacy; one can see it in P. G. Wodehouse's *Jeeves and Wooster* stories or in the dialogue of Hollywood duos such as Abbott and Costello. In those narratives, the arrival of love and marriage would destroy the dynamic and dysfunctional relationship of the male leads, and perhaps rob the protagonist at the center of the text of his foundational, wise fool innocence. In a similar fashion, Pogo and Albert remain effectively foolish and childlike because of their refusal to accept marital commitment and adult responsibility. This allows them to remain in a comedic limbo where philosophical, inconsequential banter thrives in the absence of the mundane and grounded conversations required of marriage partners and parents.

There is something slightly sexist, nevertheless, in this comedic convention where men are allowed to arrest their emotional development while simultaneously admiring women for their physical beauty, and despising them for their neediness and association with domestic obligations. It plays into 1950s male fantasies of irresponsible independence (a common theme in 1950s film comedies and Westerns) and gives female readers very little to hold onto in terms of complex comedic role models. One wishes, for example, that Kelly could have based Hepzibah on a more dynamic pastoral comedienne such as Rosalind in *As You Like It*. In that text Rosalind is allowed to engage in creative cross-dressing, smart wordplay, and philosophical investigations into the failings of men's characters. Other viable templates could include the heroines of screwball comedies—roles in the 1930s and 1940s played by actresses such as Claudette Colbert, Rosalind Russell, and Katharine Hepburn. These were funny females who displayed both physical and intellectual merits, and often bested their male counterparts in verbal slapstick. Finally, there is Lucille Ball's eponymous character from the television sitcom *I Love Lucy*. She illustrates the truly creative ways that a mid-century, mainstream comedic text can deal with a female character: Lucy is a female trickster and "liminal" figure, forever poised between the male and the female worlds, and the domestic and the social spheres. Unlike Hepzibah, Lucy, like one of the boys, gets to engage in cross-dressing, outrageous physical comedy, and funny verbal banter (Landay 166).

One is tempted to draw a connection between Kelly's limits as a creator of female characters to his real-life participation in a culture of hard-drinking, womanizing newspapermen. The ambivalence about marriage and commitment in *Pogo* certainly has its parallel in Kelly's ups and downs as a married man, and his penchant for flirtations and teenage-like infatuations with Hepzibah-like women. Nevertheless, the limited range of female stereotypes in his strip is best explained by the traditions of his field and medium. The funnies page had long been dominated by men, and as chapter three describes, the professional organizations of the field were both too slow to recognize the contributions of female artists and too eager to create newsletters and programs that objectified women in juvenile ways. Kelly's cartooning peers such as Milton Caniff, Johnny Hart, Mort Walker, and Al Capp, also dealt with female characters in similarly simplistic ways in their own comic strips (and in Capp's case, the sexism ran rampant in his personal life as well, resulting ultimately in charges of repeatedly traumatizing college-age girls with unwelcome advances). In sum, Kelly was forward-thinking and syncretically innovative in relation to most aspects of his work, but when it came to the construction of female characters, backwards traditions and personal blind spots may have arrested his creative development.

There are a great number of other interesting characters in *Pogo*, a few of whom deserve mention: Beauregard Bugleboy is a hound dog charged to be the town constable. He rarely fulfills the duties of this job, however, because he perceives the world through a romantic and sometimes epic lens, usually casting himself as the hero in whatever imaginary melodrama is unfolding in his head. There are echoes of Cervantes' Don Quixote in his character, as well as Twain's Tom Sawyer—both characters whose ability to operate effectively in the real world has been compromised by the consumption of too many romantic texts. Other secondary characters include Barnstable Bear, Miz Beaver's volatile husband; Grundoon, a baby groundhog who speaks in funny gibberish; Mister Miggle, a crane who runs the local store; Pup Dog, a lively puppy who incites the occasional crisis with his errant enthusiasm; and a trio of bats who act as a comic version of a Greek chorus, passing judgment on the behavior of the other characters or drawing cosmic lessons from the action.

Other than Deacon Mushrat, the most reprehensible social types who appear in the strip are visitors—representatives of all that is wrong with urban life, big business, or abusive government. Here is a sampling: P. T. Bridgeport, a pompous huckster who tries to sell bogus products or flawed politicians to the denizens of the swamp; Tammananny Tiger, a political operative; Seminole Sam, an opportunistic fox of the old trickster tale predator variety who continually tries to con the more guileless members of the community; Wiley Cat, a mean loner who also preys upon the regular folk; Sarcophagus MacAbre, a menacing undertaker; two cowbirds with beatnik personas and lazy, grasping habits; and Snavely, a perpetually drunken snake. Finally, there are those intruders who represent not only a generalized, disparaged social type, but also a specific public figure worthy of mockery. Over the years a great number of politicians and foreign leaders (Richard Nixon, Spiro Agnew, Barry Goldwater, Nikita Kruschev, Fidel Castro, to name a few) took on various animal forms and disrupted the peace of the swamp, but the most iconic examples of this convention in Kelly's work are Simple J. Malarkey (a caricature of Senator Joseph McCarthy) and Molester Mole (a parody of Senator Pat McCarran). Malarkey mimics on a small scale the paranoid witch hunts that McCarthy pursued in Congress, looking for subversives in all corners of American society. Mole reflects the ultraconservative politics of senators like McCarran, characterized by a "manic fear of disease, foreign ideologies, and 'deviant' sexual practices" (Kercher 68). About Mole, Kelly elaborates:

> The character "was an attempt to find a symbol for another wad of bug-eyed greed which was typified by our sudden worry about who was coming into the country as a refugee or an immigrant and who, for that matter, was going to be allowed to stay here." (Kelly, *Ten Ever-Lovin'* 80)

While Malarkey only disrupted the peace of the swamp on two distinct occasions in the 1950s, Mole persisted as a periodic intruder into the 1960s, giving Kelly the ongoing opportunity to satirize the xenophobia of far right groups such as the John Birch Society (see Figure 2.31, a strip for which Kelly also offered an alternate "Bunny" comic to prickly editors).

Figure 2.31: Walt Kelly, "You know it's treason . . . ," *Pogo*, 16 October 1964.

Some Conclusions

The core point of this chapter is that the satire and comedy in *Pogo* cannot be easily separated. The "lowbrow" humor in the strip amplifies and enables the topical satire, but it also works as a type of social criticism if we expand the definition of satire to include carnivalesque, cosmic, and deconstructive genres. But because Kelly worked at a time when the distinctions between low comedy and serious satire were so stark, he was often conflicted about what to make of this divide between the high and the low, the satiric and the comic. There were no existing justifications or templates for the interdependence of the two rhetorics in a text, and thus he would vacillate between claiming to be a mere "pie-throwin' man" and asserting that he was a serious social critic.

Kelly did, nevertheless, attempt to figure out what set his work apart from other comedic texts that contained what he considered directionless humor. He claimed, for example, that "true humor or satire" without social comment is merely "slapstick." This qualification is helpful as long as we do not limit "social comment" to the topical caricaturing of identifiable political figures; and it must also acknowledge the inherently carnivalesque and deconstructive aspects of much of physical and verbal slapstick (Kercher 59). In the following chapters I will add another distinction that gave Kelly's work direction and force: his status as an independent auteur or sateur, a businessman who used his clout and access within a popular medium—and through a popular discourse (comedy)—to engage in coherent and principled social criticism. That principled approach to the commercial and institutional side of his craft was both a precondition to, and a part of, his satiric work.

A final, helpful distinction that Kelly made regarding the qualities of a good satirist/comedian is that he or she must be ideologically engaged in order for the work to rise above mere diversion. He argued that this ideological orientation, ideally, should be to the left. For example, in 1963 he stated that the "satirist or humorist—as opposed to a jokester—is a liberal . . . against all the redundancies and stupid conservatism of the big landowners. To be a real humorist you must have skirted the edges of poverty. You must be able to look at the entrenched and say we don't like those guys" (Grove 5).

There is certainly some merit to this assertion; in our democratic tradition satire is often seen as a tool for helping the underdog in fights against those who would misuse their position and wealth to abuse the underprivileged. As a constitutionally licensed form of public attack, it can afflict the comfortable, and comfort the afflicted. One can still quibble, nevertheless, with the categorical quality of Kelly's view as well as the partisan connotations of his terms. Specifically, the distinctions between liberal and conservative are somewhat slippery or relative when one has to place a satirist within a particular historical moment, or when one looks into the unpredictable ways that people use and interpret politically engaged satire. Kelly, for example, may have been a bona fide liberal in the early 1950s, but a decade later the cultural and media landscape had changed so drastically—and his own lifestyle and business practices had drifted into such bourgeois territory—that he could easily have been considered a conservative if viewed from a particular angle. The blanket assertion that all good satirists are liberal also seems to disregard entire genres of Augustan satire (think of Jonathan Swift) that are arguably progressive (reforming society and individuals for the better), even though they used the tools of comedy and social criticism to correct foolish deviations from conservative tradition, at times, rather than to challenge a privileged status quo.

Even so, Kelly's conviction that a true humorist must be a subversive champion of the underdog is a largely effective criterion for judging the clarity and consistency of both his work and the work of his cartooning peers at mid-century in the United States. Given the conservative climate of the 1950s and the rigid strictures of the comics page, choosing to challenge the status quo or to champion forgotten or dissenting voices on the margins of society took real courage and ingenuity. The next chapter, on Kelly's business practices, describes the behind-the-scenes battles that allowed him to achieve much of that unusual success as a liberal comedic-satirist.

CHAPTER 3

Walt Kelly, Pragmatic Auteur

Of the different roles Walt Kelly played in his life, he is best loved as a comic strip artist—a craft in which he combined the skills of cartooning, comedy, and satire; few cartoonists in the history of the medium have been able to match his ability to deliver aesthetic, comedic, and intellectual pleasure in one package, and to do so consistently. But Kelly's ability to achieve such excellence in creating rich and provocative comics was contingent on his success at performing a variety of behind-the-scenes roles such as businessman, self-promoter, industry representative, and auteur (a popular artist with a distinctive style or vision who keeps creative control over his or her work). Indeed, the uniqueness of *Pogo*—its combination of topical satire, Disney-esque character construction, and slapstick verbal and visual comedy—was made possible only because of Kelly's savvy navigation of the complex business shoals surrounding the funnies page.

The newspaper comics profession in the mid-twentieth century was, in fact, an intimidating industry for artists—one that promised great wealth to the few superstars who rose to the top, but that gave little clout or independence to most creators. Like directors in Hollywood during the same era, the artist who could assert his or her unique vision in the face of massive institutional and economic pressures was the exception rather than the rule. Unbalanced contracts, touchy editors, merchandising pressures, shrinking formats, scandals in related mediums—all these factors conspired against cartoonists attempting to create strips that were aesthetically innovative, comedically complex, or satirically subversive. So an examination of how Kelly beat the system—in effect, how he achieved auteur-like clout and used it productively at times, and less profitably at others—is in order.

Despite Kelly's overall success in operating as an independent artist and satirist, the inside story of Kelly's career as a savvy businessman is not all heroics. As with any artist working in a highly commercialized field, Kelly had to make significant compromises on occasion. Most of those choices were benignly pragmatic—the essential concessions that an artist must make in order to gain access to the power and distribution mechanisms of a mainstream medium. But some might count as real missteps that reveal a side of Kelly's business persona that was too eager to please, too content to enjoy the privileges of success, or too fearful of appearing unprofessional. Interestingly, there are also a few moments when he was perhaps too stubbornly principled and thus lost out on opportunities to amplify the cultural reach of his work. Kelly, in other words, was a complicated man, driven by both an adherence to high principles and a desire to be a popular and wealthy cartoonist.

In this chapter I will explore these complexities through several discussions: a review of the principle of auteurship and how it applies to comics in general and Kelly's work specifically; an exploration of how Kelly's engagement with the craft and industry of several different comic mediums—including animation, comic books, and political cartooning—shaped his genre-defying comic strip; and an analysis of critical business choices—both good and bad—Kelly made at key points in his career. Four facets of his career as a businessman, in fact, are worthy of special investigation: his relationship with the Post-Hall syndicate, his various battles and compromises with touchy newspaper editors, his work as the president of the National Cartoonists Society, and his efforts to translate his comic strip into animated films. In each of these capacities Kelly behaved at different moments as a pioneering auteur, an opportunist, a stubborn iconoclast, and a pragmatist. A final assessment of Kelly's work as a businessman, nevertheless, has to include an estimation of how the sum of his behind-the-scenes choices affected the quality and integrity of his work. Given that criteria, one could look at individual episodes in his career and determine that the results are mixed; but if one considers his most important art and satire—his mature comic strip from about 1950 through 1965—Kelly fares extremely well.

The Auteur Concept

The term *auteur* was first applied within the film industry by French filmmakers and theorists in the early 1960s. One of the theory's principal points was that many "films produced under the most industrialized conditions [Hollywood] were held to bear the mark of an artist/auteur" (Turner 43). This concept allowed film scholars and fans to take seriously films that had previously been written off as hopelessly formulaic products churned out by art-crushing culture industries. The model also encouraged scholars and critics to recognize the signature styles of filmmakers such as Alfred Hitchcock and John Ford who worked within rigid genre categories (western, comedy, science fiction) that were traditionally seen as less worthy of celebration than "art film" by academics. Finally, critics could celebrate more fully a few extraordinary directors like Preston Sturges or Orson Welles who were able to articulate unique, sometimes subversive, worldviews in the face of the rigid economic and institutional filters of the studio system.

Since comic strips, like popular films, are categorized according to genre, created within fairly strict institutional and industrial conditions, and have traditionally been held in low esteem by both highbrow and Marxist-minded critics, the auteur concept—with some caveats—can be usefully applied to this medium in general and to Kelly's work in particular. To begin, however, one must address the limitations and flaws of the theory. For example, one critical problem with the auteur concept is that it often overemphasizes the role of a lone creator working within popular mediums that actually feature a great deal of collaboration. This is especially true of cinema, where a finished film includes the contributions of many additional figures such as screenwriters, composers, actors, producers, and others who make their mark on the film. Comic books have a similar level of collaboration because their tight production schedules require a radical distribution of creative tasks.

Given the relatively solitary nature of the comic-stripping craft, and the fact that cartoonists are called upon to do almost everything in the creation of their movie-like strips (to be at once the writer, set designer, comedian, director, editor, and so forth), the collaboration issue would seem to be less of a stumbling block in applying the concept to this field. Comic strips are surprisingly labor-intensive, however, and the successful completion of a strip on a daily basis, year after year, requires a significant amount of collaborative help; those contributions include the input of syndicate editors (especially in the strip's initial gestation phase), feedback from colleagues in the field, and the aid of assistants who deal with the business side of the craft or who help with time-consuming tasks such as inking or lettering. Defining comic strip production as a place for pure auteurship can thus lead one to ignore or undervalue these other contributors.

The fetishization of an extreme notion of the auteur's creative independence also runs the risk of accepting two earlier cultural models of artistic genius: the nineteenth-century romantic artist who creates a work of original, visionary greatness, and the avant-garde modernist who operates outside the pressures of commerce and society, and is ahead of his or her time (Fabe 122). Acceptance of the assumptions embedded within these models poses several problems. First, they trap the scholar or fan into measuring a popular work of art against the hierarchies and standards of high culture (Wexman 9). While it is true many of the best works of popular culture are created by artists who are not overly burdened with restrictions and pressures, these same creators also benefit from creative parameters, wise editing, collaborative aid, and audience feedback. Popular texts such as comic strips are refined and made more resonant, in fact, as a result of these mediations.

Overemphasizing the idea of artistic independence in the creation of popular culture also ignores the skills and intelligence required to create a distinctive and superior body of work over a number of years while still working within the restrictions of a commercial process. Orson Welles, for example, is not the best example of an auteur in the broadest sense of the term even though he behaved as "author" in the creation of his masterpiece, *Citizen Kane* (famously fighting against the strictures of the studio system, publicly mocking a powerful newspaper mogul—William Randolph Hearst—and fulfilling multiple creative roles). The problem is that he defied so many industry rules and expectations in his production of this one film that he essentially behaved as an errant, avant-garde artist, and as a result of burning so many bridges in the process of making his masterpiece, was arguably unable to sustain a long and productive career.

In the realm of comic strips, George Herriman—an independent "genius" who was celebrated by the critic, Gilbert Seldes—is also an awkward match for the auteur theory if one eschews the high art assumptions that can sometimes attach themselves to the idea of independent authorship. While Herriman's work is undeniably great, he essentially worked in a creative vacuum, untroubled by the pressures created by picky editors and fickle readers. This was because William Randolph Hearst, the greatest newspaper mogul of the early twentieth century, adored Herriman and his work, and vowed that the artist would always have a job and publishing venue within his newspaper empire no matter how low Herriman's syndication numbers fell. In fact, they plummeted to just 30 papers at one point, a number that would killed any other strip (Stewart 20). Herriman's career thus resembles an older model of high cultural production—one with patrons nurturing visionary geniuses; and this certainly seems to play a big role in Seldes's decision in 1924 to single out Herriman's work as the one truly great strip produced by this emerging American medium in the first decades of the twentieth century. Better examples, therefore, of auteurs in the broadest sense, are filmmakers like Preston Sturges or cartoonists like Walt Kelly, who worked both *against* and *within* the pressures and strictures of their mediums.

Finally, the auteur framework that favors a Romantic or Modernist notion of authorship does little justice to complex twentieth-century popular texts that are both hybrid constructions (melding visual and verbal languages) and amalgamations from a variety of genres, templates, and previous works (a text that is a "tissue of quotations," in Barthes's words) (Barthes 146). To explain, comic strips and films are rarely "original" in the avant-garde sense; they draw from existing patterns and types by reworking genre conventions, quoting previous works, and retelling old stories or jokes in new ways. This acknowledgment of the intertextuality of popular works aligns nicely with a Bakhtinian notion of sprawling, heteroglossic texts like *Pogo*—where multiple voices and modes of speech intersect in democratic, carnivalesque fashion. It also works well with the postmodern view of the artist as a sensitive conduit channeling multiple voices and energies. In sum, if one still finds it useful to talk about a filmmaker or cartoonist as the author of his or her work, that designation should acknowledge collaborative influences; it must avoid high art assumptions; and it should embrace more complex, postmodern conceptions of both author and text.

Walt Kelly as Auteur and Sateur

So how does Kelly fare according to an expanded and qualified idea of auteurship? To begin, the qualifications explored in the previous pages help to recognize some of the complexities in Kelly's work. First, many people collaborated with Kelly at different points in his career to help him create his best work: his official assistants (George Ward and Henry Shikuma); his wives, Helen, Stephanie, and Selby (to varying degrees); secretaries (who go unnamed); and syndicate editors. Further, if one takes a longer term view of Kelly's career and recognizes that *Pogo* existed in a gestational state for a number of years, then the list of collaborators could expand to included colleagues at Disney (such as Ward Kimball), political cartooning mentors like Herblock, and friends and colleagues in the comic book and newspaper fields.

There is also the more abstract notion of Kelly collaborating with his fans through letters, chalk-talks, and mock campaign rallies. If one defines Kelly as a poploric storyteller engaged in a sort of media-age call-and-response with his core readers and college students (which I do in the final chapter), then his strip—like a work of resonant folklore—reflects many of the core interests and ideologies of his avid readers. Consequently, Kelly and those fans essentially collaborated in creating a work of popular culture that effectively reflected and shaped a cultural zeitgeist.

A postmodern view of artistic production also helps one to see that Kelly's work was never "original" in the "high art" sense. Derived from a number of sources—including trickster tales, animal fables, pastoral conventions, vaudeville, blackface comedy, Disney aesthetics, and political cartooning devices, *Pogo* was an amalgamation of existing genre conventions, traditional character types, and tropes borrowed from other mediums. So although it was not groundbreaking and visionary in the modernist sense of genius and authorship, it was a work of multi-voiced, Bakhtinian complexity and syncretic vitality. Those dynamic characteristics in his work qualify Kelly as a different type of genius—a sensitive conduit and adept bricoleur, channeling and shaping familiar artistic and narrative conventions.

Given these significant qualifications and complexities, why use the auteur designation for Kelly at all? The answer is that the auteur concept still helps to set him apart as an exceptional cartoonist in several respects: as a satirist intent on communicating a clearly delineated worldview or ideology; as a savvy and independent-minded businessman; and as an artistic innovator, melding the conventions of several mediums. The auteur concept also helps to distinguish Kelly's work both from traditional works of folklore on the one side, and works of avant-garde—niche—popular culture on the other. For example, it is helpful to acknowledge the collaboration between Kelly and his core readers, but one should not confuse *Pogo* with traditional folktales that reflect collective anxieties and aspirations in a deep structuralist sense—one that assumes that Kelly has no other function than to let their collective voice speak through his art (Maule 22). While Kelly's work did exhibit folksy, poploric qualities, it was also a work of pointed satire that reflected a single author's coherent and sometimes idiosyncratic worldview. And while *Pogo* was arguably as excellent as Herriman's

Krazy Kat, Kelly did not have the luxury of creating his work in an artistic vacuum, free from commercial and institutional pressures; instead, Kelly achieved greatness despite (and because of) the pressures of having to please editors and cater to the interests of avid niche *and* mainstream readers.

The auteur concept also still allows one to distinguish Kelly from other popular culture creators content to give in to commercial and institutional pressures and strictures that either erased the individuality of their work or blocked artists from infusing their text with any degree of aesthetic innovation or satiric bite. Kelly, indeed, is one of the few cartoonists in the history of his medium who deserves the designation of being especially iconoclastic and independent as an auteur; other qualifiers might include Al Capp (*Li'l Abner*), Charles Schulz (*Peanuts*—in some respects), Garry Trudeau (*Doonesbury*), Berke Breathed (*Bloom County*), Bill Watterson (*Calvin and Hobbes*), Lynn Johnston (*For Better or Worse*), Nicole Hollander (*Sylvia*), Darby Conley (*Get Fuzzy*), and Aaron McGruder (*The Boondocks*). In Kelly's strip, like those of these select peers, the connection between aesthetics, subject matter, and worldview (the work's signature style) on one side, and the author's own personal aesthetic, intellectual, or political convictions on the other, is more tightly linked than it is in the typical mainstream strip. And that tight connection is a direct result of artists such as Kelly and these peers protecting their work from excessive commercial and institutional filtering.

Finally, the degree to which cartoonists rely on outside assistance can serve as an effective measure of how well a cartoonist like Kelly embodies the ethic of independent auteurship. For example, a comic strip artist with an auteur-like sensibility would resist the idea of farming out the most critical tasks—such as the actual writing of the strip—to other writers, collaborators, or assistants (a common practice with hugely successful strips such as *Garfield*). And when these artists die, their work would be less likely to be carried on by another artist because the strip was so thoroughly a product of the original cartoonist's personal talent and vision. The fact that the two attempts to revive Kelly's strip after his death ultimately failed seems to support this assertion.

Interestingly, auteur-like cartoonists are also more likely than typical cartooning colleagues to use some form of satire in their strips. That satire can feature political topicality in some cases (Kelly, Capp, and Trudeau), or broad, cosmic musings in others (Watterson, Johnston, Conley); it can also challenge industry conventions and prod complacent readers with parodies and commentary that critique the newspaper and comics industries themselves (Breathed, Hollander, and McGruder). Indeed, through the decades of the twentieth century, those who were most critical of draconian practices within the syndicate and newspaper industries were, in fact, satirists of some sort. The connection between auteurship and satire thus makes sense because these were the cartoonists who had the most at stake in negotiations over artists' rights, merchandising, and censorship. Their ability to create challenging social satire marked with an idiosyncratic worldview and aesthetic, and to satisfy audiences who came to expect a certain level of irreverence and topicality, hinged on their ability to operate with this auteur-like independence. These satiric cartoonists, in fact, deserve a modified designation—that of "sateur," because they embodied the ideal of a popular satirist who fights for a significant degree of economic and institutional freedom in order to engage in principled, satiric social criticism.

Before focusing too much on Kelly's resistance to commercial and institutional pressures, however, one should also acknowledge the benefits that resulted from making necessary compromises to satisfy the demands of a commercial medium—of "pandering," to an extent, to editors and a mainstream audience. Antonio Gramsci's notion of cultural incorporation provides a framework within which we can explain and judge some of the benefits or losses of "selling out." It also highlights the critical necessity of satirists achieving and maintaining an auteur-like cultural clout.

According to a Gramscian framework, the dominant culture—which, in Kelly's case, might be a cautious and conservative early '50s media culture intent on suppressing diversions from strict genre conventions and a bourgeois status quo—wants to achieve a political and economic hegemony (a controlling commercial and political interest in the culture). But in order to do this, entertainment executives—as unofficial protectors of that hegemony because of the pressure from cultural guardians and sensitive audiences—try to eliminate or censor the most unruly creators and cultural products. However, they cannot ultimately be that rigid all the time—always insisting that the entertainment they produce conform completely to rigid codes of content and form. This is because the formulaic cultural products created within the heart of the mid-century media industries sometimes only inspired a tepid level of fan devotion (think of the Hollywood studio system's early '50s decline in the face of a rising, disinterested youth culture); and thus entertainment companies were forced, gradually, to incorporate new cultural movements or artists into their offerings who could attract devoted fans because of the relative authenticity, unique markings, and appealingly subversive ideas articulated in their work. Consumers, in other words, may have predictably consumed much of the bland genre entertainment created by culture industries at mid-century, but they often reserved their most avid devotion for texts like *Pogo* that carried the marks of a quirky auteur.

At the same time, an independent sateur such as Kelly, intent on defying genre conventions, rebelling against syndicate formulae for successful strips, and bringing satire to the comics page, required the distribution mechanisms of the mainstream comics page culture in order to exert any significant cultural power. In this situation both sides are thus compelled to enter (figuratively and often literally) into negotiations. In these talks compromises are made all around to achieve the desired benefits from each side: initially, syndicates and newspaper editors are willing to let a contrarian voice into the fold because his or her work could develop into a lucrative cultural product spawning intense fan devotion. The freedom given to these creators is limited, however; the media companies expect that the artist's work generally participates in the reinforcement of "values, norms, perceptions, beliefs, sentiments, and prejudices that support and define the existing distribution of goods, the institutions that decide how this circulation occurs, and the permissible range of disagreement about these processes" (Lears 568). They would not tolerate, in other words, anything that would seriously disrupt the flow of goods and ideas that makes their industry profitable.

The media companies also naturally insist that changes be made to a text before it is given wide distribution. Editing, vetting processes, test audiences, committee reviews, and other such processes all contribute to preparing a work of popular culture for mainstream consumption. Although there may be no conscious plotting to this end, the process of creating a commodity out of a subversive work of art has the tendency to soften its roughest edges, to make it less of a threat to the hegemony of the dominant media industry's art and ideology. From the artist's end, concessions are made up front so he or she can benefit from the monies and distribution options that come from gaining access to the distribution mechanisms of the entertainment industry. These compromises could include surrendering ownership of the work, bowing to some editorial shaping, and, in general, conforming to existing rules of genre, content, and form.

There is, of course, a potential risk or downside for each participant in making these deals. The artist risks having his or her work flattened and "commodified" to the point that it no longer reflects his or her idiosyncratic aesthetics and worldview. At the same time, these media companies risk letting in an unruly artist who will defy the system, change rules in favor of artists, or even transform the cultural landscape in disruptive ways because of the broad social reach they were granted. The concepts of incorporation and auteurship now intersect, because the most interesting cases to study are those such as Kelly's where the artist is somehow able to both avoid the worst dangers that come with commercialization, *and* maximize the opportunities of participation in the mainstream entertainment industry. One could say that auteurs are artists who essentially "win" in these negotiations in the long run. They may start out their careers at a distinct disadvantage to the entertainment industry, but after building the clout that comes with broad popularity and an intensely devoted fan base, they can periodically renegotiate the terms of their contracts, protecting themselves from the worst interference that would oppressively censor their views or impinge on their creativity.

Within this Gramscian framework, it does indeed seem useful to view Kelly's career as a series of relative wins and losses in the battle between art and satire on the one hand, and commerce and institutional strictures on the other. The fact that Kelly rarely talked about his work in these combative terms, however, complicates the discussion. In fact, he stated repeatedly at different points in his career that ". . . all I'm trying to do is be friendly and maybe make a buck at it" (Kelly "Unpublished Autobiographical Sketch" 29). Of course, he also insisted on owning the copyright to his strip, arguing that "good cartoonists are subversive—they are against things," and complained openly about editors allowing the funnies page to become an "inert baby sitter for the brain," when it actually had the potential to be "the most stimulating section of the paper" (O'Sullivan 93; Kelly, *Ten Ever-Lovin' Blue-Eyed Years with Pogo* 135).

So how does one reconcile these contradictions? Is it justified to impose a narrative of struggle on a cartoonist's career when the artist himself often claimed he was uninterested in picking fights? An explanation (and justification for persisting with the art vs. commerce battle metaphor) can be made from two directions: first, by acknowledging it was strategically useful to Kelly to employ the pose or rhetoric of the noncombatant within a field that did not reward or even tolerate attitudes of subversion or defiance; and second, by recognizing that Kelly may have been conflicted in his own worldview and behavior as a result of having grown up in relatively unstable financial circumstances.

The first explanation is that Kelly essentially had to maintain the pose of being an unpretentious businessman at key moments in his career in order to allay the fears of conservative editors and cultural critics who might have perceived him as a subversive agitator using a popular medium to forward a political agenda. For example, when speaking with college students at a rally, he could be bold about his status as a satiric pundit and cartooning iconoclast but when corresponding with editors or speaking in front of conservative businessmen (such as at a Kiwanis club meeting), he would pragmatically tone down the rhetoric, sometimes even asserting that "I have no social messages" in my comic strip ("Walt Kelly Insists Comic Strip Aims at Amusement" 1). Kelly also seemed to avoid trumpeting subversive intentions or lofty designs when consorting with peers in the newspaper industry from a conservative school that emphasized working class humility and unshowy professionalism. When adopting that persona, he would modestly assert that "I come from a school of old-time cartooning. In the old days, we tried to make a buck out of drawing" (Gerson 1).

Having nurtured the dream of becoming a wealthy cartoonist from a young age, and having waited so long into his adult life before achieving any sort of financial stability, Kelly also seems to have been loathe at times to bite too hard on the hand that fed him. Indeed, as his biography reveals, he was a bon vivant who wanted to enjoy the privileges and pleasures that came with being a celebrity, and that desire often trumped loftier principles. As I chart the key moments in his career when business clashed with art, that pattern of making compromises for financial benefit will emerge. One can, of course, identify other patterns as well—for example, that of being consistent in his exploration of folk cultural forms and voices, of adhering to a coherently liberal political philosophy during a highly conservative age, and of advocating for his own auteur-like independence in a field that did not readily acknowledge artists' rights. Combined, these patterns reveal a complex artist and businessman, conflicted and compromised at times, but just as often, clear and assertive in his intentions and actions.

Kelly as Disney Animator

It might seem logical to begin this discussion of business practices with the moment Kelly signed his first contract with the Post-Hall syndicate and launched his career as a successful comic strip artist. But to achieve a complete and more complex understanding of Kelly during the mature phase of his career, one first has to go back to the early years of his professional life. There one can consider how his engagement with the business side of three other cartooning fields—animation, comic books, and political cartoons—shaped his strategies and worldview.

Kelly's desire to be an independent artist was perhaps first ignited as a junior animator within the factory-like system of production at the Disney studios. He worked there for six years, from 1935–1941, with, in his own words, "1,500 other worthies," turning out *Snow White, Fantasia, Pinocchio, Dumbo, The Reluctant Dragon* and *Baby Weems* (Kelly, "Post-Hall Promotional 1954" 1). Following a pattern similar to other Hollywood studios, Disney executives tried to create mainstream entertainment along genre patterns (perhaps with the exception of *Fantasia*) that would be reliably profitable. As a result, the creative process was ruled by committee and individual artists were generally treated as interchangeable cogs. As the critic Howard Junker has asserted, Disney "animation was unquestionably a craft, not an art. The animator was fitted in somewhere along the assembly line" (Sandler 43). Disney culture featured some progressive practices, of course. For example, artists were immersed in liberal studies, they were given opportunities to study subject matter in real-life settings, and they were encouraged to infuse scenes and characters with a liveliness and fluidity uncommon within the field of animation in general. Nevertheless, unless one was a member of the elite corps of senior animators, the work of an artist could be highly restrictive and monotonous: the inking and coloring of countless cels or the tedious "in-betweening" that linked the key drawings done by senior animators.

The fact that Kelly chafed against these arrangements was an early sign that he aspired to be a more independent artist. For example, while at Disney he was unable or unwilling to get the in-betweening right (continually trying to impose his own aesthetic, instead of following the strict model sheets); he insisted on keeping his East Coast journalist persona (bow ties and three-piece suits); and he disrupted the seemingly conformist environment with irreverent pranks and over-the-top musical performances (Andrae and Blum 135). Kelly also found himself in an awkward arrangement near the end of his tenure there. As an assistant to Fred Ward, he chose to affiliate himself with the senior animators, but he was still limited to the salary, privileges, and job security of a junior animator. From this mid-level position he could see both sides of the fence clearly: on the side of the senior animators, high pay and the ability to work as the "author" of small portions of each major film, and on the other (that of the junior animators), low pay, no screen credits, and chronic abuse within the factory-like system.

To make matters more complicated, Kelly happened to be working at Disney when tensions between management and the bulk of the studio's employees was at a peak. In the late 1930s junior animators had been asked to work long overtime hours without pay on *Snow White* with the promise they would be rewarded later for their diligence and sacrifice. Instead, many were later laid off or rehired at a slightly higher wage that simply disqualified them for earning one and half overtime if asked to work longer hours in the future (Schickel). The 1941 strike thus put Kelly at the crux of a literal battle over artists' rights and the demands of factory-like entertainment production. It also presented him with a professional dilemma since his allegiance was equally divided between the non-striking senior animators and his peers in the drawing pen. In a move that foreshadowed Kelly's later ambivalence about collective bargaining practices, he took a leave of absence to deal with an "illness in the family," thus avoiding the strike and the awkwardness of choosing sides. He secretly crossed the strike line, however, and met personally with Walt Disney to hand in his resignation and secure work back East doing comic book work for Dell, a publisher of a number of Disney titles.

Kelly as Comic Book Artist and Writer

The production of comic books during Kelly's era was usually similar to that of films in terms of the number of people who had a hand in the construction of a particular text. Work was parceled out among writers, pencilers, inkers, colorists, editors, and others—and thus the potential for a comic book to bear the stamp of a quirky auteur was often minimal. But because Kelly was working in an underappreciated (albeit high-selling) corner of the field—creating children's titles—he was given an unusual level of responsibility in both writing and drawing his features for Dell.[3] Kelly was considered a multi-talented and prolific artist by his comic book editors and peers during these years, but it is possible this unusual level of creative license he enjoyed working on the *Animal Comics* and *Our Gang* series in the 1940s may have had as much to do with the company wanting to save money, as it did with giving Kelly an unusual amount of clout or respect. Whatever the reasons, Kelly was able to flex more creative muscles as a comic book creator than at Disney, imbuing many of his comic book stories with his own aesthetic and comedic sensibilities. That sensibility did lead him to include some potentially offensive material in his comics—trickster tales, blackface tropes, and Southern dialects; but removed from the eyes of most critics and the demands of a large entertainment industry, he was able to experiment, make a few missteps, and find an original treatment of these ingredients along the way.

One of Kelly's core objectives as a thoughtful comic book auteur, however— to create layered, folk-like satiric fables—was stymied by the problematic cultural status of comic books and the narrow demographic targeting of the "kiddie" genre in which he labored. Kelly later explained he wanted to target both parents and kids through his comic books by weeding "the corn out of the action and dialogue" (Kelly, "Unpublished Autobiographical Sketch" 15). Speaking in the third person, he elaborated on the limitations of the medium:

> Comic books then were not more than a half dozen years old but they had already proven themselves to be derelict of ideas of any real worth and most of what was turned out was a bad rehash of the more sensational strips that appeared in newspapers. In many cases this was compounding vulgarity with felony and little of anything was FUNNY in them. With an eye to improving the breed Kelly tried his hand at Fairy Tale comics and the publisher said that Kelly would improve himself right out of a job. The Fairy Tales were lauded by important people, most of whom received free copies, and sold like mud pies." (Kelly, "Unpublished Autobiographical Sketch" 12)

Three problems, then, limited Kelly's ability to do something satiric and expansive with the comic book medium: first, the stigma attached to comic books— that they were juvenile entertainment for children; second, creators were expected to create stories and characters along established, rigid genre patterns that gave little room for hybrid forms or for the targeting of multiple demographics; and third, the most avid comic book buyers had little interest in layered, thought-provoking, comedic fables. Kelly highlighted this final obstacle by sharing the reaction of a young comic book fan's experience with the early *Pogo* stories: "That comic book didn't have no action in it. Nobody shot nobody. It was full of mice in red and blue pants. It stunk" (Becker 351). To overcome these issues, Kelly would either need to find a medium that targeted multiple demographics and allowed for genre experimentation—or force an existing medium to expand its parameters to fit to his original work and vision.

Kelly as Political Cartoonist

In charting the evolutionary arc of Kelly's career as an auteur, one could say that the next phase of Kelly's professional life—as a political cartoonist for a big city newspaper in the late 1940s—was a significant step in moving closer to that ideal creative independence. In this job, for the *New York Star*, he experienced new levels of artistic freedom, he was forced by necessity to refine his satiric vision, and he was introduced to additional ways to blend mediums and defy genre boundaries. Key to these steps forward was the nature of the paper for which he worked. The *Star* was an experimental paper that grew out of the famed "ad-less, leftish" paper, *PM*, that had been around since 1940; the *Star* version lasted for less than a year, running from June 1948 to 28 January 1949 (Crouch, "What do you know" 10). Because this newspaper teetered on precarious financial grounding during its brief run, Kelly, like many on the staff, was hired to perform a number of tasks. In his case, this included work as art director, spot illustrator, designer, adman, political cartoonist, and later (by his own choice), comic strip artist. All that creative shifting of gears certainly expanded Kelly's skill sets, and the weight of responsibility perhaps gave him some of the confidence required of a good auteur.

The political orientation of the paper also forced Kelly as an editorial cartoonist to find profound things to say on a daily basis about a variety of cultural issues. The *Star* was pro-labor and pro-Israel; it claimed independence from "the tyranny of slogans and color . . . [and] . . . vested interests;" and it was widely seen as the "semiofficial outlet for advanced liberal thought" put together by "a staff of indefatigable crusaders" (Crouch, "What do you know" 10). It must have been a daunting task for Kelly to develop the cartooning style and editorial voice for such a peculiar paper in a news-heavy year: a presidential election, inflation, labor issues, a building boom, civil war in China, the Olympics, and so on. In contrast to the lighthearted tone of *Pogo*, Kelly's political cartoons for the *Star* were generally sober and indignant, and his penmanship was sometimes stilted—as if he were insecure about his methods. Still, his work received some significant acclaim. For example, his series about Tom Dewey as a "mechanical man" garnered him the Heywood Broun Award for crusading journalism (Crouch, "Walt Kelly's Editorial Cartoons" 38). This success, and the general challenge of being a thoughtful editorialist on a daily basis, perhaps helped Kelly see himself as a legitimate pundit or cultural critic—a watchdog of social ills and political abuses.

It was also at the *Star* that Kelly first tried out a comic strip version of *Pogo*. At this point in the history of the medium, most comic strip artists endured a lengthy syndicate-editing and vetting process before having their work introduced to the public. But given Kelly's unusual position at the *Star*, he was able to bypass those filters and publish his strip with minimal interference. As a result, there were some weaknesses to the earliest strips that could have been remedied with good editing. It was sometimes a bit too visually dense, for example, and the "Southern" dialect was overly hammy in places. It is significant, nevertheless, that the circumstances at the *Star* gave him the confidence and freedom to create a feature that did not seem concocted by a marketing committee—that defied genre categorization. There was the highly accessible visual style at the center of his work (a Disney-esque cuteness), but the other aspects of the strip were challenging—elements most editors would see as funnies page poison: verbose wordplay, dense dialect, a dated trickster-tale setting, Freudian dynamics between characters, and flirtations with topical issues.

Kelly and National Syndication

When the *Star* went bankrupt in January 1949, Kelly took his strip to syndicates. Editor after editor rejected it on the grounds that it was too complicated and intellectual, or too verbally dense to win over a mainstream readership. Then Kelly caught the attention of the Post-Hall syndicate, a new outfit that had the emerging reputation of being artist-friendly. The youth and relatively small size of the Post-Hall organization made it an ideal fit for Kelly's genre-defying work. They informally gave Kelly free rein to pursue his vision: an animal comic with a huge cast of characters, dense wordplay, and a bit of social satire and commentary. The ten-year contract he signed was similar to the rigid documents most other cartoonists were required to sign during those years, but with one significant exception: the syndicate agreed to immediately transfer ownership rights over to Kelly at the end or renewal of the first contract.

The Post-Hall syndicate devoted a great deal of focus and energy promoting Kelly's work; he reported that they represented him with "care and ferocity" and defended him uwaveringly when editors complained about the satiric content of his work (Marschall, *America's Great* 262). On the strength of the syndicate's promotional campaigns and the inherent quality of Kelly's work, the pessimistic predictions of the other syndicates were proven wrong and an enormous readership quickly embraced Kelly's intellectual and satiric work, making it the fastest-growing strip of the early 1950s in terms of syndication numbers. This rapid rise in popularity enabled Kelly to renegotiate an already favorable contract four years before its actual renewal date. In this second round of contract negotiations Kelly essentially took legal ownership and control of the strip, and ensured that the freedom he enjoyed as a satirist would continue under a more formal, binding agreement.

There is little evidence of friction between Kelly and his syndicate during these negotiations, but it is clear Kelly was a formidable negotiator. His long experience in other cartooning fields gave him a world-savvy knowledge and chutzpah unusual for a fledgling comic strip artist. Kelly indicated as much in a personal letter he sent to an aspiring cartoonist in the late 1950s, explaining how he secured the copyright to his work: "By dint of pluck, hard work, brown eyes and twenty-five years of learning the legal shenanigans, I emerged victor" (Kelly, "Letter, August 14, 1957" 1).

A comparison of language between his 1949 contract and his renewal in 1956 indicates how adamantly Kelly was opposed to the legal conventions of a business that put the cartoonist in a subservient position and placed nearly all the merchandising, promotional, financial, and editorial decisions in the hands of syndicate editors (my emphases below):

1949: the Producer agrees . . . not to work either gratuitously or for compensation at any time during the existence of this contract for any person, association, firm or corporation in the production of any comic series, strip or feature which, in the judgment of the Syndicate, could be sold in competition with said "POGO" comic series . . . (2)

1956: **Nothing** contained in this agreement shall be construed as **limiting or restricting** the personal, artistic, literary, or commercial endeavors, activities or conduct of the Artist. The Artist shall be **free to work**, either gratuitously or for compensation, at any time during the term of this agreement, for any person, association, firm or corporation. (9)

1949: It is agreed that the legal title to all of the aforesaid comic series . . . shall be in the Syndicate, which shall have the right to copyright the said comic series . . . in its own name . . . and in all respects to have the exclusive right to deal with and make whatever use of said comic feature as seems advisable to the Syndicate. (6)

1956: **Nothing** contained herein shall be construed as a release, sale, transfer, or assignment by the Artist to the Syndicate of any right, title or interest, legal or equitable, in and to all or any part, element, feature or aspect of any daily or Sunday strip, the cartoon characters appearing therein, the word or title "POGO," or in and to any subsidiary or secondary rights that may, can and do attach thereto. **All copyrights, trademarks, trade names, patents, or other . . . rights . . . shall belong solely and wholly to the Artist . . .** (9)

1949: It is mutually understood and agreed that the Syndicate shall have entire editorial supervision of said comic series . . . and may, without notice to or consent of the Producer, make any changes, alterations, revisions, deletions or additions in or to the drawing, wording or title . . . and that all said comic series . . . shall be subject to the Syndicate's approval, whose judgment thereon shall be final. (6)

1956: Except as specifically provided . . . **the Syndicate shall have no rights of editorial supervision over the daily or Sunday strips,** . . . and the Syndicate shall not make any alterations, revisions, deletions, additions or any other whatsoever in or to said strips without the prior written consent of the Artist. **The editorial judgment of the artist shall be final and binding** upon the Syndicate . . . (3)

1949: It is further understood and agreed that the Syndicate shall have the entire and exclusive right . . . to the comic series, . . . including . . . the motion picture,

> drama, radio, television, and book publication rights therein, the right of repro-
> duction in the form of toys, novelties, games, merchandise and otherwise . . .
> and any and all characters appearing in or in connection therewith. (3)
>
> 1956: It is specifically understood that all copyrights, trademarks, patents, trade
> names or any other common law or statutory property rights in any particular
> idea . . . for such **merchandising . . . shall belong solely and wholly to the
> Artist**, and that Syndicates' sole right or interest therein shall be to receive a
> portion of the gross cash proceeds. (7–8)

The contract also asserted that Kelly's earnings would never go below $100,000 a year, regardless of the performance of the strip—an unusual guarantee in such a competitive field. Indeed, it is interesting to note how adamantly artist-friendly Kelly's language is in the revised contracts. The term "producer" in the earlier contract, in fact, is literally replaced with the term "artist" in the 1956 version. Kelly essentially achieved unprecedented power and independence in copyright ownership, freedom from excessive editorial meddling, and control of merchandising decisions or related commercial and creative projects. These concessions by Kelly's syndicate were unusual for the 1950s, and they remain unusual today. Al Capp, one of Kelly's peers, for example, had a very negative relationship with his syndicate:

> The year was 1957. Alfred had been with United Features Syndicate for over 20 ac-
> rimonious years. His original contract gave the Syndicate ownership of *L'il Abner*, a
> possession that [Capp] abhorred and fought against in increasing acrimony as his
> comic strip grew in importance. United Features had grudgingly agreed after two
> bloody decades to cede Alfred his creation. They had little or no choice. And they
> were making money from the features. ("Long Distance" *Al Capp Remembered* 111)

In the subsequent decades, there have only been a handful of artists such as Garry Trudeau, Berke Breathed, and Lynn Johnston who have wrested ownership of their strips away from syndicates. And high-profile battles between artists and syndicates over copyright ownership and merchandising decisions—such as Bill Watterson vs. Universal Press Syndicate—highlight the continued rarity of an artist-friendly contract.

The most obvious outcome of Kelly's unusual contract was the freedom to behave as a sateur—an auteur who leverages his or her clout to create challenging social and political satire. But it also had an impact on other aspects of his work. For example, he was able to be cautious about merchandising opportunities, preventing over-saturation of his characters and avoiding commercial products that would damage the quality and resonance of his comedy and satire. Close friends reported that he rejected most merchandising and advertising deals; he shunned, for instance, attempts to commercialize *Pogo*, "blowing soap bubbles or cleaning floors in a TV commercial" (Kercher 62; Ward 2). He did, nevertheless, embrace a limited number of merchandising deals that seemed to reinforce the character of the strip; this included figurines, an audio record of songs from the strip, and a variety of book collections of strips and supplemental stories. The relative rarity of these items made them highly sought-after collectibles in subsequent years.

Kelly's resistance to over-merchandising set an example for future auteurs. Watterson, for example, who never let his characters stray beyond the book collections, reflects on Kelly's wisdom in protecting his work:

> First, it interests me that for all the appeal of those cute animals in *Pogo*, Kelly did very little in the way of licensing. I vaguely remember seeing an animated *Pogo* TV special, and I have a rather poor plastic sculpture of Churchy that came with soap or something. To venture my own opinion, I think the comic strip world is much more fragile than most people realize, and that wonderful, lifelike characters are easily corrupted and cheapened by having them appear on every drugstore shelf and rack. Whatever Kelly's reasoning for refusing the glut of merchandising that was undoubtedly available to him, he set little precedent by his decision, which I think is a shame. Several fine strips have turned themselves into shameless advertisements for products. I, for one, am glad it didn't happen to *Pogo*." (Watterson 14)

Kelly as Comic Strip Artist

As cited earlier, Kelly had an ambitious vision of what the comics page could be: readers might approach it as the "most stimulating part of the paper," rather than a mental babysitter, and individual strips could be richly challenging in their storytelling and satiric content—capable of communicating "a real message" (Kelly *Ten Ever-Lovin' Blue-Eyed Years with Pogo* 135; "Pogo's Campaign Launched" 1). Using his strip as a model of what that level of creative stimulation would look like, comics could potentially feature complex verbal comedy, playful philosophizing, topical satire, genre-defying storylines, and syncretic fusions of folk forms and contemporary voices and ideas. But in challenging the conventions of the syndicate and newspaper industries that conspired against artists being able to achieve their full creative potential, Kelly ran into several significant obstacles: persistently critical perceptions among some cultural guardians of comic strips as being juvenile and lowbrow; industry practices such as censorship and popularity polling that favored lowest common denominator art and comedy; the complacency of cartooning peers; and, ultimately to a significant degree, his own opportunism.

When one surveys the critical views of cultural commentators toward comic strips at mid-century, Kelly may have been in the minority in his faith in the potential of the medium. Gilbert Seldes is often held up as an example of a high-brow critic who brought to the highly educated public's notice, for the first time, this underappreciated medium in 1927 (*The Seven Lively Arts*). But his praise was highly qualified, singling out only a few exceptional works such as *Krazy Kat* from what he considered the general dross of the funnies page. And then in 1947 Colton Waugh published the first book-length study of the medium that treated it with significant respect. But even several years later at the dawn of Kelly's career, a majority of cultural guardians and critics still ascribed to the lingering, early twentieth-century prejudice that comic strips were "infantile, brutal, un-sophisticated, and subliterate" (Hajdu 12). For example, in 1953 a writer for *The Times Literary Supplement* complained that the popularity of comic strips was a "menace to democracy;" the practice of reading them would "create a society with two classes: the thinking and intelligent minority and the strip-ridden ma-jority which is incapable of independent thinking and accepts ready-made views, if presented by badly drawn pictures." He concluded by equating comic strips with cave paintings, and warned that "Literature began with comic strips; if we are not careful, it may also end with them" (The Art of an Unknown Future" 348).

Kelly had to counter these perceptions throughout his career with pep talks to peers, editorial commentary about the history and significance of the me-dium, and promotional materials given to editors. But his most effective defense was simply producing an inspired strip, day after day, that defied those low ex-pectations. The fact that many of the great cartoonists of the subsequent 40 years, such as Garry Trudeau and Bill Watterson, cite him as a major influence, suggests that he succeeded in modeling the potential of the medium through his actual work. Furthermore, there are the testimonies of thoughtful fans—many of them children—who felt compelled to write Kelly letters in which they sound like converts to his vision:

> To find a comic strip full of endearing creatures almost devoid of violence, brim-ful of satire and a marvelous use of language—this is no longer something to be hoped for. This is *Pogo*. (Dorothy Siegel)

> I am writing to tell you how much I enjoy reading *Pogo*. Your comic is an inoffensive satire on the faults of human. Other members of my family also enjoy *Pogo*. (Karen Zacha)

> The cartoons in the paper are not just for the children and illiterate persons. One must have a knowledge of current events really to appreciate some comic strips like *Pogo*. (Samuel Casey)

> Newspaper comics to me are a means of escape from my everyday troubles and

worries. Cartoonists sometimes introduce moral, social and political happenings and ideas into their scripts, making their comics more enjoyable and often educational. (Paul Metcalf, age 13) ("Over the Transom")

Kelly was equally effective at creating devoted fans through his mock-presidential campaigns in 1952 and 1956. Traveling around the country to give both silly stump speeches and serious lectures at colleges about art and politics, Kelly convinced a generation of young adults to perceive comic strips (and perhaps popular cultural products in general) as legitimate vehicles for both entertainment and ideological expression and debate. The final chapter of this study documents in greater detail Kelly's interactions with both everyday comics page readers and the participants in these college rallies.

Kelly as Industry Agitator and Leader

Kelly's behind-the-scenes efforts to legitimize his medium and ensure the continued health of his own convention-defying work were more complex and contradictory than his relatively straightforward promotion of the medium among his core readers. Indeed, as Kelly negotiated with editors, sparred with colleagues as the President of the National Cartoonists Society, and represented his medium at U.S. Senate hearings, he alternated strategies and stands—sometimes pushing for progressive change, and at other times settling for complacent compromise. At the core of Kelly's seemingly contradictory behavior was a complex view of what kind of material the comics page should feature. On the one hand, he took a strong stand on any industry practices or attitudes that would conspire against his right to include satire or "intellectual" content in his work. On the other, he actively campaigned against the inclusion of racy or violent material he considered inappropriate for children or families.

Kelly's promotion of intellectual strips included complaints leveled at less ambitious strips, campaigns against popularity polls, and resistance to efforts by editors to censor the satiric content of his work. He was generally cautious about publicly attacking comic strip work that he considered unimaginative or inferior, but among industry friends he could be highly critical, expressing a frustration with peers who were "timorous and overly cautious" (Kercher 57). In the strip itself, he could also make his judgments clear, including generalized parodies of lame cartooning conventions such as simplistic gags, and specific lampoons of particular works such as Harold Gray's *Little Orphan Annie*, a strip he considered to be contrived and melodramatic. In return, some of Kelly's less politically engaged colleagues resented his strident insistence that good cartoonists had to be against something. Charles Schulz, for example, considered the editorializing in Kelly's strip to be too serious and "heavy-handed" for the comics page (Marschall and Groth 9).

When clashing with newspaper editors, Kelly was opposed to any practice that might limit the narrative range and creative content of comic strips. For example, he felt that crude newspaper polling would shortchange intellectual or satiric strips because the inaccurate methods of these samples would give too much clout to a vocal minority opposed to any social or political commentary on the funnies page. Kelly argued that

> Newspaper polls of readership often show so-called intellectual strips as being near the bottom of the list in popularity. All that a newspaper has to do is drop a strip so characterized and it soon discovers who answers polls. Hundreds of letters have flooded into editorial offices and switchboards have literally been plugged up with incoming calls of protest. In almost every case that I know of the strip has been restored usually with a front-page apology to the readers. To me this would prove that some large sections of the public do not respond readily to polls. And from this I would infer that there is a widespread difference in the tastes of the American public. (Kelly, *Ten Ever-Lovin' Blue-Eyed Years with Pogo* 135)

Figure 3.1: Walt Kelly, "We can safely presume . . . ,"
Pogo, 1956.

Kelly also used his comic strip to mock the crudeness of polling methods (Figure 3.1). The episode from which the preceeding frame was drawn, in fact, was published by Kelly's syndicate in trade journals as a part of a campaign used to discourage other papers from dropping the strip after inaccurate polling—and facing the resultant protests from die-hard readers.

In addition to effectively challenging these crude, lowest-common-denominator studies of audience-reading preferences, Kelly also identifies here the auteur's power to resist meddlesome strategies of censorship and cancellation. As the first chapter documented, Kelly often had to exercise that clout as editors attempted to move, censor, or cancel his strips that included topical satire; his devoted, core fans came to his rescue on a number of occasions, forcing editors to reinstate his strip after an abrupt cancellation or suspension.

Kelly and the Crusade Against Comic Books

Kelly's opposition to "inappropriate" content on the comics page may seem like a blind spot or contradiction for a cartoonist eager to expand the range of material that could be featured in comic strips, but it can be explained from two angles: first, in terms of sheer pragmatism, it would have been foolhardy to challenge that aspect of the comics page's conservatism at a time when one comparable medium—popular genre films—were severely restricted by the Hay's code of censorship, and when another—comic books—were being attacked by cultural guardians such as Fredric Wertham. And second, Kelly was a relatively bourgeois-minded family man at heart (despite his carousing habits) who was sincerely devoted to the idea that a popular medium such as comic strips (or comic books, for that matter) should not contain material inappropriate for small children or that would offend sensitive readers. This seemingly moralistic side of his character made him an awkward godfather for cartoonists of the late 1960s countercultural movement (many of whom cited him as an influence) who defied any strictures on taboo material, but it did not necessarily contradict his authenticity as the founding figure of 1960s anti-establishment ideology.

Finally, it's possible a hint of opportunism may have accompanied Kelly's adamant denunciation of inappropriate content on the comics page—because his criticisms of comic books were featured prominently in both his early promotional campaigns for his own strip, as well as his later defense of comic strips in general at the height of the anti-comic book crusades when he headed the National Cartoonists Society. In the first case, Kelly was aware of the cultural debates over whether comic book reading caused juvenile delinquency among young people. On a promotional tour in 1952, for example, he had to justify and explain his background as a comic book artist, and assure readers that his current work—though verbally dense and politically engaged—was otherwise accessible and morally acceptable: "there's no reason for a comic strip to be a despised medium; that what with blood-curdling episodes and taking off of girls' clothing, some comics had gotten so bad something had to be done about them" ("Pogo's Campaign Launched" 1). In another speech one year later, he reiterated these points: "[I was] trying to combat the terrible comic material put before children these days—burning down houses, shooting people, tearing the clothes off women—terrible stuff" (Sartwell 1).

Similar sentiments coursed through the professional community a year later. Kelly and his colleagues in the National Cartoonists Society worried in official publications that comic books, "the little problem child of the cartoon family," were going to spoil the neighborhood for everyone ("NCS newsletter May 14, 1955" 1). In addition, members were assured that "The NCS is taking part in the campaign against bad comics. Cartoonists should remember that comic books are next door neighbors to the newspaper comic strip, and you know how an undesirable neighbor can louse up the sales prospects of your house" ("NCS newsletter, July 15, 1954," 7).

Seeing how prevalent these sentiments were in trade publications within the medium, one can better understand the strategic opportunism of the NCS when they were asked to testify at the comic book hearings in New York in 1954. Kelly was president of the NCS at the time, and he had been charged with the tricky job of defending his medium in public against an onslaught of negative press about comics in general in which many critics conflated the various mediums. The bad publicity, in other words, was "rubbing off" onto strips (O'Sullivan 95). In this official capacity Kelly was highly nuanced in his arguments at times, defending free speech and satire, and even attempting to give comic books a fair hearing:

> Comic books frequently do have a great deal of value to society . . . A requirement that literature or art conform to some norm prescribed by an official smacks of an ideology foreign to our system . . . What seems to one to be trash may have for others fleeting or even enduring values . . . [Mr. Kelly has the] deeply held conviction . . . that restraints on free speech and freedom of the press threaten the liberties of all citizens and that the time to resist such restraints is when the first effort is made to impose them, even though in terms, the restraints apply to works of which we disapprove. (Kelly, "Silverman Letter")

At the highly publicized Senate hearings on the alleged connections between juvenile delinquency and comics, however, Kelly and the colleagues who accompanied him, were more unapologetically opportunistic in using William Gaines and his EC line of comic books as a scapegoat. Kelly's comic book publisher, Dell, was also in the front lines of the attack on EC. Helen Meyer, the vice president of Dell, testified as well, praising Kelly, trumpeting the wholesomeness of her firm's kid-oriented comics, and celebrating the inherent layers of censorship at work in newspaper comic strips. In effect, Kelly's affiliation with Dell—as one of their star artists—and position as spokesperson for the National Cartoonists Society positioned him doubly against EC and its line of crime and horror comic books.

Even before taking the stand to testify, Kelly went to elaborate lengths to use this excursion to the Senate hearings as a successful public relations campaign for his own medium and profession. Milton Caniff described his methods:

Kelly organized a counter-move against the negative press all cartoons were getting. In the U.S. Court House on Foley Square in New York a group of cartoonists and illustrators came early and occupied the front seats. As the hearings went on, the Congressmen became aware that we were drawing their portraits. It is hard not to "pose" when that is going on. Before it ended, the jury was hardly listening to the unhappy book artists. After the session we went from one legislator to another delivering the art. Each Congressman flew home with a half dozen drawings of himself—and a dim recall of the testimony. The Elf of the Okefenokee had cast another spell! (O'Sullivan 95)

And then in their actual testimonies in front of the senators, Kelly and his peers eagerly denounced the unwholesome content of their sister medium, making the character of their own work seem angelic in comparison. The following passage from Kelly, lifted directly from the official transcript of the U.S. Senate hearings, illustrates this strategy (my emphases):

The CHAIRMAN: Mr. Kelly, do you have some associates?
Mr. WALT KELLY: I have sir.
The CHAIRMAN: Do you want them to come and sit with you?
Mr. KELLY: I think I would enjoy the company.
The CHAIRMAN: Fine. We would enjoy having them up here. . . .
(Kelly's testimony after being sworn in:)
Mr. KELLY: We thought we would do a little commercial work here and show you some of the ways we proceed in our business . . . [Kelly's colleagues are drawing caricatures of the senators at this point] . . . I have been in the newspaper business and animated cartoons and cartooning generally since about 13 years of age . . . I got into the comic book business at one time back in 1940 or 1941 and had some experience with its early days as before the 1947 debacle of so many crime magazines and so on . . . **I decided that I would help clean up the comic-book business at one time,** by introducing new features, such as folklore stories and things having to do with little boys and little animals in red and blue pants and that sort of thing. So when my comic book folded, the one I started doing that with, I realized there was more to it than met the eye. **Perhaps this was the wrong medium for my particular efforts**. Since then I have been in the strip business, **the comic-strip business which is distinguished from the comic books.** We have found in our business that **our techniques are very effective for bringing about certain moral lessons and giving information and making education more widespread.** . . . We have about 300 members of our society, each one of whom is very proud of the traditions and I think small **nobility of our craft. We would hesitate, any one of us, to draw anything we would not bring into our home. Not only hesitate, I don't think any one of us would do it.** That is about all I have to say in that regard. (Kelly, "Senate Hearing" 44)

Kelly's friend and colleague, Milton Caniff, reiterated in his testimony the distinction between the two mediums and even celebrated the elaborate mediations through which comic strips must pass—as if saying that censorship is already an inherent process within their field:

> . . . I would like to point out here because it has not been done, we first of all represent the newspaper strip as contrasted with the comic book. It is a fact, of course, as you all well know, that the newspaper strip is not only censored by each editor who buys it, precensors it, which is his right, but by the syndicate's own editors, who are many, and highly critical, and then this censorship includes the readers themselves, who are in a position to take the editor to task for printing your material and they are quick to respond. So we are never in doubt as to our status. There will never be any question after the fact. You almost know by the time it hits the street whether or not your material is acceptable to the reader. So we are in this white-hot fight of public judgment, which is as it should be. (Caniff, "Senate Hearing" 45)

There are some disturbing disconnects here. For example, Kelly's flattering chumminess toward the senators seems falsely glad-handing for a cartoonist devoted to satirizing moralistic cultural guardians and meddling politicians. And Kelly's and Caniff's explicit praise of the layers of mediation and censorship inherent in their own industry seems disingenuous coming from two auteurs who complained bitterly in other contexts about the hassle of having to deal with meddling syndicate and newspaper editors (Block 121).

While much of Kelly's behavior and testimony at these hearings was indeed opportunistic—and perhaps even in conflict with his general advocation of artists' rights and freedoms—his position against adult-oriented comic books can still be understood, nevertheless, as consistent with some of his core political convictions. Fredric Wertham, for example, the chief witness against EC at these hearings, was also, like Kelly, progressive in his politics. The two of them were cultural guardians and critics, in a sense, whose seemingly conservative stance on lurid entertainment was driven less by pious notions of morality than by a rational interest in exposing children to the kinds of entertainment and educational materials that they believed would shape them into responsible and ethical citizens. Kelly's later efforts as a spokesman for wholesome and educational television programming for children supports this reading of these deeper possible motivations.

In sum, Kelly's efforts at protecting and promoting his medium—sometimes at the expense of comic books, the "problem child on the block"—were understandable (if not entirely admirable) from both a political and professional perspective. One ironic outcome of this crusade against EC comics in particular was that it led to the creation of *MAD* magazine, the organ of youth-oriented satire that arguably replaced *Pogo* in terms of cultural prominence in the early 1960s. William Gaines, the embattled publisher of the horror comics on display at the Senate hearings, invested his remaining resources in the aftermath of his court battles into a parody-heavy comic that avoided the heavy censorship of the new Comics Code by not classifying itself as a comic book. As a magazine, it could be more outrageous than either comic books or comic strips and according to David Hajdu, ". . . it took aim at adult society with the weaponry of the schoolyard: funny faces, cat-calls, relentless silliness, rudeness, and cruelty" (Hajdu 215). But it could also be more complex and adult-oriented than the mediums it left behind. Hajdu again argues that *MAD* "took the world more seriously than popular adult magazines of the 1950s . . . and it provoked young people to worry a great deal about grown-up matters such as the Cold War, duplicity in politics and business, and social issues such as race relations" (Hajdu 325). Meanwhile, Kelly was left to labor away in a medium that may have avoided additional layers of censorship by trumpeting its self-imposed standards of decency, but in the process may have also relegated itself to the status of being one of the most bourgeois and backwards mainstream mediums in the eyes of a rising generation of college students.

Kelly and Newspaper Editors

Kelly was famous for his generosity with editors and readers, continually sending out original strips, writing funny letters, and making time-consuming public appearances. From the contents of personal letters to editors it is clear he related to them as a fellow diehard newspaperman, sometimes even developing lifelong personal friendships. For example, he would often go out drinking with editors when on promotional tours, allowing him to develop a rapport that included nicknames, the use of outrageous profanity, and long-running inside jokes (Kelly, "Atlanta Letters"). Kelly was also famous for including the names of business associates and friends in the strip—most often as the rotating title of the swamp skiff. On the one hand, this use of flattery, good humor, and generosity to ease his negotiations with cultural guardians and editors may seem somewhat craven—the work of an unprincipled self-promoter. A more generous judgment would recognize that an effective auteur at this time in American cultural history was forced to use elaborate social niceties in order to survive. Perhaps it recalls the dynamics of a classic trickster tale in which the less powerful figure employs flattery and flowery language to distract a more powerful animal, often appealing to his or her inherent vanities or greed.

As Kelly's career lengthened into the late 1950s, his patience for these games of compromise and flattery sometimes waned. For example, Herblock, Kelly's friend, reported that Kelly disliked and often resisted functions like the national editors conventions where he would be forced to flatter editors who had censored or disliked his work (Block 121). His patience was also severely tested in 1958 when he ran a series of strips during National Education Week in which he made oblique attacks on the persistence of segregation in Southern schools (see Figure 3.2). A number of editors protested this editorializing, with one paper even changing the final panels of his strip, deleting dialogue balloons, and excising entire strips from the paper. The editor explained to readers that

> *Pogo* was given several days off—including today—because the artist became more involved in editorial expression than entertainment. This is another example of a tendency, protested by newspapers in various parts of the country for years, where comic strip artists have gotten into the realm of propaganda or editorial comment, instead of concentrating on entertaining readers. ("Desegregation and Jack Acid" 147)

Figure 3.2: Walt Kelly, "This is National Education Week . . . ," *Pogo,* 12 November 1958.

Later, the editor elaborated that "we have the right to edit, we do edit, everything that goes into the paper" ("Desegregation and Jack Acid" 148). Kelly responded with a vehement defense of his right to control the content of his strip: "Once my name and copyright are on the strips, I am responsible for what is said in them and how it is said. I'd be willing to let 519 papers go to hell if they want to insist on a right—which they don't have—to edit my copy" ("Desegregation and Jack Acid" 148).

Despite the initial and justified anger, there was still a side to Kelly that was eager to avoid long-term discord, to conform to a more "professional" newspaperman's code, and to acknowledge the right of papers to simply drop his strip if they were unhappy with its content. For example, as this controversy wore on, Kelly redirected some of his anger toward his syndicate (which had failed to intervene in the early stages of the censoring), and he ultimately sent a private letter to the editor guilty of altering his strip, attempting to mend fences:

> *Time* magazine evidently has the intention of making some sort of case out of the matter, much to my personal displeasure . . . If *Time* calls again . . . I will tell them

that I believe an editor has a perfect right to question anything that goes into his paper and to drop questionable matter if he so chooses . . . I think that anyone who is author of [copyrighted] material changed without his consent and without consultation should protest very vigorously . . . [but] If the strips had been dropped nobody in the world could have found fault, least of all me. ("Desegregation and Jack Acid" 148)

A few years later, in 1962, Kelly was again targeted by editors and other cultural guardians for including provocative and highly identifiable caricatures of foreign leaders such as Krushchev and Castro in his strip. For some editors, this material was not only inappropriate for the comics page, but potentially inflammatory; the argument was that because it ran the risk of complicating already difficult relations with Cuba and the Soviet Union, it should be censored. Kelly remained unapologetic through the controversy, responding simply in an interview in *Time* magazine that "there is a lot of fun to found in politics . . . I always do what I find to be funny at the time." The author of the article added the following coda, acknowledging how Kelly's auteur-like clout was a solid defense against such attacks: "Besides, any man with 612 newspapers on his string can afford to lose a couple now and then—especially since the defectors almost always return to the fold" (Thompson, "McCarthy, Krushchev, and Castro . . ." 93).

The overall impression from reading these various letters and reactions is that Kelly was forced to be highly flexible in relations with journalists, editors, and his own bosses. Because he was determined to defy the unwritten rules of the funnies page and benefit from the resultant status as a principled iconoclast, he also had to repeatedly defend his actions, sometimes reveling in his defiance and at others trying to appease critics.

Kelly's "Bunny Rabbit" Strips

Kelly's willingness to compromise in cases like this was arguably a survival strategy in the following decade as newspapers and syndicates continued to tighten their control over cartoonists and their work. In the aftermath of the Senate hearings on indecency in comics a strict content code had been imposed on comic books, and the aftershocks of that crackdown were felt throughout related mediums into the 1960s and 1970s. For example, "how to" literature geared toward comic strip artists started to emphasize prominently the exigency of keeping material "clean," and syndicates more aggressively analyzed a cartoonist's strips months before publication, vetting the material for potentially offensive words, images, or themes. Newspaper editors also began to censor or pull provocative strips with more regularity, and conservative readers complained with greater umbrage about inappropriate content. One of Kelly's peers, for example, complained that by the late 1950s every cartoonist knew "that he can't deal with divorce, labor, race relations or any other really challenging subject without risk-ing wholesale cancellation" (Sanders 9). Maurice Horn and Pierre Couperie, com-ics historians, elaborated, drawing from a variety of evidence including trade journal reports, anecdotes, and controversies:

> They [comic strip artists] could not include indecency . . . any suggestion of immo-rality . . . snakes (apparently offensive in some foreign contexts) . . . swear words . . . controversial topics such as God, religion, race and ticklish political questions . . . cruelty to women, children and animals . . . divorce . . . crime (and) childish pranks (which go unpunished) . . . traditional (negative) jokes about dentists, laun-drymen (etc.) . . . children's' chemistry sets that blow up . . . (and ethnic and racial stereotypes). (Couperie and Horn 135)

As a partial result of these immense pressures and strictures, Kelly adopted the practice in 1964 of providing newspapers with alternate strips to run on days his editorializing was prominent. To be clear, Kelly was not cowed into diminishing the amount of difficult, topical material he included in the strip during these years; on the contrary, he seemed to be ramping up the satire, making it less layered, and regularly running obvious caricatures of prominent national politi-cians and world leaders such as Kruschev and Castro. But faced with the pres-sures cited above, he decided that offering the alternate strip was a reasonable and professional way to give sensitive editors and publishers an easy out if they felt his commentary was "too strong" (Kelly, "The Bunny Rabbit Strips" 198).

Initially these alternate installments were referred to as the "bunny rabbit strips" because they contained throwaway gags involving a troupe of Disney-esque rabbits. Kelly gave readers clues that these were not the legitimate strips for the day by writing "special" down by the date, and by making the jokes ridicu-lously contrived and cute. An alert reader, in other words, would see that while Kelly was appeasing his sensitive publishers, he was also protesting the practice in subtle ways. In 1968, he again provided alternate strips, but these featured his principal characters rather than rabbits, and the gags were simply watered down versions of what the real satire contained. Kelly also brought less attention to the strip-swapping by writing "A" next to the date on these strips rather than "special."

Kelly ultimately abandoned this practice for two reasons: first, because of the extra work it required of him, and second, because he grew tired of catering to touchy editors. He announced after the 1968 elections that he would no lon-ger provide alternate strips; papers would have to run the strip with the topical satire intact, or not run it all ("Bunny Strips Hold the Fort" 109). The gradual decline in his syndication numbers in the subsequent years could have resulted partially from Kelly's more rigid stand on this practice, but may have also been a byproduct of Kelly's art and sensibility no longer matching the spirit of the age. Indeed, the genteel compromises Kelly made with editors, as well as the layered whimsy of his satire, began to stand in stark contrast to the flavor of other cartoon works that resonated with mid- to late-1960s youth culture: the irreverently direct parodies of *MAD* magazine, and the unhinged excesses of the underground comix movement, led by figures such as R. Crumb. In sum, being a clever auteur like Kelly—a professional artist who could navigate the commercial and institutional strictures of a mainstream culture industry through flattery and guile—became less heroic than having the chutzpah of countercultural rebels like R. Crumb who simply opted out of the system in order to draw and satirize without filters or limitations.

Kelly and the National Cartoonists Society

Returning to Kelly's tenure as president of the National Cartoonists Society from 1954 to 1956, one can highlight several areas in which Kelly's performance was highly professional, but also perhaps too eager to engage in compromise or complacency. This mixed record includes his cautious treatment of internal scandals, his tolerance of sexist practices within the organization, and his resistance to efforts to transform the Society from a fraternal supper club into an effective instrument of collective bargaining. The biggest controversy Kelly dealt with as president—other than the brouhaha over comic books—was an internal feud between Al Capp and his former mentor, Ham Fisher, the creator of *Joe Palooka*. The rough outlines of the story are pertinent to this study for several reasons: the situation involved some of the unfair practices tolerated within the field during Kelly's time, it illustrates Kelly's allegiance to public image and professionalism over significant reform within his profession, it intersected with controversies over appropriate content in comic strips, and it featured the other major satirist of Kelly's age—Al Capp—a figure whose conflicted politics and business practices compare in significant ways to Kelly's.

Capp and Fisher's feud began years earlier when Capp had worked as a poorly paid assistant on Fisher's highly successful, patriotic, and sentimental strip, *Joe Palooka*. According to Capp, Fisher spent most of his time hobnobbing with celebrities and carousing, leaving the actual drawing of his characters and much of the writing to assistants. It was rumored, in fact, that Fisher only drew the faces of his principal characters. Because he did very little of the actual work that made him famous and successful, Fisher was apparently insecure and jealous about the help he received, resulting in his vindictive and paranoid treatment of anyone who had worked in his camp. After hiring Capp, Fisher left on an extended vacation and put his new assistant in charge of doing the entire strip. Capp did fine without him, creating a storyline in which Palooka fights an uncouth hillbilly by the name of Big Leviticus.

The real trouble began shortly later, after Capp quit working for Fisher and began his own successful strip, *Li'l Abner*—a rollicking work that featured hill-billy settings and characters, including a protagonist who seemed to be a parody of Fisher's earnest Palooka. Thus from Fisher's perspective, Capp not only had stolen his ideas but was ridiculing him in every outrageous mock-melodramatic storyline he pursued. Tortured by this outrage, Fisher spent a great deal of effort in the ensuing years trying to discredit and shame his former assistant (Harvey, "Joe Palooka" 107).

Capp, in return, publicly ridiculed Fisher at every opportunity. These attacks included a Sunday installment of his strip in which Fisher was caricatured as "Happy Vermin," a greedy, abusive boss. And in an interview for the *Atlantic Monthly* in which he was asked how he thinks up his disreputable characters, Capp responded with an elaborate smear at his former employer:

> The truth is I don't think 'em up. I was lucky enough to know them—all of them—and what was even luckier, all in the same person of one man. One veritable gold mine of human swinishness. It was my privilege, as a boy, to be associated with a certain treasure trove of lousiness, who in the normal course of each day of his life, managed to be, in dazzling succession, every conceivable kind of heel. It was an advantage few young cartoonists have enjoyed—or could survive. I owe all my success to him. From my study of this one li'l man, I have been able to create an entire gallery of horrors. For instance, when I must create a character who is the ultimate in cheapness, I don't like less fortunate cartoonists, have to rack my brain wondering what real bottom-of the barrel cheapness is like. I saw the classic of 'em all. Better than that, I was the victim of it. (Harvey, "Joe Palooka" 108)

One might think that despite the obsessive bitterness of Capp's attacks, there was a heroic side to his vendetta—he was, after all, targeting the dirty secret that cartoons were often executed by poorly paid assistants while the creators went carousing. Unfortunately, that portrait is undermined by the fact that *Li'l Abner* was also largely drawn, and sometimes co-written, by lesser-paid, but more talented artists such as the great fantasy illustrator, Frank Frazetta. Capp often only drew, in fact, the characters' faces and hands in his strips, and many of his storylines were constructed in brainstorming sessions with his employees. To his credit, nevertheless, he did rise above Fisher's more reprehensible practices by at least publicly acknowledging his use of assistants, even detailing their contributions in interviews.

The feud between the two cartoonists came to a climax in the late 1940s when Fisher latched on to the already abundant sexual imagery in Capp's work, and distorted and exaggerated it by actually altering Capp's drawings. He then showed these doctored images to public officials in an effort to implicate Capp in the general attacks then being waged by cultural guardians against the content of comic books. In 1954, the National Cartoonists Society rallied behind Capp after Fisher once again tried to make the altered images public. The NCS, under Kelly's leadership, attempted to keep its own image spotless by quietly censuring Fisher and expelling him from their ranks. But behind the scenes many members of the society were equally disgusted with Capp's behavior. In private correspondence between Kelly and Capp, for example, there was evidence that the cartooning community was ready to distance themselves from Capp as well because of his immaturity and the potential that this vendetta had to disgrace the entire profession. Kelly wrote,

> . . . My duty is to the Society. We cannot entertain any foggy accusations and we will not listen to vituperation. . . in the name of all we hold dear, I feel this damned foolish harmful affair should come to an end. I am hopeful that you, with restraint, will bend every effort . . . to making an end of this nonsense. (Kelly, "Letter to Al Capp, December 16, 1954" 1)

Sadly, the whole affair ended in as ugly a manner as it began, with Fisher committing suicide soon after losing his society membership and the professional respect of his peers (Harvey, "Joe Palooka" 107). Understandably, Kelly did his best to keep the lurid details of the feud and its bitter conclusion out of the public eye. Nevertheless, his general efforts to contain Capp's unhinged qualities (the barely veiled sexual subtext of *Li'l Abner* and Capp's penchant for highly public grandstanding about abuses within the industry) effectively illustrated the general tendency within the NCS to place public image and professionalism before progressive (albeit potentially painful) reform.

This conservatism could be seen even more explicitly in Kelly's tolerance of sexist practices within the society and in his unwillingness to use the organization for anything more than a "chowder club" for successful cartoonists. In truth, the society's treatment of women during the late 1940s and 1950s was unapologetically crude. For years women had worked in the industry as both underpaid assistants and less-celebrated creators of children and teen strips, and the fact that the founding members of the NCS did not even consider admitting women into their ranks underlines the inherently sexist attitudes within that and many other professions at the time. In 1949, when Hilda Terry, the creator of the strip *Teena*, challenged the society to give her membership, the male cartoonists were divided; some welcomed the idea of female members, but a vocal minority blackballed her appeal. Regardless, after months of wrangling and multiple votes, the gender barrier finally fell.

The admission of women into the NCS, however, did little to change its rowdy, entertainment-seeking, bar-hopping nature. Indeed, throughout the 1950s the society's internal publications and meetings were full of sexist shenanigans: wink-wink jokes about the relative attractiveness of new female members (including an image of a bare, gartered and high-heeled leg entering the NCS office door); illustrations of various cartoonists' female characters in the nude; photos of male cartoonists doing nude illustrations for audiences of armed servicemen; and coverage of old-time bathing suit contests that involved the male cartoonists' wives and girlfriends. Given that Kelly was an early critic of oppressive cultural practices in the larger culture such as racial segregation, blacklisting in Hollywood, and McCarthy's brand of xenophobia and scapegoating, it is disappointing he saw no need to reform these practices either as a member or leader of the organization. It took another thirty years, in fact, before another principled sateur, Garry Trudeau, would use his clout to challenge the most blatant types of sexism in the society (in 1985, Trudeau resigned and went public with his complaints after the society leaders once again published drawings of nude female characters in the yearbook; he was especially incensed by the fact that they did this at the same yearly meeting that they had designated as the "year of the female cartoonist").

It appears that Kelly was incapable of seeing clearly the abuses regarding gender. The fact that he was famed for his own bar-hopping lifestyle and known among friends as an incorrigible womanizer probably prevented him from putting any crimps in his fellow carousers' sexist lifestyles and worldviews. And although he was not an egregious offender in terms of creating lewd drawings (any nude drawings of his two principal female characters, Mam'selle Hepzibah and Miz Beaver, are thankfully absent from those internal publications), he certainly participated in the celebrations and vaudevillian evenings that contained much of the sexist rhetoric. Furthermore, Kelly's two main female characters (mentioned above) generally conformed in unimaginative ways to the polar caricatures of women in male-produced comedy in the 1950s—the sexualized starlet and the brow-beating wife—illustrating Kelly's myopic view of these issues. In sum, when it came to gender issues, Kelly was a product of his time and profession, and made little effort to see beyond those low horizons.

As a member and president of the society during these years Kelly was also slow to crusade for collective artists' bargaining power or various artists' rights. In the years surrounding his tenure as president, the Society seemed to primarily serve as a drinking club that featured rowdy variety shows put on by Kelly and the old guard cartoonists. Kelly, in fact, was celebrated by his colleagues during these years as a supremely uninhibited performer, engaging in roasts, comedy skits, and facetious speeches—he was especially good at the mock-angry attack on a peer in which a speech that was ostensibly a tribute to a great figure in the field would degenerate into an expletive-filled rant. There is little indication, however, that Kelly used these prodigious parodic and comedic talents for much more than insider joking and garnering acclaim among his peers as a gifted performer.

While the orientation of these meetings pleased the old-guard cartoonists immensely, it grated on the nerves of younger cartoonists hoping that the Society would serve to promote their careers and protect their rights. In 1954, at the start of Kelly's tenure as president, newer members complained that he and his peers were cliquish, always sitting and gossiping together; they griped in public about the endless drinking and evenings of silly entertainment:

> The old guard (most of them) are well fixed and don't need anything from the Society except a good time. The Society will never accomplish much until the younger members who stand to benefit from the organization will voice their ideas. (Irwin Hansen)

> I joined the Society primarily to talk to other cartoonists about cartooning. There doesn't seem to be much of that kind of talk at the meetings. (John Cullen Murphy)

> I like entertainment at the meetings, but I don't like the feeling that we *have* to be entertained . . . I always feel cheated if I have to rush for a train without getting a chance to talk to friends because of a bunch of third rate acts I was forced to sit through. (Dick Wingert)

> I think the main purpose of the Society should be to *help* the Cartoonist instead of getting them high every month. (Fred Rhoads) ("Cartoonists Complain")

These complaints had been aired in previous years as well, but Kelly was not at all sympathetic to the idea that the society should be more about mentoring and advocacy than partying. The previous year, Kelly had lashed out at younger cartoonists in the organization's newsletter saying, "We're not here to help every lousy cartoonist to make a buck here. Get rid of illusions and high expectations; this is nothing more than a chowder and drinking club for we cartoonists who have made it to the top" (Kelly, "NCS Newsletter 1953" 2). Kelly's close friend, Milton Caniff, was in favor of promoting artists' rights through the general weight of the organization, but he shared Kelly's resistance to organizing the society as a device for collective bargaining: "If you are going to have a Society such as the Lambs, Friars, etc. . . . this is the Society as we know it today . . . If you start pinning editors down, you are putting your teeth into a trade union. And this *we are not* . . . and frankly I do hope we never will be" (Caniff, "NCS newsletter, June 14, 1951").

It was Al Capp, interestingly, who seemed most eager to do something more progressive and assertive with the organization. Less concerned than Kelly and Caniff about ruffling newspaper editors' feathers or making the Society look unprofessional, he saw the body as first and foremost a vehicle to reform the abusive practices within the industry. In an open letter to fellow members, he said that

> Sooner or later, the Society must justify its existence by being something more than it now is, by using its members and strength to do something affirmative for the cartoonist in the way that all associations of creative men, screenwriters, newspapermen, dramatists, and authors have made better and sounder the relationship between the artist and his business management . . . We can horse around with meetings and banquets and little stunts, add up to nothing constructive and quietly fall apart—or we can become a useful Society that devotes its numbers and its wisdom and its strength to clear up the muddiness in the artist-management relationships that keeps our profession the one important creative profession left in America with no standards, no dignity, no honest American basis. (Harvey, "Tales of the Founding" 68)

Although Capp's specific proposals too closely resembled aggressive union practices for many of the cartoonists to accept them (they did not want to offend their syndicates or subscribing papers with that kind of bold move), the society had responded to these complaints to a degree in the year before Kelly's tenure as president by setting up an ethics committee, a fund for indigent cartoonists, and a mission statement that included the general advocation of artists' rights.

It would have been difficult, of course, for Kelly to make radical changes in the organization without causing serious turmoil among many of the most powerful founding members of the club. He also had the misfortune of having to lead the society through some especially difficult situations, including the Ham Fisher affair and the Senate hearings on delinquency and comic books. Simply keeping on top of those issues, in addition to the society's regular events, would have felt like plenty of work to take on for an already busy cartoonist. The fact that Kelly did not use his subsequent emeritus status within the organization's leadership to push for greater reform in the organization or agitate for artists' rights in general is disappointing, nevertheless. And one cannot help but notice a pattern of avoiding any serious challenges to the system—unless they concerned his specific work—from his Disney days onward.

In the first chapter I ascribe this retreat from collective bargaining strategies and radical reform to a pragmatic, bourgeois mind-set that Kelly might have developed as a result of having grown up with very little money and struggled for so long in his professional career to make a name for himself. Another explanation might be that Kelly's view of himself as a maverick—"I never look back OR front. I run blind. I'm my own man"—prevented him from seeing his own professional struggle as anything more than a lone David and Goliath clash with the industry (Kercher 57). In effect, this self-focused attitude may have been a reflection of a less heroic side of the auteur mind-set: an inherent attitude of individualism. In other words, when an artist is too aggressively celebrated for his solitary production of a great work of art, for his iconoclastic stands, and for his independence from top-down control, then it is perhaps difficult for him to

imagine the need to engage in collective bargaining or to see himself as interconnected with similarly struggling peers.

Another explanation of Kelly's individualistic approach to the obstacles in
his field was that it was an outgrowth of the cautious and philosophical flavor
of mid-twentieth century liberalism. It would make sense that a liberal philosophy that had rejected the dogma and radicalisms of the pre-war Left—in favor
of skepticism, introspection, and philosophical questioning—would have little
room for strident stands and showy public protests (Pells x, 138). Kelly, as a primary articulator of this new brand of leftism, would have been more comfortable with pragmatic compromise, self-government, and cautious questioning,
than with Capp's brand of histrionic rabble-rousing. In sum, the limits to Kelly's
progressive stands as an auteur were the product of a complex melding of personal, political, and professional motivations and rationalizations.

Kelly as Animator of *Pogo*

A final episode in Kelly's career—his attempts in the late 1960s and early 1970s
to make *Pogo* into an animated film—illustrate once again some of the limitations and complexities of his career as an auteur. The first attempt to animate
Pogo was made in 1968, when Kelly was paired by his syndicate with MGM and
the legendary Looney Toons animator, Chuck Jones. Although Kelly was heavily involved in the initial stages of storyboarding for this project, he had to cede
control over the remaining production of the film because of the labor-intensive
nature of the animation process. In addition, the failing health of his second
wife, Stephanie, and the demanding obligations of his comic strip work prevented him from staying in Los Angeles to closely monitor the various stages of the
film's production. As a result, the final product, *The Pogo Special Birthday Special*,
bore little resemblance to the comic strip in either look or tone. Fans of the
strip were disappointed and Kelly was livid with Jones; he blamed Jones, in fact,
for ruining the film by imposing his own peculiar aesthetic and sensibility onto
the work. Specific complaints by both Kelly and fans included an overly sweet
soundtrack, weirdly humanized versions of the characters' faces, crude line work
that looked like Jones's signature style rather than Kelly's, and a general sweetness to the film's tone that did not match that satiric edge that defined Kelly's
work.

It is difficult to imagine how a project in which Kelly actively participated
could have gone so wrong, but the simple explanation is that a single artist's vision can easily be lost when dealing with cultural products that require so much
collaborative labor and are targeted to a generalized television audience. In other
words, the clout and control Kelly exerted over his strip could not extend to the
labor of a distant animation project headed by another artist (Jones), executed
by scores of assistants, and sponsored by a studio (MGM) concerned with mak-

ing a cheaply made product that appealed to the broadest possible demographic. Indeed, MGM had little interest in being true to the subtleties of Kelly's work since they were requiring their animators to crank out three separate films during this period, and the *Birthday Special* was only a television production—the lowest priority. According to Selby Kelly,

> The animators didn't add any 'extra' little things. If you're working at home, and you want to cut in to your own time, you can take as much time as you want to and you're paid by footage. But when you're working in a studio, you have to put out a certain amount of footage per day, or per week. If you stop, and juice it up a little and add a lot of extra personality bits so that it makes a nice scene, you're not getting your footage in. So most of the action in the scenes was down to the bedrock. They just did *exactly* what was called for. Kelly was very disappointed in the picture. (Beiman 194)

Kelly's collaboration with Chuck Jones, moreover, was complicated by that fact that Jones had himself behaved as an auteur of sorts throughout his own career, imposing his distinctive vision and style on everything he took on, from Looney Tunes cartoons to Dr. Seuss adaptations. Kelly later complained in a "towering rage," that ". . . the son of a bitch [Jones] changed it [the look and content of the film] after our last meeting!" He elaborated: "That's not the way I wrote it. He took all the sharpness out of it and put in that sweet, saccharine stuff that Chuck Jones thinks is Disney, but isn't" (Andrae and Blum 146).

In this encounter Kelly was perhaps reminded of why he had struggled in the field of animation during his Disney days: the regimented production process and the employee-studio relations had a tendency to stifle an individual artist's aesthetic style and satiric voice, homogenizing the look and tone of idiosyncratic art. At Disney, Kelly had chafed against the demands of in-betweening, following model sheets, and conforming to the regimented corporate culture. Similarly, with the MGM project, Kelly resisted creating model sheets for the animators because, according to his third wife, Selby, his characters were "very fluid and they were never planned for a whole bunch of people to draw them . . . Kelly didn't want the characters pinned down" (Crouch, "Interview with Selby Kelly" 191). These general difficulties with two animation studios—at both ends of his career—might simply be chalked up to Kelly's generally independent disposition and jealous pride in the quality of his own work; but one can read more significance into this resistance to the modes of production in the animation medium. Specifically, in addition to protecting his own work, Kelly also seemed to be protesting animation studios' regimented production lines, the cog-like status of the typical animator, and the profit-driven orientation of a medium that tended to homogenize the look of characters as well as excise the rougher, satiric edges of story material.

In the wake of the MGM disappointment, Kelly's wife Stephanie died from her long bout with cancer, and Kelly began, in a highly depressive state, to plot the making of a new film about the dangers of pollution that would articulate more accurately his satiric vision and aesthetic sensibility. It was to be entitled "We Have Met the Enemy and He Is Us"—a clear indication that its content would be more authentic. He enlisted the help of Selby Daley, a peer from his Disney days and an MGM employee on the *Birthday Special*; he said to her, "What do you say that *we* do a picture ourselves, and show them how it *should* look?" She agreed, and Kelly found an independent producer who would give him 'total control' (Beiman 194). Kelly was so determined, in fact, to exert auteur-like control on the project that he did most of the time-consuming work himself, sometimes reanimating portions several times over in order to get it right.

While successful at getting the film to reflect the flavor of the strip more accurately, he was forced to complete it on a shoestring budget, to cut it from 30 minutes to 15, and to settle for a composite of storyboard images juxtaposed with sections of full animation. Ultimately, the film was never shown as a result of a variety of negative factors: the compromised and truncated state of the film, Kelly's diminished popularity and health problems, and lackluster promotions by the film's independent production company. In sum, Kelly had successfully protected his work and achieved a level of authenticity by opting out of the flattening regimentation of the mainstream animation industry, but he also emitted little more than a cultural whimper in the end by not engaging with the far-reaching distribution channels and powers of a mainstream entertainment company. In Gramscian terms, he simply walked away from the negotiating table, resisting incorporation so completely that he was no longer participating in the cultural dialogue.

It is enlightening to compare Kelly's failed attempts in translating his comic strip into animation to the more successful efforts of another iconic cartoonist of the era, Charles Schulz (*Peanuts*). At first glance Schulz seems like a poor candidate for the label of iconoclast or auteur given his willingness to be pushed around by syndicates and editors during key periods of his career. For example, he was cowed into accepting a title for his strip ("Peanuts") that he despised; he achieved syndication in part by agreeing to have his strip run at a diminished size in comparison to the rest of the comics page; and he was never willing to ask for a sabbatical or similarly artist-friendly concessions over the course of his long career. In addition, he considered the auteur-like behavior of satiric cartoonists such as Kelly or Trudeau to be "unprofessional" (Marschall and Groth 9; Johnson 213). Specifically, he did not approve of their chutzpah as cultural critics, and looked down upon their defiant crusades in favor of artists' rights (like access to sabbaticals) or against size restrictions. Finally, he did not seem as eager or capable of protecting his strip from the overexposure and dilution of tone that can occur through aggressive merchandising.

Despite those apparent failings, Schulz was ultimately able to create a quirky and resonant strip that featured darkly existentialist undertones and profoundly cosmic satire. He achieved a high level of quality and consistency in his work too for several decades, somehow remaining relevant through many generations of young and old readers. And unlike Kelly, he also managed to translate his strip successfully from newspaper to television and movie screen, greatly amplifying the cultural reach of his comedy and characters. Indeed, the series of films he made in collaboration with Bill Melendez were somehow both hugely popular *and* surprisingly true to the melancholy tone and contemplative pace of his comic strip. Schulz did this by exerting some of the clout and control he had garnered through the immense success of his strip. For example, he insisted on control and oversight, even earning a say in the musical scores by Vince Guaraldi that aligned so nicely with the flavor of Schulz's gentle comedy.

Significantly, Schulz was also able to exert this control in spite of (or perhaps, because of) his willingness to capitalize on opportunities to work with corporate/commercial entities. For example, the relationship with Bill Melendez came about through Schulz's work on a series of Ford Motor Company commercials that featured the *Peanuts* characters, and over the years, many brand-name products provided the financial support for producing the specials. These endorsements included Coca-Cola, Dolly Madison cakes, Kellogg's, McDonald's, Peter Paul–Cadbury candy bars, General Mills, and Nabisco. The steady flow of financial support, in other words, helped give Schulz both the opportunity and the freedom to do these animated works right.

In Kelly's defense, it would have been difficult for him to find and satisfy commercial sponsors when the satiric content of *Pogo* was more explicitly anti-establishment than *Peanuts*. His final film, for example—"We Have Met the Enemy, and He is Us"—attacked the issue of pollution directly, a potentially controversial or seemingly audience-killing topic that could easily scare away advertisers.

In a final tally, Schulz, unlike Kelly, did not have dramatic clashes with politicians and industry leaders during his career; but the quality and consistency of work still qualifies him as a successful auteur of sorts—one who navigated the shoals of his industry with seeming timidity at times, but at others with serious conviction and sure navigation. Perhaps it would be fruitless to designate one or the other as a better auteur in a final tally. Both cartoonists made compromises, chose different battles, and successfully amplified their cultural influence at different times, and in different ways, gaining complicated legacies of both failure and success. Kelly was the better *sateur* in the end, however—determined always to leverage his clout into sharp social criticism, even if that meant derailing the popularity and reach of his work at times.

CHAPTER 4

Representations of Race, and Borrowings from African American Folk Forms in Kelly's Work

In January 1945 when Walt Kelly was a relatively unknown comic book artist, he unceremoniously retired one of his main characters, Bumbazine (a small African American boy), from his *Animal Comics* series. The world in which this boy had lived—a slightly softened version of Joel Chandler Harris's Uncle Remus trickster tales—lived up to the title of the comic, as it was populated by a variety of anthropomorphized swamp critters speaking in black dialect: alligators, possums, foxes, beavers, goats, and so on. As an explanation for removing the boy from the stories, Kelly pointed to the narrative awkwardness of having a human child interact with speaking animals; jokingly, he said, "Bumbazine, being human, was not as believable as the animals" (Thompson, "Returning" 7). It made more sense, it seemed, to promote Bumbazine's sidekick, Pogo the Possum, into the Brer Rabbit–type trickster role at the center of the tales.

Later in his career Kelly also admitted that excising this black character (and replacing him with Pogo) was a response to the rising sensitivity among readers at mid-century to stereotypical and denigrating depictions of African Americans

Figure 4.1: Walt Kelly, *Pogo* and Bumbazine in "Albert's Birthday," *Animal Comics* #8, April 1944.

in popular culture. He said there "was a chance for people to feel offended at the use of the little boy despite how careful [I] might be to draw the child attractively" (Kelly "Land of the Elephant Squash" 50). Kelly was perhaps wise in making this casting shift since Bumbazine—though highly three-dimensional and sympathetic in comparison to many images of blacks during this time—had an uncomfortable resemblance to the Little Black Sambo or pickaninny types that had populated early twentieth-century children's books, postcards, and comic strips.

If Kelly had never achieved significant success after this comic book work, the reshuffling of these characters would be a forgotten footnote in the history of derivative, vaguely racist American comics. But five years later Kelly used this same swamp setting, a similarly "Southern" dialect, and most of the same principal characters—including Pogo the Possum, and his nemesis, Albert the Alligator—to create one of the most beloved and culturally important comic strips of the twentieth century. This stellar success, in effect, prods one to take a second look at this early work and ask some difficult questions. For example, many observers of the Bumbazine-Pogo character shift have been content to say that Bumbazine was the last of Kelly's overt references to or representations of, African American identities, dialects, and forms in his comedy. From this perspective, Kelly effectively deracinated his work at this point from any specific ethnic markers.

In contrast, I will consider the possibility that while the physical character of Bumbazine was removed, the comedic voices and types he represented—the trickster figure of popularized folk stories who uses dialect in creatively subversive ways, and the African American types drawn from popular comedic traditions—persisted in spirit, comedic function, and political meaning as that role was transferred to the strip's main character, Pogo. In addition, because Pogo became an "adult" animal in the mature strip's fully allegorical and satirical setting, he took on additional, sympathetic roles associated with the romanticized blackface minstrel. For example, Pogo carried the minstrel's banjo, enjoyed the stereotypical pleasures of the blackface songbook, and behaved satirically as a wise fool, everyman sufferer, and wry commentator on the foibles of the more powerful characters in his society. In other words, the little possum at the center of Kelly's famous strip—the critter who ran mock campaigns for president in 1950s and 1960s, and who led the satiric charge against McCarthyism—was, in essence, if not in outward appearance, a black character.[4]

To clarify, a recognition of these connections in *Pogo* is not meant to be an exercise in revealing hidden, racist codings in Kelly's work; instead, it is an effort to trace the persistent usefulness and resonance of comedic roles and character traits that began within the conflicted dynamics of blackface and trickster tales, and migrated with the times—or were "reracinated"—into animal proxies such as Pogo. Kelly was not wholly innocent, of course, in his appropriations of black forms and identities. At his worst moments (early in his career), he could sometimes lazily recycle old caricatures or simply rehash the trickster tales and exaggerated dialect of the Uncle Remus storybook; and even at his best, his borrowings were still somewhat conflicted as he naïvely celebrated romanticized and popularized notions of black culture and identity. Nevertheless, if one judges his appropriations within a larger history of white authors and artists borrowing minority folk forms for "authenticity" and artistic energy, Kelly fares well. This chapter elaborates upon this conclusion by comparing Kelly's work to a spectrum of borrowings ranging from opportunistic and punishing distortions to progressive reworkings. Included in the discussion are Joel Chandler Harris, Mark Twain, and George Herriman, and contemporaries of Kelly, including Jack Kerouac, Pete Seeger, and Bob Dylan.

Before we discuss this history, a short preview of possible conclusions is in order. In a time where artists regularly exploited or dismissed African American forms, Kelly was not among them. An evaluation of Kelly's intentions and methods reveals he was a Northeastern, working-class liberal-intellectual who admired the "authenticity" and vitality of Southern ethnic folk life and championed the rights of African Americans—but his knowledge and reinterpretation of this culture was largely based on romantic and reductive images and ideals. Nevertheless, his best work in *Pogo* either transcended the racist types and forms from which he drew his characters, setting, and language, or it harnessed the romantic notions in which those types were still mired to progressive political ideas.

In a final appraisal, Kelly can be compared to Mark Twain in his successful reshaping of folk forms and ethnic dialects for progressive uses. Twain built upon the tropes of trickster tales and blackface minstrelsy to create room for authentic, sympathetic African American voices in American literature, and by highlighting the "fundamental heterogeneity of human nature" through a naturalistic treatment of real dialects (Sewell ix). More than five decades later, Kelly used similar means and methods to champion *ideological* heterogeneity. To elaborate, although Kelly's early comic book work was largely derivative (mired in stereotypical types and conventions), his mature comic strip was syncretic genius. In *Pogo*, Kelly modified the traditional conventions of trickster tales, blackface, and dialect comedy (adding Freudian codings, pastoral motifs, and deconstructive wordplay) to create a counter-discursive Cold War ideology that advocated self-inspection, a retreat from scapegoating and xenophobia, and a rejection of ideological dogmatism.

Theoretical Framing

As one compares Kelly's work to other borrowings of minority cultural forms, some theoretical framing and caution about word use is required. For example, an estimation of Kelly's, Harris's and Twain's relative locations on a complex spectrum between homage and exploitation should be framed within a clear view of both the benefits and limitations of using a constructed notion of *authenticity* as a critical standard or foundational ideal. As Patrick Johnson argues in *Appropriating Blackness*, "because the concept of blackness has no essence, 'black authenticity' is overdetermined—contingent on the historical, social and political terms of its production" (Johnson 3). In other words, because racial categories are already simplistic, ideologically loaded constructs, one cannot attach foundational authenticity to a generalized racial category without risking reinforcing the assumptions attached to these divisions. Moreover, one also runs the risk of fetishizing authenticity in ways that don't acknowledge the malleability of both folk and popular cultural forms, or that don't allow room to appreciate the rich fusions of cultural traditions and mediums in the twentieth century. In the end, nevertheless, it is still helpful to use a qualified and self-aware notion of authenticity as a criterion of judgment because some of the most egregious instances of cultural theft or distortion need to be judged against some foundational standard; and, as Johnson also concedes, "there are ways in which authenticating discourse enables marginalized people to counter oppressive representations of themselves" (3).

Theoretical framing in this chapter is also provided by folklorist Gene Bluestein's concepts of syncretism (a rich melding of forms and traditions in popular culture) and poplore (a cultural text that channels the energies and politics of folk culture in vital ways) that achieves popularity through organic, grassroots means, that is democratically dialogical, and that borrows and reshapes traditional folk forms in original ways (6–10). Because the concept of poplore runs counter to the mid-century modernist expectation that the only great works of art are those texts that are wholly original and avant-garde, it is an effective ideal for creating space in the cultural canon for popular works such as *Pogo* that build upon existing folk patterns in syncretic ways. While these frames help most readily in placing Kelly within a more admirable tradition of borrowings and meldings, they also allow for a richer understanding of Kelly's mature methods—the satiric, deconstructive functions of dialect, in particular, and the appeal of his liberal philosophies within the political climate of the 1950s.

Black Characters and Narrative Forms in Kelly's Work

To explore more fully how Kelly ultimately achieved the syncretic greatness and satiric complexity of his mature comic strip, we can begin by retracing Kelly's use of comedic African American character types and conventions through his early works. Along the way one can chart how Kelly's channeling of black identities and dialects developed from largely stereotypical and naïve borrowings to more original and politically progressive fusions. From the start of Kelly's career he exhibited a fascination with African American identities, dialect, and mu-sic—as mediated, of course, through popular culture. In 1936, when Kelly landed his first job with the Disney animation studios, this proclivity revealed itself in both his professional work and his everyday interactions with colleagues. For ex-ample, he collaborated with two other animators on the "jive crows" segment in *Dumbo*, a bit that celebrates, in animal form, the hipster credentials and virtuoso abilities of streetwise black musicians.

While at Disney, Kelly also engaged in interoffice musical jam sessions that referenced blackface in indirect ways. For example, in Figure 4.2, an interoffice sketch, Kelly presents himself as the black retainer from the musical *Showboat*, poking fun at the amateur musical jams he performed with colleagues. One of his fellow animators, Ward Kimball, also featured in this sketch, explained that Kelly was crazy during this time for "Southern tunes" such as *Alabammy Bound*, *Tuck Me to Sleep in My Old Kentucky Home*, and *Georgia Camp Meeting*—stan-dards that could trace their roots back to vaudeville and late nineteenth-century blackface minstrelsy (Kimball 1; Andrae and Blum 136).

Figure 4.2: Walt Kelly, interoffice sketch while working at Disney studios, circa 1941.

After leaving Disney in 1942 to work in comic books, Kelly continued to in-clude African American characters, folk forms, and dialects in his comedy. For example, some of the first *Animal Comics* stories in the early 1940s, such a 1943 installment of "Albert the Alligator," (see Figure 4.3), included stereotypical cari-catures of blacks in a corny Southern setting. These characters were fairly two-dimensional—as if they were lifted from the Stepin Fetchit playbook and old-school blackface. In another example, a black maid from one of Kelly's *Our Gang* comics from 1943 (Figure 4.4) played a stock role common in film, animation,

Figure 4.3: Walt Kelly, "Albert the Alligator," in *Animal Comics* #5, October 1943.

Figure 4.4: Walt Kelly, "The Great Our Gang Circus," January 1943.

and comic strips: the African American servant who is ignorant, easily frightened, and subjected to prankish, exaggerated violence. The fact that her figure is distorted and abused for slapstick effect (treatment usually spared Anglo female characters in the American slapstick tradition) highlights the mocking tone of the caricature (Dale 100). The two principle characters in these comic series—Bumbazine (*Animal Comics*) and Buckwheat (*Our Gang*)—were also borrowed, of course, from the playbook of pickaninny or Little Black Sambo types that circulated in early twentieth-century comedy.

From a distance, Kelly's early fascination with popularized images of black identity, dialect, and musical forms appears to be vaguely racist—or perhaps naïve and condescending at best. A closer look, however, at the cultural context in which Kelly was raised and the varied and often sympathetic uses of trickster tales and blackface forms in early twentieth-century American culture, can lead to a more nuanced assessment. To begin, Kelly's interest in African American trickster tales and vaudevillian blackface emerged at an early age. Kelly's third wife, Selby, related that Kelly described how his father initiated this love for folk stories and ethnic "fun talk" (a euphemism for black dialect, it seems) by reading Uncle Remus stories to him (Beiman 29). It should be noted that most Anglo homes had copies of these Joel Chandler Harris trickster tale compilations, as they were one of the most popular children's readers of the early decades of the twentieth-century. The working class, multiethnic nature of his hometown, Bridgeport Connecticut, also shaped in Kelly a sympathetic and democratic interest in dialect and ethnic comedy. He remembers, for example, not making a big deal one way or another about sharing a classroom with African American kids and the children of the Eastern European immigrants who worked in the shipyards. The democratic, multilingual nature of such an upbringing shaped Kelly's comedy (carnivalesque, multivocal), his left-leaning politics (a rejection of lazy xenophobia and divisive scapegoating), and his satiric sensibility (Marschall 8A). Those liberal, working-class sympathies, moreover, persisted in his personal life beyond the comic strip. Most significantly, he consistently championed African American rights in his satire and commentary throughout his career, advocating desegregation, campaigning for black hospitals, and aligning himself early on with the Civil Rights movement.

Another facet of Kelly's affinity for mediated African American forms—his love of blackface comedy and music—may have germinated in his childhood as he observed his father working as a theatrical scene painter in Bridgeport for traveling musicals and revues testing the waters before heading for the vaudeville and Broadway stages in New York. Along with comics, vaudeville featured blackface comedy and music (and other brands of ethnic entertainment) most prominently. An infatuation with musicals carried over into his teen years, as Kelly participated in variety shows staged by the youth in the Summerfield Methodist church and where he showed a "real flair for the dramatic" (Anderson 69). At the local high school he was also involved in theatre and glee club, and actually performed in blackface minstrel shows (Thompson, "Returning to Our Gang" 4). This last fact may appear especially embarrassing or incriminating to an early twenty-first-century sensibility; but ethnic comedy was ubiquitous during these decades, and performing amateur blackface revues was common within high schools, civic clubs, Boy Scout troops, and men's fraternal organizations at the time. The image in Figure 4.5—the *Our Gang* kids plotting to create their own amateur minstrel show—attests to this practice, and can also be read as an expression of Kelly's own fond memories of having participated in such productions.

Figure 4.5: Walt Kelly, "Our Gang and the Fearless Detective Agency," *Our Gang* #16, April 1945.

While the denigrating aspects of blackface are highly apparent to our current cultural sensibility, most of the participants in these amateur shows would not necessarily have felt or understood that they were participating in a wholly racist activity. Indeed, if one looks more closely at the complex intentions behind these performances, it becomes clear that they could contain a variety of meanings ranging from mocking comedy to admiring tribute. A number of scholars such as Dale Cockrell and John Strausbaugh have identified this lively mix of mockery and admiration in blackface performance, arguing that during the long history of the form the social meanings and uses of these performances ranged from racist denigration to liberating mask-wearing and sincere admiration. Blackface was a part of a larger exchange between Anglo and black cultures that amounted to a "complicated web of love and hate, fear and guilt, attraction and repulsion, mockery and mimicry" (Strausbaugh 24).

It should also be noted that the cultural meanings attached to the professional blackface performer had expanded by the 1920s and 1930s. Moving beyond the Zip Coon braggart or the Jim Crow rube of nineteenth-century blackface—stereotypes that had cast black people as the butt of the joke—new performers embodied the trickster figure, the satiric jester, the wise fool, and the heroically downtrodden everyman. These more sympathetic social meanings emerged in the 1910s and 1920s (the vaudeville and early Hollywood years) when great black comic actors such as Bert Williams or second-generation Jewish immigrant performers such as Al Jolson performed in blackface. In fact, Williams, a black man who wore blackface, was considered by many people, both black and white, to be the funniest man alive in early twentieth-century America; he is credited with infusing his blackface performances with real pathos, the barbed satire of a jester standing objectively on the margins of society, and the appeal of a sympathetic everyman.

In considering these comedic roles, and elements of tribute and attraction in Kelly's work, one could speculate that for many of the teenage performers in Kelly's high school—or the middle-aged animators tinkering with blackface songs and character types at Disney—the genre might have provided a license, in carnivalesque fashion, to vaguely scandalize, satirize, or temporarily disrupt the rigid social codes and hierarchies of genteel Anglo society. Indeed, for many of these white performers the wearing of burnt cork and the belting of sentimental songs about the South at civic events or parties was a quasi-earnest imitation of what they perceived to be admirable—albeit stereotypically "childlike"—aspects of black identity: everyman humility, irreverent soulfulness, vocal virtuosity, comic spontaneity, and emotional transparency. Handbooks published with information on how to put on an amateur blackface show highlighted these more complex intentions: "To the older fellow, the Minstrel Show holds the greatest appeal of all amateur theatricals. It gives him a chance to show his ability as a vocalist and an entertainer" (Strausbaugh 145).

Playfully channeling black identity or musical ability might have thus represented for men like Kelly an appealing escape from a corporatized and suburbanized mainstream culture—a world in which many Anglo men were growing anxious about a loss of masculinity and distinct identity in a seemingly homogeneous and straitlaced society. In addition, it could have allowed them to feel a temporary sense of emotional authenticity, cultural hipness, satiric subversiveness, and everyman heroism. In this light, the jazz-playing jive crows in *Dumbo* were not objects of ridicule; instead, they were what Kelly and his colleagues aspired to be: authentically cool, streetwise figures—independent rebels operating outside the lamely scripted "circus" of suburbia and Disney culture.

This reading can be supported by the fact that both Kelly and Ward Kimball were considered "mavericks" who had "trouble adapting to the Disney mold," and by the relish they took in razzing the sensibilities of more straitlaced fellow workers with their impromptu musical performances (Andrae and Blum 132). Kimball described his colleagues' annoyed reactions at seeing him and Kelly "stagger around the room laughing with rubber-legged glee over what [they] fancied a particularly exceptional rendition of 'Marching Through Georgia'" (Kimball 11). It is easy to imagine that the factory-like rigidity and strict hierarchy of the Disney animation system during these years, combined with Walt Disney's own conservative politics, motivated Kelly's unorthodox performances, showing an unofficial, albeit somewhat conflicted, affiliation with a more working class and "authentic" culture and political viewpoint. The fact that Kelly quietly resigned from his Disney job during the animators' strike of 1942 seems to support this reading.

Applying this more complex view of blackface to Kelly's career, one can conjecture that his enjoyment of highly mediated black images and musical forms was indeed patronizing and naïve, but it also contained elements of admiration, sincere tribute, and irreverent channeling of the anarchic energies of popularized black identities and forms. Looking to Kelly's comic book and comic strip work, we can also see how he included the sympathetic late-period blackface roles and the more progressive trickster figure functions into his construction of characters such as Buckwheat, Bumbazine, and Pogo. To begin, one can point out that the two images highlighted earlier (the *Animal Comics* townsfolk and the black maid from the *Our Gang* series) are the equivalent of comic extras or stock characters, and tertiary figures like that—of any social type or ethnicity—are often two-dimensional by nature. This does not excuse Kelly's lazy use, in this instance, of tired, ethnic caricatures, but it does encourage one to judge the significance of their appearance in Kelly's work more accurately within the conventions of exaggerated comedy. At the same time, the *principal* black characters

Figure 4.6: Walt Kelly, Bumbazine and *Pogo* in "Albert's Birthday," *Animal Comics* #8, April 1944.

Figure 4.7: Walt Kelly, Buckwheat in "Our Gang, Shipwrecked," *Our Gang* #10, June 1944.

in both the *Animal Comics* and *Our Gang* series, Bumbazine and Buckwheat, were relatively nuanced versions of a traditional trickster figure—a type with a more respectable and sometimes heroic narrative function. In addition, both Bumbazine's and Buckwheat's visual constructions (Figures 4.6 and 4.7) were relatively sympathetic and naturalistic—in comparison, at least, to more exaggerated and two-dimensional versions of the stereotype in animation, children's readers, and advertising imagery circulating at mid-century.

Buckwheat, a character Kelly inherited rather than created, was sometimes the butt of the joke in these comedies—stereotypically afraid of ghosts or pitted against animals in various conflicts—but he was also more complex than the traditional Little Black Sambo or pickaninny type. In both the film shorts and the comic books Buckwheat was often able to play the folk-wise trickster figure, outwitting greedy adults or bullies; moreover, there was a democratic equality among the kids in the gang—all of them were equally foolish at times, heroic at others. Late in the *Our Gang* series (1948) Kelly even humanized Buckwheat further, giving him a proper first name ("Alexander"), softening the exaggerated dialect, and revealing pieces of a normal home life (Thompson, "Returning" 4).

Bumbazine was a bit more problematic because he aligned, in comedic function, more closely to the glaringly racist images of black children of early twentieth-century popular culture: he lived and talked with animals, and he was always in danger of being consumed by predators such as alligators and foxes. This melding of black children's lives with harsh animal settings was sometimes

Figure 4.8: Walt Kelly, Bumbazine and Albert, "Albert Takes the Cake," *Animal Comics* #1, December 1942.

Figure 4.9: Unknown artist, "A Darky's Prayer," postcard from the 1930s.

played for laughs in postcards, children's readers, and comic strips; ideologically these texts dehumanized the children, reinforced persistent notions of Social Darwinism, and helped to justify passive neglect or active abuse of real people who faced segregation, disenfranchisement, and the threat of lynchings. So images of Bumbazine on the verge of being devoured by an alligator in these comics (Figure 4.8) brings to mind, uncomfortably, racist postcards and prints that depicted black children as "alligator bait" (Figure 4.9).

Bumbazine was, nevertheless, more than a two-dimensional postcard gag; he was also given the opportunity to behave as an intelligent trickster figure in the style of Brer Rabbit. For example, as Albert the Alligator repeatedly attempted to eat both him and Pogo, Bumbazine effectively used wit and guile—a comedic jujitsu in which the weight of the predator's foibles are used to pull him off balance—to emerge each time as the wily hero. While highly derivative of Uncle Remus stories, these tales were at least true to the "outlaw code" of earlier, more authentic African American trickster tales where word games, playing dumb, and coded ironic commentary were used to mock and subvert a corrupt dominant culture as embodied in the greed and hypocrisies of the predator (Bickley 134). It should also be pointed out that the trickster world Kelly created for Bumbazine and Pogo had none of the harsh naturalism of either nineteenth-century folk tales or the racist postcards from the early twentieth century. Albert never actually came close to eating Bumbazine, and he was equally interested in consuming chocolate cakes. There were also constant discussions of Albert engaging in "cannibalism" if he ate any of the less powerful denizens of the swamp—an early sign of Kelly's tendency to level racial and social distinctions in his satiric worldview.

In the early 1940s, the NAACP and other cultural critics began to pressure artists and entertainment companies to eliminate clearly racist images and characters from popular culture products (Sampson 2). In light of Kelly's general admiration of black culture and his progressive politics, a desire to satisfy these critics, and a sincere concern for offending readers, is most likely why Kelly decided to do away with Bumbazine altogether. In making this adjustment to the strip, Kelly essentially promoted Bumbazine's sidekick Pogo to the central role; by Kelly's own admission, he simply transferred the black boy's qualities of ". . . innocence, naïveté, friendliness and sturdy dependability" to the anthropomorphized possum (Geurin 5). Reinforcing the idea that Pogo literally replaced Bumbazine in both spirit and body was the physical transformation that occurred in Pogo during this transition: he went from looking like a beady-eyed rat—or a literal representation of a possum—to gradually resembling a small child, with an oversized head, rounded features and saucer eyes (Figures 4.10 and 4.11). In addition, Pogo spoke like Bumbazine in the 1940s—in an exaggerated African American dialect (it was only after preparing Pogo for national syndication in 1949 that Pogo switched to a more generic, Southern vernacular speech).

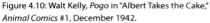

Figure 4.10: Walt Kelly, *Pogo* in "Albert Takes the Cake,"
Animal Comics #1, December 1942.

Figure 4.11: Walt Kelly, promotional drawing of
Pogo, 1956.

Many scholars of ethnic images in early twentieth-century cartoons seem to conclude that when these changes occur—when the black figure is replaced by a cute animal and when the dialect is made more generic—that the text is effectively "deracinated" from its racist, or ethnically-coded, origins (Cohen 63, Lindvall 125, Gordon 62). Ian Gordon elaborates, arguing that the general trend toward favoring animal characters in comic strips—rather than ethnic types—as the medium went national in the middle decades of the twentieth-century, was a way of maximizing the "polysemic" appeal and flexibility of a highly lucrative and merchandisable comedic character (Gordon 62, 75). In simpler terms, the animal character would appeal more broadly—and less problematically—to more people than would the ethnic type. This insight would certainly help to explain why Kelly ultimately opted for a possum as his main character rather than a Little Black Sambo knock-off, and why he softened the black dialect in his comic strip.

Nevertheless, while Gordon's analysis of commercial pressures affecting these changes makes sense, the broader observation of complete deracination is perhaps overstated. In contrast, I would assert that while the visual representation of blackness was muted after these transitions from black character to animal replacement (but not completely erased in some cases—such as with Felix the Cat), the comedic functions and stereotypical behaviors associated with African American trickster tales and blackface conventions lived on in the characters and texts. On the one hand, *visual* caricatures of blackness had become a liability by mid-century, reducing the polysemic appeal of a comic strip character; but on the other hand, comedic caricatures of a range of positive—albeit stereotypical—black *behaviors* and abilities remained resonant and appealing parts of comedic character constructions to a mainstream audience. So rather than being deracinated, these characters were simply pruned or "reracinated" in creative ways, cutting back some of the shallow roots, while reinforcing other, deeper ones below the surface.

Blackface and Trickster Figure Traits in the Mature Version of *Pogo*

As Pogo emerged as the central figure in Kelly's swampland comic book, he adopted the range of comedic roles previously attached to Bumbazine, and by extension, to other African American types in mainstream comedy. Initially, when the strip was still drawing directly from the Uncle Remus templates, Pogo was, like Bumbazine, a classic trickster figure in a Brer Rabbit role that evoked the racial and political dynamics of nineteenth-century African American folk stories. However, as the medium shifted from comic book to comic strip in the late 1940s, Kelly expanded the roles Pogo could play by modifying the trickster tale setting to include Freudian codings and the narrative and character constructs drawn from pastoral comedies; so Pogo no longer played the role of desperate prey animal trying to survive in a vicious animal-, class-, or race-hierarchy. He still had to use his wit to deal with large, unpredictable predators (Albert, a fox, and a bobcat), but the stakes were comedically abstract rather than pressingly real. As illustrations of this new dynamic, transitional strips in 1949 often featured prey-predator dynamics that included elaborate ruminations about repressing id-like impulses in a semi-civilized community of equals (Figures 4.12 and 4.13).

Figure 4.12: Walt Kelly, "What a horrible fate!" *Pogo*, 14 November 1948.

Figure 4.13: Walt Kelly, "You goin' down . . . ," *Pogo*, 16 November 1948.

Even within a year, in 1949, Pogo was gradually becoming more of a wise fool, everyman figure, and ironic observer—roles reminiscent of the expanded, sympathetic parts played by early twentieth-century blackface performers such as Bert Williams. With the shift to a gentle, pastoral setting, Pogo had the time to relax and become the gentle heart or conscience of the swamp community, acting as calming influence, arbiter of disputes, and wry, satiric commentator. The setting, too, from 1949 onward, gradually moved away from the narrow concerns of trickster survivalism to include the more adult themes of the blackface songbook. For example, the swamp became a place where stereotypical and romanticized African American pursuits such as fishing, joking banter, and banjo-playing were the order for each day.

An ironic aspect about the strategic benefits of eliminating overt racial identities in this animal allegory in the mature strip is that Kelly was actually better able to tap, unapologetically, into the lively character traits or dynamics that up until this time were associated with blackface comedy. For example, Pogo—unlike Bumbazine—exhibited personality characteristics associated with romanticized minstrel figures: a lazy, cheerful disposition; avoidance of work at all costs; an affinity for banjo-playing and impromptu singing (Figure 4.14); and a running, wise-fool commentary on the behavior of the more "educated" members in his society that included a puritanical preacher, a myopic academic, and a business huckster. Albert also abandoned the classic role of trickster tale *predator* and entered into richer comedic territory, embodying a cigar-chomping, raging id; a Mark Twain–style alazon (a character whose grand claims to knowledge and expertise are immediately undercut by an obvious ignorance); and a narcissist and oblivious buffoon. In sum, for an Anglo culture raised on racially coded comedy, Pogo remained, in his 1950s mature complexity, a vague embodiment of the positive roles once associated with the Bert Williams–era blackface minstrel: an unrepressed person who spent his time making music laced with satiric or

Figure 4.14: Walt Kelly, "What profession . . . ," *Pogo*, 17 May 1949.

parodic doggerel; a moneyless everyman who treated everyone as equals; a cultural conscience who stands objectively on the margins; and a fountain of wry, sometimes satiric, folk wisdom.

The fusion of banjo-playing, song-making, and satiric commentary also evoked an even earlier model of the black figure as a funny social critic: the West African griot, a much feared, but socially protected community jester who used music and satire to instill shame in others for their bad behavior. According to Mel Watkins, author of *On The Real Side*, "The griot combined the talents of the musician with those of the innovative poet (weaving 'his own comments, moral judgments and isolated poetic images' into his songs) and the clever trickster-jester to accomplish his ends" (Watkins 64). The point here is not that Kelly intentionally modeled Pogo after the griot—a satiric figure from another continent and cultural tradition—but that the traces of the griot's comic identity and social function made their way through African American comedy and folklore, emerging in trickster tales and the more progressive and complex varieties of blackface performance, and then finally in a cartoon character who continued the legacy of those resonant comedic roles.

Trickster Tales and the Politics of Dialect

In his borrowing from the conventions of blackface and trickster tales, Kelly also capitalized on the readily comedic and organically deconstructive qualities of popularized versions of African American dialect. As with the channeling of racially charged character types, there was potential for both missteps and inspired fusions in these practices. Before closely analyzing Kelly's particular practices in this arena, we can briefly situate his borrowings and reworkings of black speech within a broader framing of how these folk forms and dialects have been mined for their vitality by artists in both mainstream American comedy and elevated literature. Within this history of appropriation, we can see there was already a richly conflicted set of satiric and ideological tools available to Kelly when he began experimenting with these elements. Whereas some of these were blunt and offensive—used to punish and stereotype minority figures and cultures in simplistic ways—others were more benign, tending to romanticize or idealize in sympathetic, though condescending ways. Still others were highly sophisticated and deftly constructed—syncretic reworkings that transcended issues of racism to a large degree. In fact, many of these more sensitive uses allowed African American folk forms and dialect to operate in the country's oral and literary traditions as layered and organically deconstructive tools.

To begin, it should be pointed out that within Kelly's satiric universe there is a tight link between his use of dialect and the channeling of trickster tale conventions and types. These two aspects of African American folklore are interdependent in terms of their potential to engage in significant cultural or political work. In fact, as this brief review of their historical uses may suggest, it is often when they are artificially separated in popular adaptations (such as Joel Chandler Harris's Uncle Remus tales) that their originary, subversive functions are lost or distorted.

In *Black Culture and Black Consciousness*, Lawrence Levine establishes some of the original social functions of African American trickster tales in antebellum times. He argues that tales of weaker animals evading and tricking larger predators were satirically coded and "encouraged trickery and guile; they stimulated the search for ways out of the system; they inbred a contempt for the powerful and an admiration for the perseverance and even the wisdom of the underman" (Levine 132). They were, in effect, part of a covert, layered counterdiscourse that resonated with its core audience—African American slaves.

Trickster tales were also a genre of oral entertainment that developed through a collaborative call-and-response between listeners and tellers. Levine explains that "through the entire performance the audience would comment, correct, laugh, respond, making the folktale as much a communal experience as the spiritual or the sermon" (Levine 89). Because they emerged as an expression of collective ideological interests or psychological needs, the forms and functions were linked directly to the specifics of time and context (Levine 371–85).[5]

On one level, Levine's description of the folk tales' early construction and reception helps to establish the grassroots vitality of these stories in their original context and form. In turn, this allows one to see how narrative patterns and character types lost their original resonance and social functions when the form and content were flattened and repackaged for white audiences by figures such as Joel Chandler Harris and Walt Disney. At the same time, however, Levine acknowledges that these folk forms evolved and adjusted over time—radically changing conventions to suit the ideological climate for the Harlem Renaissance, for example. This acknowledgment of flexibility within the form creates theoretical space in which to apply Bluestein's conception of the vital links between folk and popular culture. In particular, rather than seeing early folk culture as pure, authentic forms that can only be defiled or wrested from their original functions (as if stepping on and crushing delicate forms frozen in amber), it suggests that they evolve or adapt over time, melding with other traditions, achieving new artistic vitality, and creating ideological resonances with new audiences.

On a surface level, African American dialect is linked to trickster tales because the stories were part of a colloquial, oral form in African American communities. On a deeper level, dialect also shaped the political functions of these tales because of its informal fluidity and playfulness. For example, wordplay often served an important function in the narratives when the trickster used semantic games to obey the letter of the law while flouting its essential spirit, or to pretend ignorance—using malapropisms or mock eloquence—to fool or ridicule a more powerful predator. Like the words in other African American folk forms such as the sermon or blues song, the dialect used in trickster tales was layered: it carried seemingly innocuous literal surface meanings while also communicating satiric subsurface messages (Davies 147).[6]

So in theory, African American trickster tales featuring satirically layered dialect expressed within their original cultural contexts feelings of discontent, ambivalence, or even served as an "outlaw code" or survival handbook for blacks in the South (Bickley 134). But because both the format of these tales and the social functions of African American dialect were later borrowed so widely by writers and entertainers beyond this original cultural setting—making their way into blackface minstrelsy, regionalist humor, modernist literature, Harlem Renaissance literature, children's books, Disney films, and Walt Kelly's satiric comic strip—these political functions were sometimes lost. Or in the most progressive cases, they were radically adjusted according to the interests and intentions of the new audience and creator.

Earlier Borrowers of African American Folk Tales and Dialect

In nineteenth-century literary canons and comedy traditions there was a spectrum of uses of black dialect and trickster tale conventions. These ranged from the condescending mockery performed by some regionalist humorists and newspaper columnists, to ideologically conflicted blackface performances, sentimental appropriations of African American folklore by Joel Chandler Harris, and the more complex, syncretic uses by writers such as Mark Twain. In the second half of the nineteenth century, when ethnic humor reigned as one of the most popular comedy genres in the nation, white newspaper columnists adopted black or ethnic immigrant personas and dialects to create comic pieces in which the minority figure and his or her speech were primarily meant to be laughed at. Of course, like blackface minstrelsy, there were varied applications of these devices that could modify and soften the comedy's most punishing tones.[7] For example, the writer could at times shift targets, capitalizing on the black character's outsider status to observe and satirize dominant cultural practices through fresh eyes.

Joel Chandler Harris is the most controversial appropriator of black dialect and trickster tales from the late nineteenth century, and superficial similarities between his work and Kelly's make him a useful model against which to measure the relative progressiveness of Kelly's own borrowings. Unlike the regionalist comedians, Harris was more of a self-styled ethnographer and literary sentimentalist than a humorist (Jones 43). This point is significant since his taming of African American folklore's more comic, subversive tones had a large impact on subsequent early- to mid-twentieth-century versions of the tales. As a newspaperman working in Georgia in the 1870s, Harris gathered dialect trickster tales and published them in newspapers, and their wide popularity encouraged him to compile them into anthologies in the 1880s and 1890s. These hugely popular collections became a mainstay in white American nurseries, embedding Brer Rabbit, Uncle Remus, and the African American trickster tale genre deeply in the mainstream American cultural imagination.

One of the most fundamental problems with Harris's appropriation of these tales is that it is hard to see it as anything other than exploitation: taking communal tales whole cloth from a minority oral tradition, softening their original ideological codings, and essentially making them his own—and earning a long career and large fortune in the process. Celebrators of Harris's work over the years have tried to defend his borrowings by arguing that whereas most cultural guardians and literary critics in the nineteenth century viewed African American dialect as a degraded, corrupt form of speech, Harris at least straddled a line between "recognition and reduction, appreciation and appropriation" (Jones 106, 100).[8] Even more generously, he was hailed by one early biographer as the first great "master" of the Negro dialect and, more recently, as one of the first writers to create sympathetic, fully formed black characters—an improvement, arguably, on the harsh, condescending treatments of the regional humorists (Bickley xi, xvi). One apologist in 1975 even suggested that African Americans owe Harris a great debt for preserving their folklore (apparently unaware that early black writers such as Langston Hughes and Zora Neale Hurston compiled less compromised collections of traditional folk tales during the Harlem Renaissance) (Bickley 131).

The few mildly progressive qualities of Harris's work were undermined by his sentimental, patronizing view of African American culture and his larger project of trying to use his depiction of an old, pre–Civil War South to heal rifts between the North and South (Blair and Hill 271). As a result of this condescending tone and ideological agenda, Harris wrested these tales and dialect from their original context and negated most of their original meanings and uses. Furthermore, the ideological codings he added no longer had sympathies with grassroots, minority, or "folk" politics, thus eliminating one way of trying to pitch Harris as a poplorist.

Harris's reworkings of particular elements of the trickster tale are also problematic if one wishes to cast him in a progressive light. Firstly, consider the construction and functions of Harris's narrator, Uncle Remus. He may have been a sympathetic figure, but like the Uncle Tom stereotype, he was a limited construction—a white person's ideal of the black slave who remained true to his master after emancipation and chose to share his storehouse of wisdom primarily with a privileged white child. And although the Brer Rabbit stories still reflected much of the trickster's rowdy, desperate world—a realm of "unrelieved hostility and danger, violence and cruelty, terror and revenge"—their meanings became muted or conflicted when framed by Uncle Remus's calm, grandfatherly delivery and Harris's nostalgic tone (Bickley 137–38).

Harris recognized that there were subversive meanings in the stories, but as the following quote illustrates, he wanted to read and present them in the least threatening, apolitical terms:

> It needs no scientific investigation to show why he [the narrator of the original tales] selects as his hero the weakest and most harmless of all animals, and brings him out victorious in contests with the bear, the wolf and the fox. It is not virtue that triumphs, but helplessness; it is not malice, but mischievousness. (Bickley 7)

From Harris's perspective, the trickster was not an outlaw or rebel fighting desperately against overwhelming odds or an unjust system, but rather a "helpless" rascal with a charmingly mischievous streak. To summarize, Harris's appropriations of folklore and dialect, at best, amounted to a simple repackaging and restating of traditional trickster tales, softening edges and giving them conflicted codings; at worst, his anthologies both artificially froze this dynamically oral story form and replaced subversive tones and codings with nostalgic, patronizing, and regressive stereotypical meanings.

Mark Twain, the other "master" of black dialect who also used trickster tale devices in his literature, fares better when measured against similar standards. As a satirist who despised civilized hypocrisy, Twain had a natural affinity for folk wisdom and unschooled honesty. Thus in his personal life he developed a sincere admiration for the emotional honesty or "authenticity" of African American spirituals, and admired Frederick Douglass's simple, effective, honest speech (Fishkin 6–7). In his writings Twain was able to use colloquial speech—most famously in *The Adventures of Huckleberry Finn* (1884)—to create a new form of polyphonic literature and also to harness the naturally counterdiscursive qualities of African American vernacular.

Twain's use of dialect varied from character to character; at times, in fact, it served as a marker of ignorance, degeneracy, or pretension (as with Huck's dad, for example). But in the case of the principal characters in *Huckleberry Finn*, Jim's and Huck's dialects were used to dissect the pretensions, contradictions, and rationalizations of the dominant culture. Huck, who can be read (according to Shelley Fisher Fishkin) as a black voice, was a humorless questioner of corrupt moral codes; and Jim, playing the trickster, alternated between feigned ignorance and calculating flattery in order to navigate safe passage through a minefield of literal and figurative dangers.

Twain's reputation as a dialect writer has fared better than Harris's because he used dialect to satirize rather than sentimentalize, capitalizing on the inherently layered, subversive qualities of colloquial African American speech for many reasons; because his literature was syncretic (fusing folk forms and dialect with regionalist humor and satire, and using the picaresque story structure); because he was a poplorist (catering to a popular audience, but articulating an ideology in his satire that had a progressive, grassroots resonance and resembled in ideological spirit the African American folk form from which he borrowed); and because his tricksters remained true to their outlaw heritage (existing on the outskirts of society, and questioning core social orders). As a result, many black writers, including Langston Hughes and Ralph Ellison, hailed him as an enabler or path-maker rather than appropriator. In 1991 Ellison argued, for example, that Twain "made it possible for many of us to find our own voices" (Fishkin 4). Finally, Twain was perhaps the first writer to capitalize fully on the "counterhegemonic" qualities of African American dialect, described by Gavin Jones:

> The antagonistic power of black English is also rooted linguistically in its creative, improvisational disruption of accepted norms, its skill in masking subversion within a seemingly common tongue, its counterhegemonic capacity to "take the oppressor's language and turn it against itself." Black language does not simply stand for a wider cultural subversion. It demonstrates [that] . . . dialect can be an act of political resistance in itself. (Jones 213)

Moving into the twentieth century, George Herriman, creator of the comic strip *Krazy Kat* (which ran from 1913 to 1944), deserves special mention because of the way his work built upon Twain's legacy and was later echoed in Kelly's work. Herriman was part African American—from a Louisiana Creole heritage—but hid his ethnic identity in order to ease his way through a predominantly white newspaper culture. He did this by being quietly self-effacing, by posing as a "Greek," and by wearing a hat to hide his kinky hair. Issues of black identity and speech, however, emerged in *Krazy Kat* in codedly complex and subversive ways. The basic plot structure of the strip echoed trickster tale conventions by featuring an eternal, cyclical competition/love triangle between three characters: a black cat of ambiguous gender who spoke in a creatively mangled dialect and was in love with a malicious white mouse; a criminally minded mouse who despised the cat and continually punished her/him by flinging bricks (which the cat misinterpreted as affection); and an authoritarian police dog who loved the cat and hated and persecuted the rebel mouse.

It seems reasonable to read into the fable-like, cosmic satire of *Krazy Kat* some of Herriman's own struggle with double consciousness and possible distaste for the restrictive norms of the dominant culture.[9] His use of dialect, although more ambiguous and playful than Twain's, also took advantage of the potentially subversive tools within ethnic, vernacular speech. As Figure 4.15 illustrates, the comic strip's humor was principally driven by wordplay—malapropisms, double meanings, creative spellings, characters speaking past one another, and so on. The disorienting effect of these linguistic disruptions was reinforced by a continually mutating, surreal desert setting, and a metafictive, graphic playfulness. In sum, in less directly political ways than Kelly, Herriman used modified trickster tale conventions and the comedic tools within vernacular speech to highlight polyphonic cultural complexity and to satirize rigid social norms.

Figure 4.15: George Herriman, *Krazy Kat*, 6 January 1918.

In the first half of the twentieth century, black dialect was also called upon to perform interesting cultural work in the realm of high, modernist literature. In *The Dialect of Modernism*, Michael North analyzes T. S. Eliot's and Ezra Pound's use of Brer Rabbit references and dialect to articulate defiance of literary norms. In effect, the use of black dialect and comparisons of themselves to the trickster became metaphors for subversive acts of literary experimentation, of visceral, authentic freedom triumphing over "dead convention." In North's words, "the dialect in modernism [was] a model for the dialect of modernism" (North 78).

At mid-century, the Disney studio made its mark on the history of these appropriations by featuring black dialect as comic relief in films such as *Dumbo* (1941) (the hipster crow scene discussed earlier in this chapter) and by adding to Harris's legacy of condescending and sentimental uses of folk forms in *Song of the South* (1946). This second film, a partially animated adaptation of Harris's Brer Rabbit tales, even further softened (beyond Harris' treatment) the rough, naturalistic, and political edges of the stories by reducing the animal characters to cute, stylized, cartoon types. Although some of Harris's original story structures are still there—woven into a medley of interconnected tales—the desperate life-and-death comedy and drama of the trickster's world is undercut by the glossy, day-glo, rubbery-resilient quality of the animated animals, and by the sugary pastoral setting that teems with flowers, songbirds, and butterflies. Moreover, Harris's sentimental and stereotypical treatment of Uncle Remus is amplified in Disney's version as this character cheerfully sings that he "cain't open [his] mouth without a song jumpin' right out" and sees everything as "satisfactual."[10] If *Song of the South* had something politically progressive to say in this reworking, or if it were somehow a rich syncretism of white and black cultural forms, it might qualify as poplore; but as an apolitical (at least *consciously* apolitical), committee-constructed Disney confection that was targeted to a broad, generic audience and that essentially reworked already softened Brer Rabbit tales (with no apparent effort to reconnect in any meaningful way to the original folk forms), it is little more than an extension of Harris's brand of exploitation. Perhaps the most disturbing aspect of Disney's common practice of reworking traditional tales and folk forms is that the Disney interpretation effectively becomes the dominant version of these forms in the cultural memory or imagination, eclipsing most other variations or reworkings.

Within the emerging folk revival and beat writers movements at mid-twentieth century, one can find more sympathetic—albeit still conflicted—borrowings of African American vernacular forms. While these movements did not borrow the trickster tale format specifically, they did mine African American dialect and other related folk forms such as the blues and bebop. Some figures in each movement, moreover, are similar to Twain and Kelly in the way they harnessed concepts of authenticity to articulate countercultural political agendas or capitalize on the naturally counterdiscursive qualities of vernacular forms. For example, Harry Smith and Alan Lomax, the archivists who helped to initiate the folk revival movement, had a purity of purpose that seems to exempt them from charges of exploitation. Smith's packaging of blues and folk songs from the early decades of the century into sellable albums was a labor of love rather than an opportunistic commercial endeavor (he essentially did it below the radar of the mainstream music industry), and he largely allowed the original forms and creators to speak for themselves. Lomax, too, as a field archivist, had little interest in personally profiting from the transmission of folk forms to a broad audience. His work, in fact, seemed to function as an antidote to the homogenized appropriations on display within mainstream entertainment; specifically, by going into the field and directly recording blues singers and storytellers, he could acknowledge the work of the originary culture and creators, and create a standard of authenticity against which commercial borrowings could be critically compared.

More problematic were the commercial songwriters and folk singers who were introduced to vernacular forms of white Southern and African American cultures by Smith and Lomax. On the least authentic end of the spectrum are highly popular acts such as The Kingston Trio that one is hard pressed to classify as poplorists because of how they softened the rough edges of blues songs and folk ballads into sweet-sounding, apolitical ditties. Like Harris, they repackaged vernacular forms for a white audience while neither attempting to be true to the outlaw spirit of foundational forms, or to create significant, syncretic additions or variations. On the other hand, Pete Seeger and other more politically engaged folk revivalists of the late 1950s and early 1960s—those singer songwriters and groups involved in the Newport Folk Festivals—were more poploric in their respect toward issues of cultural provenance and authenticity of form and in the way they used vernacular forms as tools for political expression.

However, as the much-discussed rift between Bob Dylan and the folk revivalists illustrates (when Dylan "plugged in" at the 1965 Newport Festival and scandalized the core musicians and fans of the movement), some folk revivalists may
have fetishized concepts of authenticity and purity to the point that the forms
could no longer develop to fit new cultural moments; migrate into more popular,
commercialized realms; or fuse with other emerging vernacular genres. To be
fair, it could also be argued that when Dylan parted ways with the folk revivalists, he also abandoned some of the political dimensions of folk forms; in his
subsequent career he traded the direct, Guthrie-esque political agitation of his
early years for the broader appeal of being a country-inflected, popular rock performer. Ironically, it is his later, largely apolitical work that has introduced broad
audiences to, and amplified the significance of, the forms and politics of his early
political work and that of other folk revival purists.

Finally, Jack Kerouac offers an example of another one of Kelly's contemporaries who made both missteps and deftly original moves in the process of
appropriating, appreciating, and modifying black cultural forms. One could argue that Kerouac's spontaneous prose style was syncretically dynamic as it drew
from a variety of sources including Freudian concepts of psychic automatism
and stream-of-consciousness narratives, Jungian notions of mining the cultural
subconscious for resonant archetypes and difficult truths, and the counterdiscursive musical structure of bebop jazz. It is with this final influence, obviously,
that Kerouac draws from African American vernacular forms by alternating between long sentences, and short, percussive declarations, and by allowing his
thoughts to wind out like long, improvisational riffs, giving verbal form to bebop musical motifs. But this was not simply a borrowing of musical structure—
it was also a harnessing of the subversive power and connotations of the genre's
cultural "dialect." To explain, because bebop was a musical form created largely
by black musicians attempting to counter the popular, gentrified sounds of big
band jazz, it was perceived by both its creators and appreciators as an intentionally difficult and authentic kind of artistic and cultural expression—one that
ran counter to packaged, mainstream music and entertainment. This countercultural attitude was evident in the identities of its stars (Charlie Parker, John
Coltrane, and Miles Davis), in its cult following, and even in the logic of its musical form—its disruptions of conventional notions of time; its unrestrained—
"unrepressed," perhaps—"blowing"; and its improvisational communication of
rebellion and individuality.

We see, then, that at the same time Kelly was creating his strip (the late 1940s
and early 1950s), Kerouac was engaging with bebop jazz in large part because of
its status as the latest manifestation of "outlaw," black, vernacular culture. For
example, in *On the Road* Kerouac used the performance or appreciation of bebop
jazz as a metaphor for evading or challenging the dominant white culture's ethos
of materialism, the corporate clock, cultural regimentation or conformism, and

the normative ideals of the suburbs. He labeled it the "sound of the night," suggesting that it existed on the margins of mainstream culture, prodding and countering the rigidities of daytime, corporate life (Kerouac 12).

In *On the Road*, Kerouac also articulated a general admiration for black vernacular culture through his fictional alter ego, Sal Paradise. Beyond idolizing bebop jazz musicians, Sal also pined for the seeming authenticity of identity and experience that would come from living in a "raggedy" African American neighborhood—a place where he perceived time moving at an alternating flux and flow that would echo the freedom of action and experience to which he aspired (Kerouac 180). There are similarities here to both Mark Twain's use of African American folk culture—the admiration of the spontaneity and authenticity of black experience and arts; his protagonists' adoption of a quasi-African American voice and identity as he explores from the perspective of the margins the breadth and variety of American experience—and the construction of counter-discursive, syncretic literature that draws upon a type of folk dialect—the literary equivalent of bebop jazz, in Kerouac's case. However, Kerouac's missteps in the politics of appropriation are more dramatic than Twain's. Specifically, while Twain indulged in some mild romanticization of the authenticity of black language and experience, Kerouac's admiration relied on caricatures of black authenticity that were patronizing at times. Specifically, Kerouac romanticized the poverty and marginalization of mid-century black culture, seeing those qualities as a facet of black authenticity; he also used blacks as props in his narrative—useful others through whom he and his alter ego could self-authenticate.

Kerouac revealed this strategy in Sal's aspiration to become black: while walking through a black neighborhood, Sal imagined being able to touch the "knee of some dusky, mysterious, sensual gal," and wished he "could exchange worlds with the happy, true-hearted, ecstatic Negroes of America" (Ibid., 180). There is the aestheticization of poverty here as well as the condescending projection of an earthy sensuality onto black women; and Kerouac's emancipatory project, imagined through the filter of black experience and voice, is ultimately more existential and individualistic than Twain's collective, democratic vision.

Walt Kelly's Use of Trickster Tales and Black Dialect

So how does Kelly fare when the same criteria are applied to his uses of black forms and dialect as he went from Disney animator and children's comic book creator, to forerunner of the countercultural movement, and engaged in cultural borrowings that spanned the spectrum of attitudes and methods highlighted in the preceding pages? His early missteps resembled those of opportunistic borrowers such as Harris; and even later in his career, his lack of direct understanding of African American culture led him to romanticize African American identity, forms, and "authenticity" in naïve ways. Nevertheless, like the best poplorists in other mediums, he harnessed the organic vitality of black, vernacular forms to create vital, syncretic variations on trickster tales and dialect comedy that fit the needs of core readers at a particular cultural moment; and like Twain, he was ultimately true to the outlaw heritage or politically subversive qualities of the forms he borrowed and modified.

Initially, Kelly's *Animal Comics* work, in terms of dialect use, was very similar to Harris's appropriations in the Uncle Remus tales. In many of the early tales Bumbazine and Pogo spoke in a relatively hammy, unnuanced African American vernacular, saying things like, "Don't want no truck wif dat goo' fo' nothin' ol' 'gator." Strangely, however, there is no clear arc of crass uses of dialect gradually evolving into more syncretic texts in these comic book stories. For example, the earliest Pogo and Albert adventures from 1942 followed fairly traditional Uncle Remus-style storylines but featured dialect that downplayed the rough edges of colloquial speech; characters said things like, "Oh, don't eat me first—I don't deserve the honor." But then in installments just one year later, the exaggerated dialect was in full force, while the storylines increasingly softened the relationship between the predator (Albert) and his prey (Bumbazine and Pogo). The flux and shift of both narrative patterns and dialect in these stories suggest Kelly was vaguely aware he had not yet found his voice or moved beyond derivative treatments. It also anticipates Kelly's more thoughtful and constructive tinkering with conventions once the mature comic strip began to connect with its core audience.

It was during the next stage of Kelly's career—during his time at the *Star*, when he first tried out *Pogo* in comic strip form—that Kelly gradually began to behave like a true poplorist, moving beyond opportunistic appropriations of tired trickster tales and exaggerated dialect to becoming an innovative and politically engaged satirist. The shifts in storylines, character construction, and politics in the strip during these years chart this transformation.

First, the departure of Bumbazine—as the storylines went from comic books to comic strips—was an essential step in leaving behind the no-longer-resonant conventions of antebellum trickster tales. When Bumbazine was present in the comedy, the animals in the swamp were limited to behaving as two-dimensional, storybook types; but when Pogo took on the lead role, the storylines became more explicitly satirical as all of the characters began to embody more complex, adult social types. Nevertheless, Pogo did exhibit vestigial traits of the desperate trickster figure during his first couple of years as protagonist. For example, during the strip's run at the *Star*, Pogo had to constantly use his verbal wit and guile to avoid becoming dinner for two resident predators—a fox and a bobcat. But significantly, he was now buddies with his earlier nemesis, Albert; there were still echoes of the old predator-prey dynamic in their friendship, but any true aggression was sublimated into verbal banter and accidental attempts at "cannibalism." This original variation on the trickster tale dynamic marked Kelly's entry into syncretic territory—a comic world featuring Freudian treatments of animal interactions and motivations; a shift toward a pastoral setting where characters exhibited relatively benign foibles, in which the only serious dangers were invading forces of malignant dogmatism, greed, and scapegoating; and uses of dialect that emphasized the dialogical nature of society and the need for tolerance of human foibles and ideological differences.

Dialect and Ideological Heterogeneity in *Pogo*

When the strip went into national syndication in 1950, Kelly made additional changes that pushed it further into more original, syncretic territory. For example, Kelly adjusted the dialect in the strip after getting negative reader feedback and hearing from a skeptical editor who explained to Kelly, "It's funny [the strip] after you explain it, but believe it or not we now have 165,000 readers and you're going to have a hell of a time running around. . . ." (Kelly, "Biographical Sketch" 17; Andrae and Blum 138). Thus, in the name of clarity Kelly did away with the elaborate phonetic spellings and Uncle Remus–style black vernacular.

In this seemingly gentrified iteration of the strip, however, some traces of the minstrel's voice in Pogo's homey drawl and wise fool behavior remained, and the speech of all the characters still fell within a broad range of generalized Southern dialects. As with Twain's use of dialect in *Huckleberry Finn*, there was a dialogical richness and specificity to each character's choice of slang, malapropism, and neologism. This linguistic variety in both Twain's and Kelly's texts emphasized the creolized complexity of American society and allowed the word choice of individual characters to speak volumes about their worldviews and peculiar foibles (Dillard 191). For example, the speech of both Pogo and Huck was the most "common" and unadorned within their respective satiric communities, indicating that they were the resident truth-tellers who could see and speak outside of society's falsely constructed moralities. And that of buffoons like Albert—and in Twain's case, the Duke or Dauphin—were the most full of embarrassing slips, self-aggrandizing neologisms, and ignorant misreadings.

Taken as a whole, the strip's language also retained in its modified form many of the malleable, disruptive qualities of black, colloquial speech. Free from the grammatical rules and constraints of "proper" English, it became an "improvisational disruption of accepted norms," capitalizing on the potentially satiric and "counterhegemonic capacity" of malleable slang and dialect (Jones 213). In effect, Kelly's fluid, verbal improvisations were fueled or inspired by African American dialect in the same way Kerouac's anti-establishment prose style was modeled after the structure of bebop jazz.

Kelly further highlighted the flux and variety of language and meaning—and the shifting perceptions of truth and reality, by extension—by signaling the tone and ideological intentions of each character's dialect with a creative use of evocative typefaces. For example, Deacon Mushrat (Figure 4.16) spoke in pretentious Gothic script, and P. T. Barnum, an ursine huckster, spoke in the amplified font of old-timey advertisements. Other characters, such as Albert and Churchy, spoke in a more generic typeface that was appropriate for their folky ignorance—rife with creative misspellings and malapropisms.

Figure 4.16: Walt Kelly, ". . . a flair for foreign relations." *Pogo*, 3 November 1950.

By highlighting these competing dialects, Kelly could pack each strip with multiple throwaway puns and create situations where the reader enjoyed the dramatic irony of being the only one within the babel privy to each character's intended meanings or blatant misunderstandings. On a more theoretical level, this cacophony of voices and worldviews illustrates nicely the Bakhtinian concept of democratically dialogical literature (Bakhtin 426). Like a master novelist, Kelly channeled the voices of different representative social types and gave his work a heteroglossic complexity by meshing primary "narration, secondary voices, different genres, oral everyday speech . . . stylistic, individualized speeches of characters," parodies of different genres, literary allusions, and metafictive devices (clever acknowledgments of the constructedness of one's writing or art) (Bakhtin 263). But for Kelly this complexity was not in the service of a superficial or gratuitous literary game, as can be seen in some postmodern literature. Instead, he grounded it with Pogo's truthful common speech and harnessed it to a core satiric point—that we all see and experience the world differently and should thus be slow to judge and condemn.

Kelly highlighted this point in several ways during one of the most famous runs of the strip—the storming of the swamp by Simple J. Malarkey (a caricature of Senator Joseph McCarthy) in the early 1950s. In physical appearance he resembled the old-fashioned trickster tale predator: he was a bobcat with a blocky, simian build; pupiless eyes; rough clothes; and a shotgun. In methods, however, Malarkey was a more complex predator—one that reflected more accurately the fears of the core audience of the strip. Rather than trying to literally consume individual animals, he attempted to replace the political system of the swamp—an organic democracy—with a police state that controlled its citizens through fear, division, and scapegoating.

Malarkey's methods, in fact, highlighted the coercive and divisive ways words, language, and texts can be used. When he arrived, his ostensible purpose was to help Deacon Mushrat and Mole MacCarony with their bird-watching club (a euphemism for Red-hunting), but Malarkey quickly took over the club by force, doing away with free elections, tearing up the club constitution (so that he could dictate a self-serving and variable legal code), and intimidating the other members at gun point (Figure 4.17). Once in control, he proceeded to rename the club the "Bonfire Boys" and mounted a campaign to tar and feather—both literally and figuratively—all the community residents.

Figure 4.17: Walt Kelly, ". . . new member . . . ," *Pogo*, 5 May 1953.

Malarkey's somewhat faulty logic was that feathering all the denizens of the swamp would make it easier to tell who the birds (Reds) were. He would force upon each individual, in other words—as if they were a text to be manipulated—an external signifier that would reinforce his simplistic, predetermined view of a social order made up only of subversives and patriots. After failing to tar and feather one of the most innocent citizens of the swamp, a puppy, he quickly turned on his friends. In his attempt to get Deacon and Mole feathered up, he fell into a pot of boiling tar himself—a suiting punishment that echoed traditional trickster tale conventions (predators falling prey to their own cruel devices and vices). Then, in one of the darker episodes ever to appear in the strip (both visually and narratively), a tar-covered Malarkey chased Mole through the darker reaches of the swamp with a huge ax. After this episode, Pogo and his friends assumed that Malarkey was dead, and for many months he was not seen in the swamp. However, he resurfaced a year later, caused more mayhem, and was eventually driven out for good by Sis Boombah, one of the few prominent female characters in the strip.

Returning to the core point of this discussion, we note that while Twain used linguistic variety—with an emphasis on African American vernacular—to engage in a form of organic deconstruction of the dominant culture's hypocritical logic, pious justifications, and conflicted ideologies, Kelly in these early '50s strips went deeper into intuitive poststructuralist territory by highlighting multiple splintering dialects and emphasizing the resultant instability of language as a truth-carrying instrument. While Twain highlighted the "fundamental het-erogeneity of human nature" through a naturalistic treatment of real dialects, Kelly emphasized ideological heterogeneity by amplifying, stylizing, and exag-gerating the flux and variety of a generalized and splintered black dialect (Sewell ix). On an applied political level, this acknowledgment of the messiness of lan-guage translated into a more skeptical view of dogma and dominating ideolo-gies. While one of the dominant ideologies of the early 1950s—McCarthy's con-servatism—insisted on ideological unity or conformity, Kelly's alternative realm allowed for the acceptance of messy, decentralizing views and voices (Bakhtin 274).

Kelly and Black Cultural Authenticity

Now that we have an idea of the political methods and vision of Kelly's mature strip, we can continue the discussion of the political significance of Kelly's no-tions of black cultural authenticity in *Pogo*. Since Kelly constructed an artistic identity as a folk-wise storyteller for the media age, his methods can be com-pared to those of folk revivalists such as Pete Seeger—in particular, the way they inspired college students to take an interest in political issues through an ap-pealing, vernacular form. Like the revivalists, Kelly used the cultural power of claims to authenticity as they related to African American forms and identity to construct an appealing persona and make his strip's settings and characters resonate with his core audience. As a popular artist connected to engaged read-ers, Kelly stood outside the mechanisms of culture factories like the Hollywood film studios that created products preconfigured to affirm conventional, bour-geois values. Further, the "authentic" pastoral folk setting of his strip offered an imaginary ideological refuge for college students and liberal readers who were vaguely opposed to the superficiality of mid-century commercial culture, to the perceived homogeneity of suburban life, to the rigidity of corporate culture, and to the oppressive politics of McCarthyism.

Significantly, however, Kelly proved in the end to be less tied to constructed notions of pure authenticity than the folk revivalists, and this allowed his work to evolve in a dynamically syncretic fashion. Whereas Seeger and other purists in the folk revival movement were dogmatically committed to notions of pure instrumentation and traditional musical forms—thus limiting, ultimately, their ability to evolve syncretically and reach a truly broad popular audience—Kelly allowed himself to modify forms and conventions to adjust to the needs and interests of a truly large readership (this included not just dissenting college students and liberal adults, but children introduced to the world of politics for the first time through a comic strip, and readers of different political opinions encountering Kelly's politics who were initially drawn to the more readily ap-pealing qualities of his cartoon art and slapstick). Perhaps a comparison could be made between Bob Dylan and Kelly: just as Dylan was able to expand the reach of the progressive politics of the folk revival movement by fusing folk forms with rock instrumentation and beat lyrics (while in the process losing his membership among the purists), Kelly brought the inherently progressive politics of folk forms and dialects to a popular audience by fusing them with the broadly appealing qualities of cartoon-cute drawings and easily consumable comic strip comedy.

In summary, Kelly's earliest work bore similarities to that of Harris as he appropriated folk forms and conventions in derivative and generally condescending ways. Early on he also resembled Twain, the folk revivalists, and Kerouac in his romanticization of the seeming authenticity and spontaneity of black culture. In his mature years, when his admiration was perhaps less naïve, his commitment to black rights more sincere, and his use of authenticity harnessed to a brand of progressively democratic politics, this practice took on more admirable overtones. In a final accounting of his mature comic strip when he created an original, syncretic variation on vernacular forms, and in poploric fashion interacted with and addressed the needs of, a highly engaged audience, he aligned himself most closely with Twain's progressive legacy. His borrowings at this point seem like more original variations on core conventions. And in the end, even though Kelly radically modified trickster tale conventions and carried the use of dialect into aracial, postmodern territory, his goals remained ironically similar to those of nineteenth-century African American folktale artists. Within a relatively oppressive cultural and political context, he created a resonantly coded animal allegory through a collaborative call-and-response with emotionally and ideologically invested readers. And like the political allegories in those early folk tales, his layered satire addressed the real emotional and political needs of this core audience. Acting as a media-age fireside raconteur, he created for them a set of embraceable, pragmatic alternative ideologies—perhaps what might be considered an "outlaw code" for liberal intellectuals navigating their way through the treacherous cultural waters of the McCarthy era.

CHAPTER 5

The Aesthetics of *Pogo*

Kelly's greatness as a satirist and comedian was matched by his excellence as an artist. Indeed, *Pogo* was an unusually vivid and eye-arresting comic strip because of the dynamism, solidity, and rich array of values and textures in his visuals. Because of these aesthetic qualities, *Pogo* is widely considered by comics scholars to be one of the best works of art to ever appear on the funnies page. R. C. Harvey, for example, describes the art in *Pogo* as a "cathedral of accomplishment" and argues that Kelly's

> comic strip achieved the maximum of which the medium is capable, a zenith of high art. If we accept the definition of comic strip art as a narrative of words and pictures, both verbal and visual, in which neither words nor pictures are quite satisfactory alone without the other, then we must say that Kelly welded the verbal and visual elements together into a comic chorus so unified, so mutually dependent, that it crystallized forever the very essence of the art. (201)

Harvey's estimation seems right on target, and one could add that this codependence between the visual and verbal elements of Kelly's work often has the quality of a sweet-and-sour counterpoint. On the one hand, the verbal satire in *Pogo* can often be aggressively pointed in its topicality, or melancholic in its view of incorrigible human nature; and on the other hand, the visuals in the strip are cutely dynamic, full of entertaining and strategically distracting dynamism. In a simplistic sense, then, the visuals in *Pogo* are sometimes the sugar that helps the medicine of social commentary go down easy. At other times, as I will illustrate, the art of the strip is provocative and complex in its own right, acting as an integral element of the satire or performing its own metafictive commentary.

Harvey's assertion that the visual and verbal elements of *Pogo* are inextricable echoes a similar point this study has made in several places: that the various elements of Kelly's career and work—whether it be business, art, comedy, or satire—cannot be readily separated. There is such a high degree of organic fusion among influences and overlapping comedic and aesthetic tools in the execution of *Pogo*, in fact, that one must be flexible and creative in the construction of theoretical frames that will do justice to its peculiar complexity. When it comes to the work of this chapter, for example—a study of the visual construction of *Pogo*—this translates into looking to some of the following sources and ideas for help: the history of animation, given both the cinematic qualities of comic strips in general and Kelly's training as an animator in particular; the visual conventions of other related mediums such as comic books and political cartoons—additional fields that shaped Kelly's aesthetic; approaches to comics that consider the interconnectedness of words and images, and the way that visual symbols in comics function as a type of "readable" syntax; and frames that acknowledge the visual/aesthetic qualities of the seemingly "non-art" elements of the strip, such as typefaces and panels.

Kelly and the Disney Aesthetic

To begin, one can look to Kelly's training as animator for both an explanation for why his visuals stood out on the comics page, and for how the art of *Pogo* reinforced the verbal elements of the strip's comedy and satire. As the first chapter described, Kelly received his liberal arts education at Disney, a company that wanted its animators to be well-grounded in art history, diverse cultural aesthetics, and the canon of world folklore. But unlike a traditional university liberal arts curriculum—which would be largely abstract and theoretical in its exploration of arts and ideas—Disney's program was vocational, channeling that learning immediately into the construction of popular art. Kelly appreciated the applied nature of this training, stating that "color, moods, movement, staging, ballet technique, music and timing became, not book learning, but the life's blood of the Disney craftsman (Kelly, "Unpublished Autobiographical Sketch" 7).

The Disney studios asked for a great deal in return for that training. Unlike the often crude and slap-dash productions of their competitors, Disney films emphasized realistically constructed backdrops (often painted in richly nuanced watercolors), fluid and dynamic motion in the characters (requiring a greater number of stills per minute than the typical cartoon), sensitive line work from frame to frame, and a broad palette of nuanced colors (demanding an enormous number of junior animators to execute the details in each cel). This perfectionism effectively elevated Disney animation in the eyes of many critics; their films were "'art' as opposed to the less respected products of Warner Bros. and MGM, which were considered 'mere cartoons'" (White 38–39).

There was a less positive side to the elevated Disney aesthetic, however. The sheer scale of the factory-like process of construction needed to create such elaborate films, for example, resulted in unfair and sometimes abusive working conditions. Within the hierarchy of the Disney corporation there was a small corps of relatively well-paid and pampered, senior animators, and then a vast army of junior animators and colorists (many of them forgotten female laborers) who were underpaid and overworked. So, while the Disney method of production may have created some classic films, it also resulted in ugly defections within the ranks, bitter unionizing efforts, and rancorous labor strikes. The perfectionism inherent in Disney's large-scale animation processes also had a tendency to result in a sometimes homogenized look; the rigid rules surrounding individual artists following strict model sheets often subsumed those artists' spontaneity and quirky aesthetic sensibilities into a look that could appear corporately bland. There are exceptions to that assertion, of course; at times senior animators were given license to infuse a scene with their sensibility, and in a few rare cases a writer-artist, such as Bill Peet, was allowed to imprint his particular style on an entire film (*The Reluctant Dragon*).

The profit-driven orientation of such a large Hollywood studio (huge investments coupled with blockbuster expectations) also conspired against the Disney aesthetic achieving any kind of gritty and nuanced richness. In particular, that capitalistic ethic encouraged both writers and artists at Disney to create highly commodifiable art, softening the rough edges of both the content and aesthetic look of fairy tales and myths that had long served as richly dark, cautionary tales in the folklore canon. As a result, wild things were domesticated and often made to look irrepressibly cute within the Disney universe. That softening of sharp edges, in fact, took on a literal meaning in the visual construction of characters, as the repetitive, multi-artist construction of their heads and bodies—and the emphasis placed on creating highly merchandisable products—resulted in forms that were rubbery and round, with dynamic and slickly polished line work (Shickel 51–52; and Solomon 49).

Even with this training, Kelly and his work were not wholly products of the Disney machine. It is well documented that he behaved as an incorrigibly independent artist while at Disney—struggling to conform to model sheets, imprinting his own aesthetic on everything he did, and rebelling against corporate conventions (Andrae and Blum 135). Kelly's position as a junior animator gave him little opportunity to imprint his own aesthetic sensibility on the texts he helped construct, but his iconoclastic behavior hinted he was already thinking like an auteur, imagining opportunities to assert his own voice and style. Before we look to the other fields where Kelly further refined his independent aesthetic—comic books and political cartoons—a brief cataloguing of some of the specific visual tropes borrowed from animation that Kelly ultimately used in his mature comic strip is in order. These elements included elaborately constructed backdrops, a cinematic flow of action, and a construction of character heads and bodies within the general outlines of a Disney aesthetic.

As with Disney films, *Pogo* featured a backdrop executed with detail and atmospheric nuance. Whereas a majority of comic strip artists in Kelly's time (excepting, perhaps, Al Capp) treated backgrounds as an afterthought, providing only minimal and sometimes careless outlines of trees, buildings, or other inanimate objects, Kelly constructed a swamp environment that seemed to breathe and live. The trees, for example, were realistically twisted and three dimensional, as if caught by Kelly's brush in mid-growth (see Figure 5.1). Kelly's care, in fact, in using rich shadows and varied line work to describe their organic growth pat-

Figure 5.1: Walt Kelly, "The New Fort Mudge Memorial Dump," *Pogo*, 2 November 1969.

terns, three-dimensional structure, and rich surface textures, suggested he had studied his material from real life—or mimicked the trees drafted by other Disney animators that were based on direct observation. The execution of other seemingly unimportant elements in the background too—such as water, grass, furniture, and tools—was done with similar care. Each object had heft, texture, dimension, and judicious eye-focusing detail.

At Disney, a general devotion among animators to construct realistic, eye-pleasing backgrounds served to elevate their product above that of competing studios that did not have the same budget or institutional practices for creating such high-quality art. It effectively made Disney's films more escapistly entertaining as well—they seemed like an "extension of Hollywood live-action cinema" as they suppressed "many of the signals that would remind audiences that what they were watching was, in fact, a cartoon" (White 42–43). For Kelly, a comic strip artist working in a more blatantly two-dimensional and comparatively static medium, there was no possibility of transporting readers to that degree.

Scott McCloud has suggested, nevertheless, that print comics that feature elaborately constructed backgrounds juxtaposed with more simply drawn characters (works such as *Tintin*, certain brands of manga, and *Pogo*, for example) invite much reader engagement and identification. The solidity and breadth of the setting convinces the reader of the "reality" of this imaginative world, and then the spare construction of the principal characters provides for both quick reading of core emotions and an easy entry for the readers to project themselves into the comedy and philosophy of the work. In summarizing those strategies, McCloud writes, "One set of lines to see [those constructing the background]. Another set of lines to be [those delineating the characters]" (42–43).

The care devoted to the backgrounds in *Pogo* also reinforced the various narrative functions of the Southern swampland. The gnarled trees, hanging Spanish moss, and gentle bayou waterways conjure the mythic qualities of a Southern rural lifestyle, removed from the rat race of modern life; it also evokes the perfect setting for enjoying good company, music, and food. The Sunday installments, in particular, with their inclusion of full color and panoramic frames, celebrated that vision of Southern pastoral leisure. One could say that the visual and narrative elements of the strip worked in collaboration: the authentic quality of the various visual elements in the setting reinforced notions of authenticity, sincerity, and spontaneity that often accompany a Southern rural locale in fiction.

Kelly also evoked deeper pastoral associations in his strip by softening the edges of this swamp environment. Brambles, thickets, and bogs are replaced with gentle paths, soft mounds of grass, and meandering but easily navigable waterways. Because the violence and competition of the natural world has been tamed both aesthetically and literally, the characters are free to enjoy food, music, and comic-philosophical discussions while living in some kind of carefree golden age. The few times that the natural elements actually appear menacing coincide with the arrival of serious predators such as Malarkey and Mole—as if their presence corrupts the pastoral placidity of the swamp (see Figure 5.2).

Figure 5.2: Walt Kelly, "Okay, I'll go in . . . ," *Pogo*, 10 June 1953.

Kelly also borrowed from Disney, and animated films in general, various methods for making the action in the strip flow in a fluid and dynamic way. The great Russian filmmaker Sergei Eisenstein admired the Disney's studios devotion to giving their films that headlong, visually lyrical thrust; he described it as the "inner flow of the music" made manifest in the exterior visuals (White 39). *Pogo* seems to have some of that internal music driving the action of its characters as well. Whereas most comic strips feature static, stationary characters engaged in verbal banter, Kelly's characters are perpetually in movement, gesticulating with their whole bodies, reacting with exaggerated pleasure or alarm, or racing from frame to frame in a fugue-like flow of bodies, heads, and limbs. But true to his Disney training, there is always a restrained, lyrical quality to that action—none of the extreme exaggeration associated with Looney Tunes or Tex Avery–style animation.

The lyrical, dynamic movement of characters in Disney films was an out-growth of the company's training methods. Animators engaged in "action analysis" that required them "to observe a model executing a complete movement and then to sketch from memory, creating an *impression* of the movement rather than duplicating the movement in photographic detail." Walt Disney also believed that "exaggeration was important . . . in capturing the impression of movement," but animators were trained to keep that distortion within reasonable bounds, learning "the importance of balance to a body in motion, the ways that folds in clothing are formed by anatomical stretch points, and how to give weight—physical presence—to their characters" (Harvey 189, 191). The movement of characters in the mature version of *Pogo* exhibited this same effective balance between dynamic, slightly exaggerated movement, and restrained, realistic treatment of anatomy, gravity, and clothing (see Figure 5.3).

Figure 5.3: Walt Kelly, "*Pogo*, I resents yo' insinuations . . . ," *Pogo*, 4 February 1953.

Kelly's proficiency in drawing dynamic figures allowed him to feature a great deal of vaudeville-style slapstick in the strip as well: funny visual disguises, pratfalls, tugs of war, chase scenes, and a healthy number of comic blows. And as with other animated animals in a comedic allegory, no serious injury ever incurred from that mayhem. The characters' rubbery and resilient bodies always seem to recover within a frame or two.

Finally, Kelly's construction of the contours of his animal characters was deeply animation-influenced. To begin, the fluid and varied line work conveying the contours of each character's body parts and face was a signature Disney convention. Artists in lesser animation studios tended to use flat, unvarying lines in the construction of figures, but Disney animators were trained to imbue the line work in their characters with a painterly dynamism, using gestural strokes and nuanced widths and values. Kelly's mature work was executed similarly with dynamic brushwork that infused every limb and feature with movement and nuance. For example, looking closely at the characters in *Pogo* one notices that the lines narrow at joints (communicating movement), thicken on the underside of various features (suggesting shadow and heft), and ebb and flow according

Figure 5.4: Walt Kelly, "Hot dog!" *Pogo*, 20 October 1950.

to the specific movement or gesture of each moment (see Figure 5.4—Albert's snout, in particular, in its construction with thick and thin, tapering lines).

The generally rounded shape of the heads and features of the characters in *Pogo* also owes a debt to animation and Disney aesthetics. In his book *Enchanted Drawings*, Charles Solomon explains that many animators engage in a type of rounded "shaping" of features that is a result of drawing methods peculiar to the medium: "the more often an artist draws a particular shape, the more rounded it becomes as the muscles of the forearm move through an increasingly familiar pattern" (Solomon 49). He adds that artists are further encouraged to emphasize this rounded aesthetic because of its inherent psychological appeal, making characters more broadly accessible and commodifiable:

> . . . humans react favorably to creatures with soft, rounded forms. The Disney artists discovered that characters with the proportions of a human baby would be perceived as cute: a large head with big, low-set eyes and a small nose and mouth; a little, rounded body; chubby limbs with tiny hands and feet . . . The rounder, jovial Mickey in "Brave Little Tailor" (1938), whose proportions Fred Moore had redesigned along these principles, has an immediate appeal and charm that the more angular Mickey of "Steamboat Willie" lacked. (Solomon 49)

John Canemaker, another animation scholar, makes similar observations and speculates further on the psychological appeal of these distilled, childlike character forms:

> Felix is a radical abstraction of "cat," as Mickey is a symbolic distillation of "mouse." Both characters exhibit a childlike cranial bulge with big round eyes atop a small body, an image which triggers people's innate feelings of affection for babies. The construction of both Felix and Mickey is based on interlocking circles, a shape that

subconsciously connects with sensual, pleasurable imagery. In addition, the circle
symbolizes infinity and eternity; it denotes wholeness and continuity—survival.
There is a feeling of reassurance about it. (Canemaker 7–8)

The mature Pogo (Figure 5.5) in particular resembles Mickey Mouse and Felix the
Cat in this respect: saucer eyes, perpetual smile, and highly rounded features.
Albert too, and most of the other main characters, exhibit some of the characteristics of animation's softening, "shaping" methods. In contrast to Disney, however, there are many secondary characters in the strip whose faces resemble with
great specificity the real animals upon which they are based. The most loath-
some characters, in fact, could not even be described as cute; they look like real
predators, with sharp teeth, a generous amount of hair, and angular features.
In the early 1950s, when a woman complained about the presence to two "ugly"
predatory animals in the strip, Kelly defended their inclusion, arguing that they
effectively represented the "ugliness of the world" ("Pogo Creator Kelly Spurs
Fight for Survival" 1).

Figure 5.5: Walt Kelly, *Pogo* in the 1950s.

That dose of ugliness helped temper the cuteness of many of the main characters and it infused the strip with a darker, more mature tone than can be seen
in most Disney features—one that acknowledged the presence of real, mundane
evil (as opposed to fantastical villains) in the world. The contrast between Pogo's
cute, mask-like simplicity and the ugly realism of the more reprehensible characters also served to invite readers to identify more powerfully with the strip's
protagonist. As McCloud suggests, the iconic distillation of a cartoon protagonist's cute features has the psychological effect of inviting reader identification;
like a welcoming, semi-blank slate, the readers project themselves into the role
of protagonist, experiencing the world of the comic character with powerful di-

rectness. In fact, on a spectrum that McCloud uses to quantify cartoon characters' level of simplification and power of identification, he places Pogo toward "meaning," away from reality, and far from abstraction (McCloud 53-53). That means that Kelly bases Pogo's look on distilled human features that are effective carriers of meaning and portals for identification. Moreover, there is neither too much slavish devotion to depicting the face realistically (it embraces a simplified cartoon syntax), nor is the depiction so abstract and stylized that it draws attention to its own constructedness in a two-dimensional, avant-garde way.

At this point one can see an example of the interconnectedness of Kelly's "cute" aesthetics and his social criticism: the mainstream, endearing look of Pogo's rounded persona helped Kelly achieve a breadth of popularity with readers inclined to embrace characters that resembled the professionally polished and rounded look of Disney-style animation. The iconic simplicity of Pogo's features, moreover, could have encouraged readers to identify in a profound way with his protagonist; they empathized with Pogo, sharing his worldview and seeing the foibles of the other characters through his eyes. Once attracted to and engaged with those aesthetics, readers were then given a consistent diet of social and political satire. Through Pogo's persona they were also introduced to a coherent worldview or code of behavior—an ethic of self-inspection and tolerance that served as an effective counter to many of the reactionary politics of the day. The result was a comic strip that was visually pleasing, emotionally engaging, and potentially transformative in an ideological sense.

Walt Kelly and the Aesthetic Conventions of Comic Books

Strangely, the earliest version of *Pogo* did not resemble the Disney aesthetic. When Kelly first left the company in 1943 and began working in the medium of comic books, he employed a homier and grittier style—more akin to the images found in turn-of-the-twentieth-century children's books than mid-century animation. Moreover, Kelly's drafting and inking skills as a comic book artist initially appeared somewhat rushed and amateurish at times. One problem was that he appeared to be trying too hard to construct his characters—both animal and human—with a literal, illustrative naturalism. His first attempts at drawing the kids in the *Our Gang* series, for example, exhibit too much fussy shading and awkward line work, suggesting he attempted to render features in exacting detail. There is also a shaky inconsistency to the faces from panel to panel—revealing, perhaps, the types of problems that must have gotten him into trouble as a junior animator at Disney in following model sheets. The earliest images of Pogo, too, were somewhat unpleasant. He wears a dirty nightshirt and resembles a beady-eyed rat with a down-turned scavenger's snout—not exactly the type of cutely iconic character that one could imagine running a successful mock-campaign for president someday (see Figure 4.1).

Interestingly, the only characters in these early 1940s comic books that initially looked polished and confidently constructed were the black stereotypes: Bumbazine, Pogo's companion, and the other African American characters that made cameo appearances. Perhaps this exception could be explained by the fact that Kelly was building upon existing templates in this case—the ubiquitous images of pickaninnies and hipster musicians that populated animated shorts and comic strips in the first half of the century. Despite that obvious borrowing from existing images, Kelly still somehow imbued those types with a degree of naturalism and sympathy that was uncommon to the more simplified ethnic stereotypes in other comic mediums.

So why and how did Kelly refine his art over the course of the next decade before making a splash on the national stage through the medium of comic strips? The most obvious answer is that he produced a great amount of material during these comic-book years. Drawing the characters over and over allowed him to engage in that "shaping" that leads eventually to the rounded, dynamic, and polished look common to animation. That refinement of technique can also be seen in Kelly's line work. Early images of Albert look lumpy and unnatural: the line tapers at odd points, weird bumps emerge at random places on his head and back, and there is a messiness to how the brush strokes intersect or resolve their endpoints. With time, however, Albert's features became more iconic and bold, and Kelly's line work started to exhibit economical flair and confidence.

The changes in aesthetic can also be explained in terms of the narrative shifts in *Pogo* over the course of fifteen years. The early versions of *Pogo* in comic book form still resembled Joel Chandler Harris's Uncle Remus tales. Harris's story anthologies contained watered-down versions of the authentic trickster's world dating back to slave communities in antebellum times, but that world was still a frightening place, with predators in constant pursuit of weaker animals. Kelly initially borrowed directly from the Harris stories, perhaps, even including a subtle mimicking of the grittier cartoon illustrations that accompanied Harris's stories at the turn of the twentieth century.

As Kelly moved away from those borrowings and their brand of allegorical naturalism in the late 1940s and toward Freudian codings and pastoral motifs, the aesthetic of *Pogo* exhibited two shifts. First was a domestication of rough edges, malicious facial features, and the most extreme expressions of cartoony violence. Second, the line work and figure construction became more polished and mature; it appeared as if Kelly were trying to communicate that pastoral calm through a steadier hand. So it would be inaccurate to say that the strip simply became sweeter over time. More accurately, it excised the corny tone, the awkward drawing, and the naturalistic roughness, and replaced them with a tameness, professional refinement, and cuteness of character construction that reflected both the Disney aesthetic mentioned earlier and the pastoral ideals Kelly embraced in his mature work.

As described in the preceding chapter on race and dialect issues in *Pogo*, these shifts are seen most dramatically in Pogo the character's transformation over time. As the possum replaced Bumbazine as the star of the strip, he also took on more child-like, human qualities: the large and rounded head, the saucer-shaped eyes, and upturned, blunt nose. Kelly's line work for the character of Pogo also became more economical—less detail and more polish, making every stroke count in his protagonist's iconic construction. These changes made Pogo both more commercially viable and polysemically flexible (Gordon 62, 75). And the more generic qualities of his persona (less rat or even 'possum than anthro-pomorphized/generic animal protagonist) allowed Kelly to take advantage of the amplification through simplification and reader identification that McCloud associates with simplified cartoon faces. Finally, it gave Pogo the opportunity to play a variety of comic-satiric roles—ranging from trickster to everyman and wise fool—and to operate as a generic, open-ended icon that could appeal to children, college students, and casual adult comics readers.

Although it's hard to identify and quantify the various aesthetic conventions Kelly borrowed from comic books, one can see a few obvious influences, such as the visual flow of information associated with longer narratives, a text-heavy storytelling style, and effective use of the gutters between panels to commu-nicate continuities and shifts in action. To begin, whereas most gag-oriented comic strips offer stand-alone vignettes from day to day with isolated punch lines, Kelly's strip resembles comic book storytelling in that each comic/dramat-ic arc takes place over several weeks, like a short story or novella. Visually, this translates into a style that is dynamic, forward-moving, and varied in its use of shifting backdrops or contexts. Accustomed to the generous amount of informa-tion communicated in the comic book medium—passages of exposition, the in-trusion of a narrator's voice, internal thoughts, elaborate back-and-forth banter, and recurring themes—Kelly also made his comic strip highly text-heavy. For some modern-day readers, in fact, the combination of Kelly's rich visuals and dense speech balloons might seem like too much data to process; accustomed to the visual minimalism and verbal brevity of today's postage stamp-sized strips, they balk at the effort required to engage with Kelly's work.

The gutters between panels in *Pogo* also owe a debt to the medium of comic books. Unlike animation, which allows for a continual flow of action, comic books feature panels containing discrete images that indicate particular, key moments in the flow of the narrative. Each moment must be both a readable, believable segment in the narrative flow, as well as a stand-alone vignette featuring a key action or expression. The best comic books do this with a logic and economy that allow one to read seamlessly, filling in the gaps of action or imagining the cause and effect that occurs between frames.

Because Kelly created sprawling narratives in which multiple characters interact with both verbal and visual mayhem, one should not underestimate how hard it was to translate those skills of linking panels across gutters. He had the added difficulty, of course, of working in a medium that provided only a handful of panels per day and offered the challenge of configuring those few panels into both an installment in a long-term narrative, as well as a stand-alone gag— and Kelly accomplished this masterfully. Significant physical action often occurs between several panels; the size of the characters remains consistent despite radical shifts in action and perspective at times; there is a logic to the visual, narrative flow; and Kelly even capitalizes on the limitations of his medium to create visual gags. Those devices include surprise reveals, a deadpan freezing of the action, and moments of visual irony (in which the reader sees something significant that is lost on the characters within the strip).

Kelly and Political Cartoons

Kelly's tenure as a political cartoonist at the *New York Star* in the late 1940s also shaped certain aspects of his mature comic strip aesthetic. Those influences included the use of varied line work to create an array of rich values and textures, and the distillation of recognizable public figures into iconic caricatures. Because of the limitations of black and white newsprint, editorial cartoonists have had to devise ways to communicate an array of values within their cartoon simulations of reality. Early etchings and woodblock prints in the late eighteenth and early nineteenth centuries featured crosshatching, shifts in line width, and stippling to create those effects. Later, in the Gilded Age, cartoonists working for popular cartoon weeklies such as *Puck* used lithography—a medium utilizing a wax crayon capable of communicating highly nuanced values and lyrical shapes—to create more layered and naturalistic cartoons. In the twentieth century artists used pen and ink methods that updated the crosshatching and line work of early prints, and many artists adopted an additional method—the use of Ben-Day dots, sheets of transparent plastic featuring fields of dots of varying density—to suggest shifts in value.

Aside from the Ben-Day dots, Kelly dabbled in all of these methods during his stint as a political cartoonist. Some of his images were executed in lithography, while others relied entirely on line work and crosshatching. There was often a tentativeness to his lines in these images that suggests he struggled to find a signature style during this short tenure, mimicking other cartoonists at times, trading tools, and perhaps holding back. There are other points, however, when one sees signs of confidence and virtuoso ability. In some of the lithographic cartoons, for example, there is a flow of imagery that feels free and expressive, like some of the best illustrations from social realists such as George Bellows or John Sloan (Figure 5.6). Additionally, in some of his more traditional pen and brush

Figure 5.6: Walt Kelly, "Human Stupidity," *New York Star*, 1948.

Figure 5.7: Walt Kelly, "It wasn't so much the" *New York Star*, 1948.

cartoons—such as the one shown in Figure 5.7 in which he features an ailing globe—each line is made to count in creating a range of values and in modeling forms in ways that appear both dynamic and realistic.

On 4 October 1948, when *Pogo* first appeared in comic strip form—printed alongside Kelly's political cartoons in the *Star*—the strip displayed some artistic weaknesses. There was an occasional stiffness to the line work, for example, and backgrounds were sometimes too detailed and prominent, competing with the main characters for attention. In general, there is a fussy attention to unnecessary detail in these early cartoons that distracts the eye. But when the strip went national, Kelly seemed to settle on some methods that capitalized on the best qualities of both his lithographic and pen and ink cartoons. The characters were executed, for example, with a flowing, calligraphic line that one might associate with a fluid medium like lithography, but also with a rich array of values one associates with direct brush and pen work.

That confident line work is one of the marvels of *Pogo*. The boldest strokes, executed with a brush, communicate the contours of characters and major elements in the landscape. Through subtle shifts in the thickness of those lines, Kelly indicates shadows and the play of light across features and limbs (see the construction of Albert's snout in Figure 5.8). Narrower lines were used to indicate essential details and create textures and values. But unlike some political cartoonists who use a literal crossing of hatches to suggest gray values, Kelly created parallel hatches with both brush and pen that aligned to the contours of forms and flowed seamlessly from density to sparseness, depending on the value desired. The resulting effect is one of dynamic movement and subtle shift

Figure 5.8: "Nothin' but?" *Pogo*, 9
February 1959.

in value from inky black to the most sensitive grays. The fact that Kelly did not
have to resort to mechanical-looking Ben-Day dots or fussy stippling to create
these effects is a miracle to many fans of the cartooning craft. What's impressive
about these aesthetic effects is that not only are they distinctive as a work of art,
they become seamless supports to the action, immersing the reader in the emotional and satiric world of *Pogo*. In other words, the aesthetic and satiric aspects
of Kelly's art once again work in tandem.

The caricaturing of recognizable figures is another aesthetic tool Kelly developed as a political cartoonist, and one should not underestimate the difficulties
of this skill. Recognizable caricatures occupy a visual zone between realism and
cartoon distortion that adheres to these rules: the individual must be recognizable, the target's features should be exaggerated and stylized for comic effect,
and, ideally, those exaggerations should be amplifications of the figure's internal
character flaws. Jonathan Swift helped to establish that last rule, arguing that
making fun of a target simply because that individual is fat simply amounts to
unjustified, gratuitous mockery, but making fun of a target's obesity is justified
when he or she has a selfish or greedy character (Swift 529). In that case, the
physical flaw can work as an effective visual metaphor or amplifier of the person's more abstract personality flaw.

In some cases, the target may lack distinctive physical qualities that can be
used for satiric effect. In those cases, the cartoonist can assign a metaphorical
identity with its own visual punch and satiric logic. During his short run as a
political cartoonist, Kelly famously succeeded in doing this with Thomas Dewey,
a milquetoast politician with bland features. He depicted Dewey as a "Mechanical Man," incapable of thinking and acting independent of a mechanized script.
That Kelly garnered significant attention and awards from these cartoons attests
to the success of his chosen metaphor.

When Kelly entered the world of comic strips, there was little precedent for
including recognizable caricatures of politicians on the funnies page. Strips such

as *Li'l Abner* (starting in 1934) included generic political figures who resembled identifiable leaders in oblique ways, but no one had attempted to introduce editorial caricature as directly as Kelly. First, he had to defy the unofficial taboo against including topical politics in the medium, but there were also challenges achieving that stylized distortion within the compact frames of a comic strip. How does one juxtapose, for example, a relatively detailed caricature of an identifiable public figure with iconically simple cartoon characters without destroying the fiction of the strip?

The fact that Garry Trudeau, the only other significant cartoonist to attempt this strategy, essentially failed, highlights the difficulties Kelly faced. To elaborate, Trudeau was unconcerned about the taboos against fusing editorial cartooning with comic stripping, but his efforts at creating recognizable caricatures fell flat. Images of figures such as Donald Trump, for example, were somehow both too fussy in their construction and not entirely recognizable, and the real cultural figures felt out of place in Trudeau's stylized world, where almost all of the characters have heavy-lidded eyes or sharp noses. Trudeau ultimately found a fix to the problem by distilling his political targets down to cartoon icons: feathers, cowboy hats, floating waffles, and so on—symbols that embodied or amplified the figures' core failings.

Kelly's most famous attempt at political caricature that conformed to all of the requirements above was also his most successful. His image of Malarkey as Senator Joseph McCarthy was recognizable, but stylized and distilled enough to mesh with the iconic characters around him. In order to fit seamlessly within the animal universe, he had to be a critter as well, and the ready-made category of swamp predator (bobcat, in his case) was a perfect assignment since the residual trickster tale associations with that character type—grasping, short-sighted, and authoritarian—amplified the Senator's public persona perfectly.

Kelly made Malarkey recognizable, moreover, with a few deft details that communicated both the particularities of McCarthy's physical appearance, but that also kept Malarkey visually situated within the surrounding characters' range of iconic construction (Figure 5.9). For example, Malarkey had stooped shoulders, narrowed eye slits, a squatty and aggressive brow, and a perpetual five o'clock shadow. That uncouth swarthiness of his face offended some readers—even prompting one editor to whitewash the whiskers—but Kelly's decision to exaggerate those traits was justified in a Swiftian sense in that it communicated McCarthy's rampaging incivility in the Senate and his unhinged, hyperaggressive public demeanor. The devastating power of this McCarthy caricature—the way that this distilled cartoon image of the man became the default image of the senator in the public eye—was a relatively rare achievement in the history of cartooning.

Prominent cases that compare favorably are few; they might include Thomas Nast's images of Boss Tweed, Herblock's depiction of Nixon as a sewer-dwelling

Figure 5.9: Walt Kelly, "Simple J. Malarkey . . .," *Pogo*, 1 May 1953.

creature, and Trudeau's distillation of George W. Bush to an asterisk within a cowboy hat or battered Roman helmet. Because of complaints he received over the inclusion of a recognizable politician in his comic strip, Kelly had some fun with the second installment of Malarkey episodes by placing a bag over the character's head. Readers were familiar enough with the original images that they could still identify the Malarkey's identity through his physique and actions, and Kelly had the added bonus of readers making the visual association between the gunnysack and the white masks worn by McCarthy's ideological cousins, the Ku Klux Klan (Figure 5.10).

Figure 5.10: Walt Kelly, "I'm afeared . . .," *Pogo*, 8 October 1954.

Later caricatures of other prominent political figures in *Pogo* were only partially successful. Kelly displayed the occasional flash of brilliance in assigning the proper animal identity to a political figure (Kruschev as a loutish pig or J. Edgar Hoover as a bulldog, for example), but he also lapsed into the habit in the 1960s of giving these characters too many particularized details. The resulting caricatures—as illustrated in Figure 5.11, the drawings of President Lyndon Johnson—were often too realistic, with the head not quite meshing with the animal body, and the character in general standing out with too much specificity against the iconic simplicity of *Pogo*'s cartoon world.

Figure 5.11: Walt Kelly, ". . . old opinions . . . ," *Pogo*, 16 April 1968.

Other Influences

As an avid reader and largely self-taught student of art history, Kelly's aesthetic sensibility was also shaped by a broad range of artists working in high and low mediums. Writing in the third person in an unpublished autobiographical sketch, he lists some of those influences:

> The artists who had impressed him were mostly cartoonists and the list included Ernest Shepard [most famous for the classic *Winnie the Pooh* illustrations], Rackham [art nouveau style illustrations of *Alice in Wonderland* and various fairy tales], Herriman [*Krazy Kat*], Roy Crane [*Captain Easy*], Matisse, Picasso, Daumier, David Low [political cartoonist with a fluid brush stroke], Henry Kley [German artist creating fantastical, cosmic political cartoons], Sullivant [turn of the century gag cartoonist specializing in highly detailed, anthropomorphized animals], C. A. Voight [a "pretty girl cartoonist"], Cliff Sterrett [*Polly and Her Pals*], Peter Arno [New Yorker cartoonist with a bold brush stroke and a flaneur's view of urban life], and DeBeck [sports cartoonist]. He began to be impressed by the cartoonists over the years who have bridged the gap between the avant-garde in art and the meat-potatoes and whiskey school enjoyed by so many Americans. He was further impressed by the economy of line and word which generally goes into most comic strips. (Kelly, "Unpublished Autobiographical Sketch" 26)

It is difficult to generalize about such a varied list of artists. Kelly's eclectic taste is evident, of course, and he makes a point of highlighting his willingness to draw from both "high" and "low" art traditions. A few additional points stand out, nevertheless. First, there is an iconoclastic quality to many of the artists listed here; creators such as Herriman, Sullivant, Kley, and Arno, for example, stood out in their chosen field, either pushing their mediums to new levels of complexity, or happily following their own peculiar aesthetic visions. With forerunners like this in mind, Kelly could have felt emboldened to defy the traditional strictures of the funnies page.

Many of these artists, such as Matisse, Daumier, Low, Kley, and Sullivant are also especially adept at describing human and animal forms with lyrical, expressive brushstrokes or pen lines. Kelly spoke admiringly of Sullivant in other interviews, as well, celebrating the artist's unusual ability to create animals that were highly naturalistic in their physical anatomy, lyrical and dynamic in their movement, and still vividly anthropomorphized and comedic in their expressions. Those expressive brush strokes—and that same dynamism and personality in character construction featured in Sullivant's work—were also some of Kelly's core strengths. It was perhaps his mimicking of Sullivant that elevated Kelly's methods to a level higher than the Disney aesthetic—adding details and textures more common to pen and ink illustration, and reining in some of the most cartoony and rubbery tendencies of the animator's rounded treatments of animal forms.

Two other artists in Kelly's list—Shepard and Rackham—represent the classic era of children's book illustration when artists created work that rivaled fine art in its expressive qualities and complexity. Kelly had similar aesthetic ambitions for comic strips, hoping to bring greater legitimacy to a medium that, like children's book illustration, was often disparaged as overly commercialized or cute. It should also be noted that the great majority of the artists on this list did not simply engage in gratuitous visual fireworks. Shepard, for example, knew how to imbue his spare virtuoso line work with a humanity and gentle sense of humor that seamlessly wed the visuals to the text of *Winnie the Pooh*. Herriman, the creator of *Krazy Kat*, also found ways to ground his visual cleverness to emotionally complex characters and deep cosmic themes. Their art, in other words, did not overshadow the comic and narrative richness of their writing; instead, it amplified and deepened the non-visual aspects of the work.

Kelly's work epitomizes that melding of great art with narrative richness and comedic depth. One can admire the visuals and revel in the deft brush work and attention to significant detail—or enjoy the ample array of values and textures on display. But as with Shepard's work, Kelly's comic strip has a lasting appeal and impact because the art is melded, inextricably, with the personalities and inner lives of the characters, the larger meanings of the swamp context, and Kelly's humane view of human foibles and differences.

The "Non-Art" Elements of Kelly's Visuals

A full discussion of Kelly's aesthetic techniques should include his nuts and bolts working methods as well as an analysis of the less flashy aspects of the strip's visuals, such as lettering and panels. To begin, Kelly worked on a slanted drafting table, using the cartoonist's traditional tools: T-squares, illustration board, and inkwell pens and brushes of varying widths. It should be noted that Kelly's use of brushes to achieve his thick and thin, lyrical lines is a dying craft among both editorial and comic strip artists. There are a few traditional holdouts with this skill—artists such as Pat Oliphant or Bill Watterson—but most cartoonists have switched to mechanical pens that are much less expressive in their line quality. That shift is a result of shrinking formats (less room for visual inventiveness); the dominance of a homey, minimalist aesthetic; and a general diminishment of the craft surrounding the profession (fewer people coming out of bullpens or animation studios where they might have learned those skills).

The size of Kelly's originals is quite large—approximately 6" x 15", fully twice the size of the printed strip. The practice of drawing the originals much larger than the end product has been common throughout the history of the medium; it benefits the artist in that it allows for the freedom of working in large strokes, and it improves the final look of the comic as the reduction process sharpens details and eliminates subtle mistakes. The drawing of the strip itself—including all panels, figures, and lettering—was first done by Kelly with a blue-leaded pencil (Figure 5.12). The blue sketches did not reproduce later in the copying process, and thus no elaborate erasing was required; the inking could be executed directly over the penciling. This resulted in Kelly being able draw in a more organic, free, and fluid manner.

Initially Kelly executed every aspect of his strip, from sketching and lettering through to the final inking. When the strip became highly successful, however, and Kelly was swamped with additional traveling and lecturing obligations, an assistant, George Ward, was hired to help with certain tasks, such as inking the

Figure 5.12: Walt Kelly, "Yoo hoo!" *Pogo*, 22 September 1968.

lettering and finishing backgrounds. The most prominent aspects of the strip, however, such as the inking of the contours and faces of the characters, Kelly reserved for his own special touch.

Although finished by an assistant, the lettering in *Pogo* is still a reflection of Kelly's general aesthetic vision, and the same complexity and nuance evident in other aspects of his art is present here as well. The lettering varies from one speech balloon to the next, differing in angle, width, boldness, and font. There is a sort of sans serif default script in the strip that is all caps, but even that foundational typeface can display an italicized slant or extra-bold line to connote anger or a shift in voice inflection (Figure 5.13). A bit of that variation within lettering was common to other strips of the same time period as well, but Kelly was unique in introducing entirely different fonts for different characters' voices. P. T. Bridgeport, for example, speaks through the overwrought lettering of advertising broadsheets, suggesting the huckster-like hype and superficiality of his speech (Figure 5.14). And Deacon Mushrat communicates through a Gothic script that connotes his darkly puritanical voice and mind-set (Figure 5.15). The typefaces, in other words, acted as extensions of the character's persona or social type, a perfect melding of visual and verbal elements to register a satiric point.

The varying typefaces also reinforced some of the prominent philosophical themes in the strip: the multivocal nature of a healthy (albeit cacophonous and carnivalesque) democratic society; the value of open-ended civil discourse and debate, where competing worldviews and ideologies mingle; the instability of language, as individuals use words that splinter and shift in their meanings from individual to individual and from one context to the next, and so on. These ideas are not presented in a heavy-handed manner; instead, the shifting typefaces and varied lettering emphases communicate both visually and organically—a seamless part of the strip's verbal-visual satire.

The panels that surround and frame the action in *Pogo* are also a significant, seemingly "non-art" aspect of Kelly's work. One of the first things a reader no-

Figure 5.13: Walt Kelly, "An' it's a partridge . . . ," *Pogo*, 23 December 1952.

Figure 5.14: Walt Kelly, "*Pogo* in person!!!" *Pogo*, 28 April 1952.

Figure 5.15: Walt Kelly, "Naturally," *Pogo*, 27 May 1952.

Figure 5.16: "Rring . . . ," *Pogo*, 7 February 1952.

Figure 5.17: Walt Kelly, "Congratulations." *Pogo*, 8 March 1968.

tices about these panels is that they are drawn with a looser, more spontaneous hand than the typical cartoon border. The lines ebb and flow in their width and angle, and Kelly occasionally breaks the panel or gives it a little jog, as if mimicking the texture of bark (see Figure 5.16). The emotional impact of this organic motif is significant, if subtle; whereas the rigidity of most cartoon panels suggest some sort of mechanical, controlled containment of the action, Kelly's panels connote authenticity, open-endedness, and reinforce the music-like flow of action and voice from panel to panel.

The malleability of Kelly's panels also takes on a metafictive slant when he displays characters' leaning against the panel walls, gently bowing the lines, or talking from behind speech balloons or across the gutters between panels, drawing attention to the artificiality of those visual separations (Figure 5.17). The only other artist who was equally inventive in his self-deconstructive use of panels and other cartooning conventions was George Herriman, an artist who introduced playfully surrealistic visual games into his two-dimensional cartooning syntax. It is interesting to note that both these artists harnessed those visual games to larger theoretical themes. In particular, they both articulated a liberal-postmodern concern with the subjectivity of perception. To elaborate, by deconstructing their own texts—playfully revealing their creative hand in the physical form of the strip—they modeled how other popular texts could be viewed as visually and ideologically constructed texts as well. In other words, those texts can be recognized as artificial constructions of a particular artist's (or committee's) worldview rather than a timeless reflector of unassailable conventional wisdom.

The End of Kelly's Aesthetic Style and Influence

By the late 1960s Kelly's very strengths as an artist—the virtuoso line work and general visual complexity—made his work seem out of touch with the emerging zeitgeist. Whereas Kelly's dynamism and layeredness had contributed to the potency of his satire in an early 1950s cultural climate, it was perceived as old-fashioned in the next era, which favored a minimalist and sometimes unshowy aesthetic. Four distinct drawing styles, in fact, overshadowed Kelly's comic strip during its last years: the stylized and angular look of cheaply produced UPA animation; the spare minimalism of strips by Schulz and Hart (*B.C.*); the anarchic zaniness of *MAD* magazine and Warner Bros. animation; and the self-taught amateurism of Trudeau (*Doonesbury*).

The minimalist aesthetic dominating comics and animation in the 1960s was pioneered in large part in the 1940s and 1950s by an animation studio, the UPA (United Productions of America). UPA introduced an alternative to Disney's elaborate cinematic realism—it was a method of "limited animation" that featured "fewer and less detailed backgrounds; created fewer animated movements—often only the movement of eyes, mouth and functional limbs on key characters; and employed simple, repeatable movement cycles and stressing sound over some aspects of action" (Wells 64). Significant works coming from this studio included the *Mr. Magoo* shorts, *Gerald McBoing Boing*, *The Tell-Tale Heart*, and *Unicorn in the Garden*. Some critics celebrated this brand of "reduced animation" for its modernistic distillation of forms and its potential to be used more effectively for metaphorical or political uses. Gilbert Seldes, for example, appreciated the UPA aesthetic's "primitive" directness and "impudent and intelligent approach to subject matter and . . . gay palette, a cascading of light colors, the use of color and line always to suggest, never to render completely, a great deal of warmth, and an unfailing wit" (Maltin 330).

Other animation studios noticed UPA's innovations as well, and eventually adopted a similar look, if not the same limited methods. Warner Bros. and MGM, for example, introduced stylized backgrounds into their work by the mid 1950s, and many of their characters began to exhibit a more angular, edgy look. Disney also got on the bandwagon, adopting a distilled, modernistic aesthetic in films such as "Pigs Is Pigs" (1954), "The Truth about Mother Goose" (1957) and "Paul Bunyan" (1958) (Solomon 207).

The animators at UPA were largely those Disney employees that had fled the company during the 1941 strike—the same troubled episode that led to Kelly's departure from the company. Their gripes with Disney and its methods helped to shape their aesthetic:

> Their sophisticated artistic views were supported by strong, liberal political beliefs and a conviction that the arts, including the art of animation, could be used as a tool for social reform. These young men chafed at the restrictions of Disney animation—the traditional, almost Academic style of drawing; the animal characters; the emphasis on humor; the familiar stories. They wanted to expand the medium, to explore contemporary graphic styles and different kinds of storytelling. (Solomon 226)

Given that Kelly's art still contained much of that old-fashioned Disney aesthetic in the 1960s (the dynamic line work, the animal characters, the humor, and the grounding in a mythic site), it is no wonder that his work began to seem out of touch in comparison to the seemingly more avant-garde animation in the surrounding culture. Kelly also suffered from some guilt by association, as Disney fell out of critical favor in the 1960s because of a general failing of creating art and stories that were too cute and bourgeois in their narrative and artistic treatment of stories:

> . . . critical opinion began to shift away from Disney and toward Warner Bros. and, to a lesser extent, MGM (especially the cartoons of Tex Avery). This shift, which continued into the seventies, has been attributed to the general irreverence and "antiestablishment" attitudes of the sixties and early seventies . . ." (White 38–39)

The contrast between *Pogo* and the stylized and more irreverent aesthetic of 1960s animation became even more acute as Kelly's style gradually became more visually sedate and comedically philosophical as the 1960s wore on; it was as if Kelly were becoming fatigued, or the pastoral tone of the swamp had finally excised all of the vaudevillian carnival and trickster tale violence of the early strip. Kelly's gradually failing health may have had an impact on the look of the strip as well, with images becoming more spare and static as the strip neared the end of its twenty-year run. This gradual tamping down of visual energy created an even greater gap between Kelly's calm aesthetic and the "the anarchic brashness" of Bugs Bunny and Warner Bros. animation (White 41). The outlaw code of traditional trickster tales had found another revival in viability—this time within an anti-establishment era that liked to see mainstream animated shorts in which bland authority figures, such as Elmer Fudd, were physically abused in vividly exaggerated ways.

Minimalist styles also overshadowed Kelly's aesthetic closer to home on the comics page, in the work of emerging artists such as Charles Schulz and Johnny Hart. In addition to reflecting aspects of the general trend toward reductive stylization, their simplified aesthetic was an outgrowth of a number of other trends: financial crises in the newspaper industry that resulted in cost-cutting measures on the comics page; the growth of suburban papers and decline of urban dailies; and a general emphasis on highly accessible, inoffensive, blockbuster strips (Friedman 50). The comics page had seen reductions in the 1930s and 1940s in response to economic crises and newsprint shortages, but the early 1960s crisis prompted draconian changes, such as the elimination of niche strips in order to limit the daily comics to one page and the introduction of standardized frames that would allow editors to stack strips into space-saving columns or squares (Chillino 64). Schulz's strip, in fact, was originally run as an experimentally small, space-filling cartoon. In order to make his images readable within those narrow confines, he was forced to draw squat figures within a spare context.

Schulz's sensibility too—one of calm, melancholic irony—contributed to the static aesthetic of his strip as well, and matched the reduced dimensions nicely. In contrast, Kelly's strip did not read well at a reduced size. The visual complexity of *Pogo*—its high level of detail, the density of his word balloons, the organically shifting panels, and the dynamism of his moving characters—did not register with the same clarity as the minimalist strips. And the carnivalesque busyness of the strip began to read a bit hammy, perhaps, in contrast to the visual and emotional restraint of strips like *Peanuts*.

After the introduction of the Comics Code in the late 1950s and the shift in demographic targeting in the early 1960s (away from urban readers toward the less multiculturally diverse readers of the new suburban dailies), the comedic and aesthetic tone of the comics page also trended toward the bland and safely contained. *Pogo* and *Li'l Abner* were perhaps the two significant holdouts from an earlier era of carnivalesque and satiric comics. But Capp's drift into reactionary politics in the 1960s and Kelly's polite layeredness—which included the introduction of alternative "bunny strips" for squeamish editors—made them a poor match for the youth generation that had a taste for more rebellious verbal and visual entertainment.

MAD magazine, which did not have to bow to the strictures of the Comics Code or answer to touchy suburban newspaper editors, was able to deliver the more directly anti-establishment aesthetic that fit the zeitgeist. The anarchic parodies in the magazine were illustrated in a zany style by artists such as Harvey Kurtzman who favored in-your-face visual gags and grotesque exaggeration over Kelly's brand of lyrical restraint. Some of the carnivalesque energy that had once coursed through the comics page was also redirected into the underground comix movement. Anti-establishment artists such as R. Crumb saw no place on the increasingly mediated funnies page for their art and satire. He explained that he

> abandoned my childhood dreams of becoming a big-time professional cartoonist because by the time I was a senior in High School I clearly discerned that the medium had become constricted, formulized, locked to a strict set of stifling commercial standards. I considered myself inadequate to meet those standards. (O'Sullivan 136; Zwigoff)

There were tradeoffs, of course, in abandoning a mainstream medium that had developed editing processes that also helped to refine comedy and art in positive ways. Crumb's work was bracingly rebellious in its treatment of taboo subject matter and his densely crosshatched art had a gritty, naturalistic complexity that would not have worked in the visually constrained funnies page; but the lack of any editorial filtering resulted at times in work that was gratuitously offensive, reveling in Crumb's quirky fetishes and curdled misanthropy. Some of the parameters placed around a work like *Pogo*, in other words, had a positive impact on the work's comedy and art, pushing Kelly to create a style that walked the line between mainstream accessibility and idiosyncratic innovation.

Another aesthetic that emerged at the tail end of Kelly's career was an amateurish, do-it-yourself look that one associates most closely with Trudeau's strip *Doonesbury*. In Trudeau's case, that untutored approach was an extension of his satire and ideological orientation. He explained, "My style was so unprofessional—it was this kind of urgent scrawl that played into the marketing of the strip as something that was supposed to be dispatches from the front. It looked like it had been created in a frenzy, and that gave it a kind of authenticity (Bates 62). This homey aesthetic legitimized him, in other words, in the eyes of young people who distrusted mainstream entertainment that was too slickly produced, too squarely evocative of their parents' taste in polished musicals, cute cartoons, and overproduced music. Ironically, then, it was perhaps Kelly's original strengths as an artist—that polished, Disneyesque style and virtuoso brush work—that may have caused him to seem square and outdated by the early 1970s.

In Trudeau's case, the use of amateurish, unfinished drawings aligned nicely with his intentions as an anti-establishment, truth-telling satirist, but sadly the trend did little to benefit the funnies page in general. Trudeau half-jokingly admitted, "I've always thought my main contribution to the comics page was that I made it safe for bad drawing, that *Cathy* and *Bloom County* and particularly *Dilbert* would have been unthinkable had I not challenged the assumption that competent draftsmanship was prerequisite to a career in cartooning" (Astor 31).

That combination of the do-it-yourself trend in drawing and the persistent neglect by newspapers of the medium in general (shrinking formats, eliminating pages entirely, and favoring only the simplest types of art and satire) has meant that beyond Kelly's heyday only a few strips in the field can be celebrated for aesthetic quality. If tempted to see the currently depressed state of the mediums' aesthetics as inevitable, one only has to look to Europe for comics traditions that defy that narrative. In countries such as France and England, magazines and newspapers feature strips, such as Posy Simmond's work, that meld great satire and elaborately fluid and dynamic art; moreover, comics such as *Pico Bogue* (Alexis Dormal and Dominique Rocques) and *Le Retour à la Terre* (Manu Larcenet and Jean-Yves Ferri) in France feature lyrical art and still somehow effectively straddle the fence between adult and youth sensibilities, much as did Kelly's *Pogo*.

And so with no room for expansive and innovative art on the funnies page in recent decades, there has been little opportunity for artists to return to Kelly's template, to revive his methods and style. There are a few exceptions, however, worth highlighting. First, there is the most obvious heir to Kelly's status as one of the greatest artists to ever work in the medium: Bill Watterson, the creator of *Calvin and Hobbes*. Not only has Watterson achieved the same level of visual lyricism, but he also harnessed his art to profound cosmic satire. Watterson, in fact, cites Kelly as a major influence, and one can see many obvious similarities in their art: vividly and economically constructed characters full of personality and dynamic movement; detailed backgrounds juxtaposed with iconic faces and figures; and varied, lyrical brushwork that infuses even inanimate objects with the pulse of life. Watterson's Sunday installments compare especially well to Kelly's best work. Watterson took full advantage of the expanded size and inclusion of color in Sunday supplements, creating panoramic scenes from nature or going on fantastical visual flights that included dinosaurs and space travel. It is interesting to note that Watterson, much like Kelly, had to continually assert his rights as an auteur—sometimes engaging in direct combat with syndicates and editors—in order to create work that was so innovative and expansive.

Second, there are other artists less obviously influenced by Kelly who have managed, despite the current strictures of the medium, to create highly detailed and aesthetically detailed work. Four standouts are Lynn Johnston (*For Better or Worse*), Darby Conley (*Get Fuzzy*), Richard Thompson (*Cul de Sac*), and Aaron McGruder (*Boondocks*). Johnston defied the minimalist trend, creating a naturalistic family strip that featured fully drawn figures executed in a flowing, expressive line. Conley has a tighter drawing style that features dense textures; it is amazingly detailed for the reduced dimensions of the comics page, and works effectively with his deadpan animal-human domestic comedy. Thompson's nuanced aesthetics (expressive, sketchy linework and muted colors) amplify perfectly the strip's situational humor grounded in sympathetically neurotic characters.McGruder has introduced onto the comics page an entirely fresh aesthetic: Japanese-style manga animation with an angular, stylized treatment of bracingly uncute African American characters—a refreshing contrast from all of the buffoonish caricatures of blacks on the comics page that preceded them.

One can also look for traces of Kelly's legacy beyond the comics page, in related mediums that have not experienced the same visual depredations. Jeff Smith, the creator of the *Bone* series in graphic novels, for example, cites Kelly as an influence. And websites that feature exchanges between animators, political cartoonists, and comic book artists often celebrate Kelly as a significant father figure as well—a comic artist whose aesthetics have bled across mediums in the same way his art defied easy categorization. In sum, despite all the trends that have emerged in the years following Kelly's passing, fans and practitioners still return to Kelly's art as something to savor and celebrate. True artistic ability and genius of that level can only go out of style for so long. *Pogo*'s art has a lasting appeal and power that has secured its position as perhaps the best drawn feature in comic strip history, and has ensured its potential to influence budding cartoonists in a variety of mediums for decades to come.

CHAPTER 6

Walt Kelly, Mid-Century Poplorist

One of the core points of this study has been that Kelly and his work defy easy categorization. As an iconoclast who exerted an auteur-like clout, he transcended genre and medium conventions, melding the technical methods and narrative conventions of animation, political cartooning, and comic books. His role as a cultural creator was equally complex. Not content to quietly churn out a strip while holed up in a studio, Kelly led a high-profile public life, reveling in chalk-talks, stump speeches, punditry, interviews, and vaudevillian variety shows. As a result of this border-defying creativity, his significance as a cultural icon has to be considered from several angles. This final chapter attempts that task; it moves beyond the narrow description of Kelly as a comic strip artist and considers his larger public significance as a politically engaged public intellectual, media-age raconteur, and poplorist.

The United States, unlike some European countries, lacks a rich tradition of celebrating erudite intellectuals and social critics as cultural superstars. Whereas academics, philosophers, and serious novelists are often given top billing on talk shows and treated like celebrities in countries such as France and Italy, they barely register on the cultural radar in this country. The United States has long preferred "organic" or folky intellectuals—figures such as Mark Twain, Will Rogers, or Garrison Keillor—whose self-deprecation, homey wit, and democratic worldview qualify them to opine about the foolishness of our collective values and practices. The lack of pretension in their critiques and use of vernacular speech reinforces their ideas as authentic—an outgrowth of folk wisdom untainted by the jargon of academia, the partisan rhetoric of politicians, or the bland corporate-speak of bureaucrats. Kelly fits nicely within this legacy as a self-taught intellectual who employed colloquial language, a playful wit, and a self-inspecting ideology to chide American readers.

While Kelly's persona was drawn from this seemingly timeless American template, the values and ideologies articulated in his speeches and satire were in sync with a particular brand of Cold War liberalism grounded in existentialist ideals and that aligned nicely with various anti-establishment ideals such as those championed by early Civil Rights Movement proponents, Beat poets, rebel comedians, and folk revivalists. Historian Richard Pells nicely describes the foundational convictions of Cold War liberals such as Kelly. He suggests that the history of European and American societies in the early twentieth century had "disclosed the lethal consequences of utopian fixations" and the dangers of any brand of extremism or fanaticism including that of their fellow leftists. As a result, they were "wary of messianic dogmas, [or] apocalyptic thinking," and for them, "ideology had become a dead end." They developed, thus, a "preference for asking questions instead of inventing answers" (Pells x). Kelly's embrace of this worldview was directly reflected in the daily flow of multivocal comedy and drama in his fictional swamp, where "pragmatic compromise" was the operating philosophy, where sometimes humble silence was better than arrogant pontificating (Figure 6.1), and where the virtues of ethically and happily engaging in "day to day living" were the chief concerns (Pells 138). As in Voltaire's *Candide*, which also embraces a pragmatic pastoral ethic (at its conclusion), the characters in *Pogo* follow the modest ethic of bettering the world by "cultivating their own garden" (or, in their case, "fishing in their own swamp").

Figure 6.1: Excerpt from "Monday school . . . ," *Pogo*, 7 December 1962.

Kelly's distaste for dogma, fanaticism, and their byproducts (scapegoating, rigid hierarchy, hypocrisy, etc.) was also a reflection, perhaps, of the popularity of existentialism among mid-century liberal intellectuals. If one embraced the tenets of existentialism—that the concept of God is a fiction (or that Christians had irredeemably warped their God into a vindictive, divisive, and joy-crushing figure), and that there is largely no overarching set of truths that shape or rule mankind's existence—then a healthy skepticism toward authoritative institutions, dogmatic ideologies, and overly confident metanarratives is in order. In addition, one might be compelled to respect the validity of a variety of ideological positions, given the subjective nature of perception and knowledge. In Kelly's case, this blanket skepticism toward dogmatic philosophical or religious systems

Figure 6.2: Walt Kelly, "You got a goin'-picnic . . . ," *Pogo*, 7 May 1964.

fueled, most famously, his prolonged attack on McCarthyism, but it also made him an equal-opportunity satirist, ready to attack blindered stridency wherever it emerged. He attacked communist dogma, for example, in his cowbird sequences and took a swipe at the Black Muslim movement in the United States in 1964 as well (Figure 6.2).

In the art of cultural creators as diverse as Joseph Heller, Lenny Bruce, and Allen Ginsberg, that skepticism also resembled a type of early postmodern deconstructionism. Through playful monologues, stream-of-consciousness poetry, and comedic writings that emphasized the instability of language, these social critics highlighted how institutions and political parties use ideologically loaded discourses and authoritative but contradictory texts to enforce dogma and control individuals in society. Kelly participated in that agenda as well, using his dialect-driven, verbal slapstick to question the divisive ideologies of 1950s conservative culture and politics. And like any good existentialist, Kelly insisted that a basic set of moral principles could be imposed on life and society by principled humanists: the golden rule, authentic behavior, and self-critical introspection.

Kelly's existentially tinged intellectualism certainly struck a chord with college-age students who were beginning to question the dogmas of their parents' mainstream values; the immense popularity of his Pogo-for-president campaigns attest to that resonance. One also should not underestimate how deeply his worldview resonated with everyday readers. Stephen Kercher argues that middle class Americans in the 1950s were more interested in hearing dissenting voices than most depictions of the era would have us believe. In reality, college-educated, middle-class individuals actively sought for "oppositional spaces" in the entertainment and reading they consumed, and were inclined to be highly self-critical. Quoting Morris Dickstein, Kercher argues that "relentless self-criticism . . . not complacency, was the key to postwar culture." Popularized existential theory—with its goal of "exposing reality" and questioning the "suffocating banality, artifice, and hypocrisy infiltrating American life and culture"—helped to satisfy that inward impulse to at least question, though perhaps not abandon completely, the foundational ethics of one's middle-class, suburban life (Kercher 3–4).

That relentless questioning and self-castigation emerges repeatedly in the core themes of Kelly's strip. Albert is continually worried about his motives as his bodily appetites compete with his head and heart; Pogo quietly questions each characters' justifications for their actions, including his own; and Porky Pine insists that it is everyone's foundational right to make "dern fools of themselves." Kelly reinforced that self-critical philosophy in both interviews and punditry as his career progressed. In a 1958 interview he asserted that ". . . we shouldn't ever expect too much of ourselves because we're frail and we're inclined to break very easily" (Kelly, "London Calling" 94). And then, by the late 1960s, he elaborated on this worldview in complex ways, giving full form to ideas that had been there all along in simpler, more comedic form:

There is no need to sally forth, for it remains true that those things which make us human are, curiously enough, always close at hand. Resolve, then, that on this very ground, with small flags waving and tiny blasts of tiny trumpets, we shall meet the enemy, and not only may he be ours, he may be us . . . Hold yourself at arm's length and examine closely what you see. Who is the one who loses the car keys, forgets to pay the crucial bill, scatters your socks beneath the bed, spills the red wine on the prized tablecloth? You can blame it on the dog, if you have one, or on your wife or husband, if you have either half of the set. It is easy to blame anything on someone else. The world is an available scapegoat. But when you have the time, go to a phone booth, call up any stranger, at random, and confess. You did it all. (Kelly, "Zeroing in on the Polluters" 224)

Even without the help of Kelly's journalistic elaborations, many readers from various backgrounds could identify the oppositional space created by Kelly's philosophy of liberal, existential questioning of both oneself and a complacent status quo. On the mild end of the spectrum, children's fan letters talk about "brave teachers" who were "supporters" and "defenders" of *Pogo* in small-town schools, or "egg-headed" parents who enjoyed the strip as much as they, the kids, did ("Over the Transom"). On the sharper end, college students at Kelly's Pogo rallies would recall that the strip resonated with readers because they "were really pissed off at the forces of repression, at the status quo, the blind faith with the powers that be" (Boatner 90). In sum, *Pogo* acted as a "nexus through which ideologies may be actively reorganized"—an accessible starting point for imagining ways to dissent from mainstream ideologies or political dogma (Woolacott 217).

Kelly as Poplorist

Given both the coherence of Kelly's satiric worldview and the powerful reach of his ideas through a highly entertaining, mainstream medium, one must look for additional concepts to describe his cultural clout and significance. In addition to operating as an auteur, for example, he achieved the status of sateur by leveraging his industry clout and independence into social criticism. Furthermore, his popularity as a performer on the lecture circuit also prompts an expansion of his designation from mere comic strip artist to media-age raconteur, a sort of mid-twentieth century version of Mark Twain—a public lecturer who effectively used his vivid public persona to amplify his satire.

Perhaps the concept that best embraces Kelly's unique qualities as national storyteller/jester is a model of cultural creator presented in the introduction— that of poplorist. In these closing pages, a few more words about how this concept applies to Kelly, especially in relation to his interaction with fans, is in order. Gene Bluestein, a folklore scholar, coined the term and concept of poplore, in part, as a way of legitimizing the art of pop culture creators who are unusually well-connected to their audiences and the spirit of their times. In other words, much like the auteur concept, poplorists formed a new category of artists that exists between the divide of supposedly pure and authentic high or folk cultures on the one side, and crass, factory-produced mass culture on the other.

The criteria for classifying a creator as a poplorist include the following: their work should achieve a breadth of popularity through grassroots means; it revives "stylistic elements and values from the matrix of traditional culture"; and it should be created through a collaborative call-and-response between creator and engaged readers. As a result of that engagement, the work is often dialogical, containing voices that linger from the traditional forms that inspired the work, or that are included when the readers/collaborators lent a hand in the creative call-and-response process. Unlike many cultural products that feel bland and mass-produced, poploric texts actually address the ideological interests and psychological needs of a core audience and often articulate a brand of democratic, progressive politics sometimes associated with folk forms (Bluestein 6, 8–10).

Kelly was a poplorist in almost every respect: although a savvy self-promoter, his strip achieved its breadth of popularity largely through grassroots means; it revived "stylistic elements and values from the matrix of traditional culture" in its syncretic recasting of trickster tale and pastoral motifs; and because of Kelly's avid interactions with fans on lecture tours and through correspondence, one could say that the strip was partly created in a collaborative back and forth between Kelly and core readers. Finally, because of that lively give and take, Kelly's strip ultimately addressed the interests and needs of a core audience, articulating a brand of democratic politics that contained echoes of the subversive resistance to dominant cultural ideals that is sometimes a characteristic of folk forms or discourses.

A closer look at some of Kelly's interactions with his readers serves both to underscore this idea as well as add some qualifications and complexities to the argument. To begin, Kelly was famous in cartooning circles for the sheer volume of fan mail he received. Anecdotal evidence, which included casual comparisons between members of the National Cartoonists Society at the height of Kelly's popularity in the mid 1950s, suggest that he had the highest volume of letters among all of his peers (Rodgers A21). A great deal of that enthusiastic response can be attributed to the inherent qualities of Kelly's work, of course—no strip at the time rivaled *Pogo* in terms of comedic richness, satiric heft, and emotionally engaging characters. But Kelly also stimulated extensive fan devotion and interaction through several labor-intensive methods. For example, he religiously responded to any fan mail; he did this with personalized messages (as dictated to a secretary) and gifts that included book collections, original strips, and casual drawings. That generosity was so rampant, that archivists have been distressed to find that very little of Kelly's original artwork remains to be catalogued. Personal appearances at hospitals, high schools, colleges, and civic clubs—where he would lecture, give chalk-talks, sign books, and receive customized awards—were also part of his promotional strategy. That traveling would reach a peak during presidential campaign years when Kelly used his "I Go Pogo" campaigns as a vehicle for connecting with fans and attracting new readers.

Kelly's college visits were specially structured and calculated to elicit enthusiastic engagement from both devoted fans and casual readers. For example, before embarking on these tours Kelly would assign an assistant to study college newspapers and then make up a list of issues and concerns currently of interest to students (Walt Kelly Collection, Box 2 Folder 14). He would then send out packages of materials (Figure 6.3) with explicit instructions to the editors of local or college newspapers that helped him maximize the effectiveness of his visits:

> Presentations of buttons to prominent businessmen and other outstanding local citizens during the I GO POGO drive offers [sic] obvious picture possibilities. And I am sure that some of your staff won't be long in coming up with other local angles. Here's to more and more readers for your newspaper. (And my comic strip.) Through the I GO POGO campaign, as outlined, I would like to contribute to that end." (Kelly "'I GO POGO' campaign letter to editors" 185, 186)

Figure 6.3: Walt Kelly, promotional material from 1956 mock-presidential campaign.

From a distance that level of calculated promotion may seem to undermine the idea of Kelly achieving his popularity through grassroots means. In a media age, however, when one's audience is potentially enormous, far-flung in their cultural sites, and diverse in their demographic makeup, the mechanisms and networks for transmitting one's persona and stories have to take advantage of the broadcasting reach of various mechanized media and established promotional systems. One cannot fetishize, in other words, some kind of pre-modern mode of grassroots communication where single individuals have contact with a cultural creator and then recruit, at ground level, additional devotees (although certainly some of that was going on with Kelly's frequent public appearances). Moreover, the fact that Kelly's promotional methods did work effectively—often beyond his own hopes or expectations—supports the notion that there was still an authentically popular reaction to his work. If the strip itself had not resonated deeply and immediately with its core readers, it would have faded in importance in the same way that so many even more aggressively promoted comic strips and films have quickly fallen off the cultural radar over the years.

One can also support the grassroots claim by highlighting the fact that Kelly did most of this promotional strategizing and labor by himself. While his syndicate effectively promoted him with "care and ferocity," they did it in accordance with Kelly's wishes and often followed his lead as he imagined ways to amplify his reach on college campuses (Marschall, *America's Great* 262). The revisions to his 1956 contract underscore the auteur-like clout and authority Kelly exerted in issues related to promotions and merchandising (see chapter 3).

One of Kelly's objectives in promoting his work so aggressively and in tying his public persona so explicitly to his strip, was essentially to "convert" readers to *Pogo* in a heartfelt way—as if they were becoming part of a club or interpretive community of which he was the head. He readily admitted this in an interview, asserting that, "The cult aspect of the strip is intended. It's a whole way of life that was created to become part of the readers' lives. That's the one thing I aim for" (Crinklaw 1). Fan letters and various newspaper reports from the time suggest that he was highly successful in this effort. Children's letters, for example, describe how their entire family read the strip and discussed its significance; how they organized *Pogo* reading clubs with their friends; and how their teachers in school read and "support[ed]" Kelly's work ("Over the Transom"). Some of those organized reading clubs would look for hidden messages in the strip; others, such as a group that called itself the "*Pogo* Protection League," would monitor and combat any efforts by editors to cancel or censor Kelly's work (Kercher 65; Crinklaw 5).

Several of those activities suggest an unusual level of engagement with a popular text. The notion of "supporting" *Pogo*, and Kelly in particular, indicates that many of the core fans of the strip felt they were part of an embattled community with a shared ideological agenda. Like the traditional storyteller or minstrel

and his engaged audience, a sense of solidarity or common purpose emerged between Kelly, his comic strip, and his avid readers. The battles or challenges faced
by this interpretive community may not have been as literal as those confronted
by listeners of antebellum trickster tales, but they perhaps felt almost as daunting in an abstract sense: the divisive rhetoric of a paranoid political landscape,
the formulaic and homogenized entertainment cranked out by a floundering
Hollywood studio system, and the dehumanizing effects of powerful corporate
and commercial cultures that were becoming an increasingly dominant force in
people's lives.

The story of Kelly's intimate engagement with his core readers is not completely heroic, however; there were issues that complicate an overly enthusiastic
assertion of poploric collaboration. At certain points in Kelly's career he seemed
to loathe one-on-one encounters with fans, for example—especially in the late
1960s when he appeared to develop an edge of impatience and misanthropy
(Crouch "An Interview with Selby Kelly" 192). It was as if he could muster the
energy and enthusiasm necessary to play that role of national storyteller when
on a stage, playing a hammy role and receiving generous applause, but when
required to patiently connect with a lone individual, his tolerance for receiving
adulation and for simply behaving in a friendly manner became exhausted.

Despite all of Kelly's success in understanding his core readers and articulating a resonant ideology, there were times when the ins and outs of that collaboration baffled him. Responding, perhaps, to the varying results he received
when mounting his mock presidential campaigns over the years, he complained
later in his career to his friend Milton Caniff about the "fickleness" of college students; he mused that despite his continued, "great popularity on campuses, [he]
couldn't understand for sure exactly what students wanted from his comic strip"
(Crouch 112). Some of that confusion could have been the result of a changing
zeitgeist in the 1960s, when college students began to prefer direct, authority-
questioning social protest over the allegorical and inward-looking satire of Kelly's strip. And Kelly's anxiety over this issue—though not the state of mind one
would expect of a confident poplorist—can still support the idea that he placed
a premium on the collaborative nature of his work. How many other writers or
artists would even wrestle with such issues?

One could also qualify the idealized notion of Kelly as a folkloric articulator
of collective social fears and desires by pointing out that some of the popularity
of *Pogo* can be explained by the wildfire-like mechanisms of entertainment fads.
While over 50,000 college students did indeed request "I Go Pogo" buttons in
anticipation of Kelly's rallies, 150 colleges embraced Pogo as their official candidate, and student bodies turned out in massive droves for the cartoonist's stump
speeches, it is reasonable to speculate that only a portion of those individuals
(albeit a significant portion) were true *Pogo* fans. That kind of enthusiastic band-
wagon-jumping can be explained by considering the potential college environ-

ments have for fostering entertainment crazes. Because of the captive nature of this youth demographic—everyone attending the same classes, sporting events, and so on, and actively and anxiously observing and mimicking each other's entertainment and fashion choices—it is easy enough for a cultural product, once it reaches a critical mass of interest, to sweep through virtually every dorm. That kind of monolithic craze is less likely to happen in our age, given the sheer number of cultural trends that course through the Internet and other mass media, but in Kelly's time, comic strips were one of only a half dozen mediums capable of that level of popular penetration.

In addition, the general status of *Pogo* in the media as a comic strip for intellectuals and eggheads—a perception that Kelly intentionally promoted at times and tried to undermine at others—probably added to the cachet of being a fan (a fair-weather one in this case) for some students (Rodgers A21). There was cultural capital, in other words, in affiliating one's self with the *Pogo* craze or campaign. Indeed, perhaps the strip's association with dissenting politics during the McCarthy era added to the value of a young person saying they loved the strip and its main character; for many students flirting with liberal political views for the first time, it would be the equivalent of saying that you rejected the provincial and dogmatic politics of your parents' generation.

In light of this clear-eyed view of the meaning of Pogomania at the height of Kelly's career, one can take a second look at the rowdy Harvard rally mentioned in the opening pages of this study. While not dismantling this concluding chapter's construction of Kelly's status as an engaged poplorist, it does add some complexities to the discussion, highlighting political and class issues that muddy the waters. To begin, the raw numbers suggest that this mock rally was an eruption of bubbling political discontent: 1,600 people showed up; three police wagons, eight patrol cars, and twenty-five policemen arrived to try to control the scene; and a mêlée ensued in which twenty-eight Harvard students were arrested (Boatner 90). The official interpretation of the events from the authorities' perspective was that the sheer number of students and their raucous behavior amounted to a public hazard, and that the police's "efforts to bring a semblance of order to the big square went almost unheeded by the students." That refusal to cooperate resulted in the arrest of those twenty-eight students for "disturbing the peace." Apparently those bookings were also complicated by a series of physical struggles in which three officers received minor injuries ("Police Seize 28" A5).

A closer look at some of the rhetoric used by the city leaders and arresting officers, however, reveals that the incident had as much or more to do with existing animosities between city and campus—and accompanying class divides—than it did the excesses of a mock-campaign rally. A city councilor quoted in an article in the local municipal paper, for example, described the behavior of the students as "shocking," and complained that ". . . the entire city is without pro-

Figure 6.4: Kelly speaking at Harvard, 1952. Copyright © Okefenokee Glee & Perloo, Inc. Used by permission.

tection as all of the police officers have to be called to entertain these guests of the city who are supposedly here to obtain an education." He warned that future clashes with students would be met with even greater force, including the use of firefighters who would push the "rioters" back with a hose (Ibid., A5).

The Harvard newspaper gave a different portrait of the events, describing how the police aggressively attacked students with clubs and fists, even kneeing one student in the groin. It was reported that a particular officer loudly declared that "Getting arrested will teach you Harvard bastards a lesson!" ("Students Claim Mishandling" A1). Kelly, according to this version of events, showed up just after the mêlée was settled and was appalled by the reports of police brutality. He could not believe that the police had nothing better to do than to harass students at a playful political rally for a fictional character. As Figure 6.4 illustrates, he apparently was able to give his stump speech after all, despite the chaos of the preceding hours.

The councilor's contemptuous description of the students as "guests" of the city, and the police officer's epithet of "Harvard bastards" suggests that the town-gown split in Cambridge was acrimonious at this time, with the community leaders perhaps seeing the school as a bastion of privilege and assumed superiority. Students, on the other hand, could have been using the *Pogo* rally to express frustration against a stifling status quo—one that in the heat of the conflict might have found representation in the stodgy local government and its overly aggressive police officers. The fact that the councilor entertained the idea that hoses should be used to force back rioting students fits the rhetoric of the times, as identified by scholars of the Cold War era: on the one hand, an older, more conservative segment of society that felt that rebellion from norms needed emergency "containment"—in the same way that the government was trying to contain the spread of communism on many fronts; and on the other hand, an emerging youth demographic unwilling to be corralled by authority figures and reactionary politics (May 14).

Despite the particular local factors that complicate the meanings of this one specific rally, the general "I Go Pogo" phenomenon, with its series of equally enthusiastic (if less overtly violent) rallies across the country in 1952 and 1956 supports the notion that Kelly had achieved a poploric clout and reach with his satiric work. The general intensity of fan devotion found a literal, physical outlet in these rallies. And one could posit that these events took on carnivalesque social dynamics and meanings in light of the general ethic of "containment" in the 1950s. To explain, carnivalesque cultural experiences, according to Mikhail Bakhtin, can provide a temporary liberating release from the pressures and rigid rules of everyday life. For those carnival moments, the social strata of society is inverted, with the fool and the king reversing roles; dialogical entertainment replaces the monological lecturing of the official culture; the distinctions between performer and audience in a folk-cultural sense are dissolved, allowing for a highly participatory experience; mask wearing and new identities are tried out; and earthy, irreverent humor reigns for the day (Bakhtin, *Rabelais* 6–7).

For college students living in an era that celebrated cultural conformism and seemed to operate according to mechanisms of top-down social control, a bit of carnivalesque release in the guise of a mock-political rally must have sounded especially appealing. One could forget classes, homework, and various social pressures; everyone could let loose with an enthusiasm usually reserved for sporting events; people were given the license for that afternoon and evening to participate in parades, chanting, and cheering, achieving a dialogical and participatory frenzy; one could elevate a literal fool (the wise fool of Pogo) into the place of authority (the presidential candidate); and a student could even imagine a new identity for himself or herself—a politically engaged enthusiast, devoted to a set of real ideological ideals. The images of Kelly surrounded by eager students at these rallies seem to support the idea that the events carried a playful, participatory, and expansive carnivalesque tone (see Figure 0.1). Furthermore, student recollections of their motivations in attending the rallies suggests that the act of participating carried real ideological meaning for some—that it represented an effort to affiliate themselves with an alternative ideological ideal: "Pogo represented a fair handshake among people trying to do good in the world. Pogo, along with his friends, was a terribly imaginative and evocative character; he was an optimist no matter what he found in the way of ignorance and opposition and resistance among others" (Boatner 90).

In estimating the libratory power of carnivalesque experiences in the medieval era, Bakhtin posits that they were politically ambivalent, serving as a steam valve of social discontent, and perhaps reinforcing the status quo in conservative ways (Bakhtin 9). But those dynamics could differ in a twentieth-century American context where the social strata were much more fluid, where political dissent and satire could thrive and exist beyond isolated carnival moments, and where individuals were free to reinvent themselves. Carnivalesque experiences could thus be truly liberating moments, opportunities to glimpse "alternative possibilities" for one's identity and ideological orientation, and for the configurations of the surrounding social structure (Connery 127). The potentially mind-liberating qualities of Kelly's mini-carnivals were amplified by the ubiquity and accessibility of his satiric work. The rallies themselves, in other words, were concentrated carnival experiences, but highly engaged readers also had access to *Pogo* on a daily basis in comic strip form and in book collections, and could thus regularly dip into that alternative world of dialogical playful comedy and progressive political ideals.

Kelly Compared to Other Poplorists

The significance of Kelly's status as an authentic and effective poplorist at mid-twentieth century can be showcased by comparing him to other cultural creators who achieved a similar resonance in their creative work and collaborative rapport with their core fans. These figures include some of the rebel comedians of the 1950s, the folk revivalists of the same era, and Al Capp, the only other comic strip artist from Kelly's generation to match him in terms of satiric output and flamboyant public persona. Capp, in particular, provides a productive comparison and contrast because of how much the two cartoonists' life stories paralleled each other, how similar their comic strips were in terms of setting and satiric ambition, how they both engaged directly with college readers, and how strikingly different their politics and public personas turned out to be in the end.

The emerging "rebel comedians" of the 1950s—figures such as Mort Sahl, Danny Thomas, and Lenny Bruce—shared some similarities with Kelly in terms of relationship with audiences, the use of folky and vernacular satiric tools, and the general political orientation of their social criticism. Flouting the canned joke-telling of the previous era of "square" comedians like Bob Hope, these alternative performers used first-person storytelling, dialect, and stream-of-consciousness rants to deliver their satiric take on society. As Gerald Nachman describes them, "They were more folklorists than jokesters, creating characters and scenes, kissing cousins of America's humorists, with a distinct point of view" (Nachman 25).

Mort Sahl, in particular, shared some common attitudes and devices with Kelly. He articulated a comedy of dissent at a time of seeming national conformism;

he created a "casual campus" wardrobe and persona, gaining popularity with students and intellectuals; and he created satire that was multi-voiced and verbally dense. The verbal complexity of Sahl's comedy resembled the heteroglossic flavor of Kelly's strip, in which he channeled so many different voices from various segments of society, often using differing typefaces to signify shifts in rhetoric. As Nachman describes it, "Sahl mastered the contemporary argot—the empty phrases, circumlocutions, euphemisms, and platitudes—not just of politics and show business but of the military, media, academia, feminism, psychology, [and] relationships" (Nachman 67).

Sahl, like Kelly, was also especially engaged with his audience, attempting to create resonant comedy through a call-and-response with his listeners. He described that interaction to a reporter:

> I never found you could write the act. You can't rehearse the audience's responses. You adjust to them every night. I come in with only an outline. You've got to have a spirit of adventure. I follow my instincts and the audience is my jury. If I try a joke and they like it, I extend it. The audience is bright, you have to believe that, and they'll know how to find the nugget in the story. The audience will always find the joke . . . (Nachman 64)

Figure 6.5: Kelly giving a mock-political stump speech in 1956. Copyright © Okefenokee Glee & Perloo, Inc. Used by permission.

At first glance, Kelly's back and forth with his fans seems to be less immediate—it was largely mediated by letters, editors, and syndicates, after all—but if we consider the sheer number of chalk-talks, high school visits, and campus stump speeches he gave, he begins to resemble these rebel comedians more closely (Figure 6.5). Like them, he had the opportunity to take the pulse of a youth generation through direct contact, hearing their laughter and approval as he articulated a set of ideological ideals they could embrace.

Interestingly, Kelly may have also shared a weakness common among these alternative comedians: their tendency to take themselves too seriously, to allow their careers as effective humorists to be curdled by idiosyncratic, strident, and sometimes misanthropic satire (Nachman 29–30). Lenny Bruce, for example, was famous for his combative relationship with audiences, and Mort Sahl often grew impatient with his fans, alienating many of them with his strident and overly personalized rants. In Kelly's case, late in his career, he simply lost the balance between engaging comedy and indignant satire. As a result, some fans may have grown tired of his lecturing stridency, and he, in return, became confused by their fickleness.

One significant difference between Kelly and these comedians is that they largely remained niche entertainers throughout their careers, while he achieved a mass popularity more in line with mainstream comedians like Bob Hope. Kelly's medium, of course, allowed for this greater reach; he had a national stage that penetrated almost every home, while they had to eke out a career on fringe comedy stages and the occasional television appearance. Kelly's willingness to "pander"—in the most positive sense of the word—also amplified his popular appeal. By pairing his dissenting comedy with cute and polished visuals and a highly engaging alternative world, he gave fans from a variety of cultural formations the opportunity to stick around for a while, reveling in his welcoming comedy and storytelling first, and perhaps his pointed social criticism later.

As a poploric reviver of folk stories and forms, Kelly also shared much in common with the musical folk revivalists of his era. They, like Kelly, connected with disaffected intellectuals and college students, offering them "authentic" and politically resonant cultural products, and interacting with them in call-and-response fashion at campus sing-alongs and music festivals. While the politically engaged central figures of the movement—folk purists such as Pete Seeger—seem to be the best candidates for the designation of poplorist, it is Bob Dylan who makes the most interesting comparison with Kelly. To explain, the core revivalists of the folk movement fetishized concepts of authenticity and purity so thoroughly that the music they played could no longer develop to fit new cultural moments; migrate into more popular, commercialized realms; or fuse with other emerging vernacular genres. It lacked syncretism, too, as figures such as Pete Seeger tried to freeze the folk music within a block of nostalgic amber.

Dylan, in contrast, was willing to "plug in," both literally and figuratively, as he embraced amplified rock music and melded traditional folk lyrics with beat poetry. That syncretic innovation and embrace of mainstream forms and means of distribution make him comparable in poploric terms to Kelly. *Pogo* was also a syncretic fusion of folk storytelling themes and conventions with pastoral and Freudian codings; in addition, it was "plugged in" in the sense that it took advantage of a mainstream medium—comic strips in this case—with an immense national reach. Dylan, like Kelly, also experienced moments when that call-and-response with fans broke down—derailed by the fickleness of the shifting cultural moment. In Kelly's case, however, it was the youth culture charging ahead, while in Dylan's case, it was him challenging or outpacing the traditionalists in his live audiences.

Walt Kelly and Al Capp

In closing, a comparison with fellow cartoonist Al Capp is useful in highlighting the uniquely successful ways that Kelly exercised his poploric tools. Some of the similarities between the two men's careers are uncanny: both grew up in the same town, Bridgeport, Connecticut; both suffered from debilitating childhood sicknesses or injuries (in Capp's case, the loss of a leg from a run-in with an ice truck); both chose at a young age to pursue cartooning as a career; both attended the same high school—Warren Harding High; both created strips based in the American South that channeled voices and conventions from folk culture; and both became prominent auteurs and satirists in the field of comic strips. Finally, these two friends—and sometimes combatants—shared a similar proclivity for hard-living and womanizing.

The differences between the men's biographies are also significant, and may go a long way in making sense of the ultimately divergent orientations of their poploric satire. Capp, for example, was much more bold and bombastic than Kelly as a young man; his parents had difficulty controlling him as a teenager, and in school he showed a lack of respect for authority, feeling little motivation to succeed according to traditional standards (Capp 79–81). Where Kelly had been a socially talented teenager involved in plays, journalism, and singing groups, Capp was placed into remedial classes, failed geometry, drew nude pictures of his female teachers, and ultimately dropped out of high school. Like, Kelly, he did not go to college, but he never had the benefit of the kind of mind-expanding liberal arts education the Disney studios offered. Instead, he learned to be a cartoonist simply by moving to New York, jumping into the field as an apprentice, and teaching himself.

The two artists' differing temperaments persisted into their adult professional years. Kelly was forever smoothing ruffled feathers and nuancing his way through difficult situations such as the Disney strike or various crises in the National Cartoonists Society; Capp, on the other hand, seemed to be continually embroiled in feuds with editors and peers (such as the Ham Fisher affair described in chapter three). In most cases Kelly's social skills made him the better businessman and more universally beloved cultural figure. Occasionally, however, Capp harnessed his combativeness to righteous causes, such as the reformation of the clubby practices of the NCS. In contrast, Kelly's efforts to gloss over difficulties in various NCS scandals or to protect old-boy privileges within the "club," undermined his integrity as a principled sateur.

The professional lives of the two cartoonists intersected most obviously in the subject matter and satiric nature of their strips. Both cartoonists chose to create visually dynamic comic strips set in the American South, that gathered avid readerships through grassroots means, and that challenged the general restrictions of the comics page in terms of topical satire and the breaking of genre conventions. And like Kelly, Capp received generous accolades for this work. While Kelly was compared most commonly to Mark Twain, Capp was linked to Daumier, Hogarth, Voltaire, Sterne, Cervantes, Rabelais, and Swift; John Steinbeck even suggested in 1953 that Capp was "the greatest contemporary writer" and that the "the Nobel Prize Committee should give him serious consideration" (Becker 187–89; White and Abel 31; Coupiere and Horn 73).

Capp's strip, which began in 1934, was also embraced by a mass audience, and although it has been out of syndication for over thirty years, it continues to be a cultural force today. The many popular manifestations of the *L'il Abner* universe, including film and Broadway musical versions, have enshrined elements of the strip as cultural fixtures or symbols (Sadie Hawkins Day, a load of colloquial words and phrases, and some of his satiric creations such as "Shmoos" and "Kigmies"). His work does indeed deserve some of the praise it has received, since it did feature an exuberant brand of Juvenalian satire that contrasted brilliantly with the bland tone of surrounding strips on the comics page. Capp also dared to push against the limits of content and tone while creating a consistently funny storyline that included attacks on abstract public figures and a generalized mockery of human foibles. Capp also deserves kudos for his efforts to protect the medium against censorship and editorial practices that would have further limited creative artists' freedom.

Celebrations of Capp's work, however, tend to overlook some of the more disturbing facets of his career, satire, visual aesthetics, and storyline. Those aspects include Capp's burlesque, ribald preoccupations in the strip—often to the point of eclipsing the tone or point of the satire; his use of hillbilly stereotypes, settings, and dialects as relatively unnuanced comic devices; the vindictive, self-congratulatory tone of some of his satiric attacks; the ambiguity of some of his best satiric symbols and devices; and Capp's combative—and sometimes abusive—relationship with his college fans near the end of his career. I will consider some of these aspects of his satire and career as they intersect with Kelly's work.

To begin, the two artists' treatment of their Southern settings differed in significant ways. On the one hand, Kelly used a Southern pastoral swamp popu-lated by diverse animal types (or "ethnicities") as the allegorical site for his sat-ire. This mythic site served as an imaginative escape from the social strictures and commercial development of mid-century mainstream America. Capp's strip, on the other hand, featured a more literal depiction of a Southern landscape that carried less positive associations in the collective imagination—an Appalachian community of poor Southern whites. Lacking allegorical distance and ambigu-ity, it worked as a site for mocking laughable others—in this case, Caucasian people who seemingly had no excuse for not capitalizing on the educational and commercial opportunities that seemed to be lifting so many families into the ranks of the middle classes at mid-twentieth century.

Within this setting Capp created a rollicking, picaresque satire in which his protagonist, Abner, a naïve young rogue, serves continually as the butt of for-tune, wandering from mishap to adventure, the "eternal fool" (Berger 63). But whereas Pogo behaves as a wily trickster or wise fool, Abner is a gullible buf-foon, sometimes undermining the plans of greedy and malicious intruders to his backwoods community, but always doing it obliviously, unwittingly. In this respect, Capp follows a venerable comic tradition of using the country rube as a foil against the evil machinations of representatives of the outside, "civilized" world, but because Abner possesses little folk wisdom or native guile, the satire never achieves the complexity associated with poploric works that channel the subversive energies of traditional folk forms.

To elaborate, Capp's Rabelaisian comic strip, with its oblivious protagonist, outrageous caricatures, and physical slapstick, could have served as a "deformed text" that challenged readers to read and interpret actively, seeing more clearly than Abner, identifying the contradictions in characters' behavior, and creative-ly interpreting coded images and layered satire. On the less progressive side, Capp, unlike Kelly, did not attempt to contrast the goodness of Southern, rural, pastoral life with the depravity of the big city. Instead, his satire is pervaded by a "Falstaffian" tone that included "mocking burlesques" and "devastating parodies" of all social types and worldviews, including those of his protago-nists (Becker 190). Moreover, he depicts his core figures as contemptible "oth-ers," broad caricatures or stereotypes of a dysfunctional hillbilly culture ruled by laziness, moonshine, ignorance, animalistic behavior, poor hygiene, shotgun weddings, and poverty. The humor in the strip often emerges from those conde-scending assumptions. In one typical Sunday strip from the late 1930s, for exam-ple, Mammy, Abner's mother, is the butt of the joke. Abner gives her a radio for a present and Mammy carries on conversations with the announcer "inside the box." She ends up kicking out the contraption when the fellow she's attempting to address refuses to resume playing the music she prefers. The strip ends with her reconciling with the box and trying to follow a beautician's advice on how to make herself attractive for men. Since she does not have powder and rouge, she substitutes corn meal and strawberry jam. The humor in this installment could appeal to the average reader's own fear of ineptness, but on the surface it operated primarily as an exaggerated stereotype that ridiculed less educated, marginalized social groups, and congratulated suburban readers on their relative sophistication.

The worst villains in Capp's strips tended to be wealthy and powerful industrialists, aristocrats, and politicians. They are forever invading Dogpatch, trying to exploit people and resources. Capp reserved some of his greatest contempt, however, for his protagonist, Abner (Figure 6.6). He referred to him as a "stupid lout" or imbecile rather than naïve country boy. With Capp's treatment of Abner devoid of any sentimentality or sympathy, his lead character comes across as goofy, childish, and often monomaniacal. His obsessive pursuit of various silly objectives, for example, often serves as a fun parody of the common narrative of the rugged individualist in society making his way from rags to riches, but Abner remains the eternal fool at the end of the adventures, settling for a ridiculous version of his intended goal, and defeating evil only by chance or stupidity.

Figure 6.6: Al Capp's *Li'l Abner*.

Capp's treatment of these targets in *Li'l Abner* can be categorized best, perhaps, as "Hobbesian": a comedy "based upon a feeling of superiority" (Berger 94). It often runs counter to one of the foundational rules of good satire in a democratic culture—that it be used as a tool for protecting the powerless against the powerful, rather than as a means of scapegoating or ridiculing peoples that have little or no voice and who might be economically and socially disadvantaged. Another weakness is that rarely does this type of satirist dish out the abuse equally to all deserving recipients; a certain group is often spared the satirist's disdain— an elite cadre of superior readers that include the satirist. In Capp's case, he exempted himself and his core, middle-class readers who followed the satire of his strip most closely. These readers are spared any discomfort, as the characters on both the high and low of ends of society are depicted as archetypal, laughable "others." To elaborate, the typical reader might be socially sandwiched between the two class-based targets in the strip—the upper classes on one hand who were the principal villains, and the ignorant working class whites on the other—thus leaving them with a sense of satisfaction about their own middling level of privilege and affluence. Another way of putting it is that these educated middle-class readers, having escaped from the lower classes, but still anxious about losing their precarious social position, or falling prey to the cultural diseases of the aristocracy, could take cathartic pleasure in having the distance and otherness of these two extremes explained to them in exaggerated terms (Coupiere and Horn 70).

In contrast, Kelly's work avoids Capp's brand of condescending contempt and misanthropy in several ways. First, Kelly sympathetically identifies with his protagonist, Pogo, and sets him up as an admirable everyman and viable candidate for a humane set of values. Second, Kelly gently mocks the foolishness of his secondary characters, but reserves his most devastating mockery for the true villains in his world—conniving invaders such as Malarkey. In addition, the allegorically distanced world of cartoon animals in *Pogo* prevents his caricatures from being read as direct scapegoating of an identifiable demographic. And while Capp's setting features a brand of punitive satire that emphasizes the pleasures of schadenfreude and superiority, Kelly's mythic Southern landscape features the progressive codings of trickster tales and pastoral comedies—genres that either champion the underdog or invert the social order in progressive ways. Finally, Kelly's ethic of self-inspection before the mockery of others, which resembles the biblical maxim of seeing the beam in one's own eye before looking for the mote in another's, prevented his satire from ever degenerating into Capp's brand of condescending mockery.

The comparison between Kelly's introspective, self-targeting satire and Capp's comparatively Hobbesian and self-congratulatory tack has been a largely abstract exercise to this point. One can see the vivid, real-life ethical import of these satiric worldviews, nevertheless, if one examines the two creators' poploric interactions with college fans. On the one side, Kelly tried to engage with college students' psychological and intellectual needs, meeting them halfway, in a sense, by doing research on their interests and fraternizing with them at mock rallies. While the satire he created in the end was an outgrowth of his own worldview and sensibility, it was also customized, to a degree, to resonate deeply with these most avid fans. It would be impossible to quantify which aspects of *Pogo* are an outgrowth of this media age call-and-response, but one could conjecture that the strip's gradual shift in the early 1950s from traditional trickster tale conventions into more philosophical Freudian and pastoral themes was an aspect of that collaboration. And the strip's core ethic of tolerating ideological heterogeneity and engaging in healthy self-inspection matched the emerging countercultural zeitgeist among 1950s intellectuals.

Capp's relationship with college students was radically different. While the political orientation of *Li'l Abner* had seemed vaguely left-leaning for the bulk of its run (mocking icons of big-business and puritanical cultural guardians on a regular basis), it took a reactionary turn in the mid 1960s. Capp attacked youth culture and the peace movement with a vehemence that essentially reduced his strip to an angry polemical tract. Students were portrayed as filthy, violent animals that attracted hordes of flies. He labeled their movement S.W.I.N.E.: "Students Wildly Indignant About Everything"; and he targeted leaders in the movement, such as Joan Baez and John Lennon, as conniving hypocrites.

Capp defended his work by arguing that he was attacking the "status quo" as he always had, and was still "for" the underdog. He said in an interview near his retirement,

> I don't think my politics changed. You see, I've always been for those who are be-ing shamed, disgraced, ignored, by other people. That group has changed. Now it's the poor bastard who's rich—well, I don't mean rich, and of course I always had Bull Moose [his caricature of an evil capitalist]—but the poor son of a bitch who worked, who was being denounced by the liberals. (Marschall 15)

Capp continues, describing a run-in with Harold Gray, a notoriously reactionary cartoonist from the previous generation. The two seemed to share an affinity for the type of far-right paranoia that one associates with McCarthy or the John Birch Society:

> The only time I met him [Gray] he took me aside and said, "You're making some money now. Buy a farm and build a great big stone wall around it because they're coming—the bums and the Russians." "Well," I said, "Thank you very much," and promptly bought a farm! (Ibid. 15)

With these political views as motivating factors, Capp initiated his own tour of college campuses—in his case, to engage in one-way attacks instead of open dia-logues. The strip itself illustrated these encounters, with Capp portraying him-self as the put-upon defender of common sense, patriotism, and morality, and caricaturing his audiences as smelly, hippie Neanderthals. There may have been a kernel of merit in Capp's "conservative" working-class perspective on some of the contradictions and hypocrisies of the countercultural movement, but that reason was lost amidst the self-congratulatory, harsh, polemical nature of his at-tacks. Indeed, despite Capp's flattering depiction of himself, the reality of these encounters was that he could become viciously combative, taking glee in using hyperbole to denounce the youth movement. An excerpt from Capp's speeches on campuses during this period reveals how thoroughly his misanthropy and his use of savage hyperbole and distortion had pervaded his satiric vision:

Princeton has sunk to a moral level that a chimpanzee can live with, but only a chimpanzee. It has become a combination playpen and pigpen because it disregards the inferiority of the college student to every other class. . . . President Nixon showed angelic restraint when he called students bums. . . . Colleges today are filled with Fagin professors who don't teach, . . . they just corrupt. (Anderson 88)

Interestingly, Capp's behavior on these visits also highlighted one of the possible by-products—hypocrisy—of social criticism or satire that is primarily punishing and scapegoating, rather than self-reflexive. To explain, the core message of Capp's reactionary stump speeches and mock debates was the need to return to common sense and morality in the country. But after Capp would attack "immoral" students in the day, he would often spend his evenings luring unsuspecting coeds to his room so that he could expose himself and then proceed to chase the young women around the room and attempt to molest them; they usually got away or locked themselves in the bathroom because he was slowed down by his false leg. Like Kelly's indiscretions, these public scandals were initially overlooked, but syndicated essayists like Jack Anderson were able to dig up some of the details from these encounters. The following is a description of such activities the day before Capp was scheduled to give a speech at the University of Alabama in Tuscaloosa:

Late that afternoon, a coed, active in the arts program, went to his room at the Stafford Hotel to deliver . . . materials he had requested for his speech the next night.

Capp told the young woman he was impressed with her and discussed the possibility of hiring her to help produce the "Capp on Campus" radio series, then in progress. Then, according to the girl, he began making forceful advances toward her and exposing himself to her. She tried to leave but found she could not get the door open. She said she finally broke free and locked herself in the bathroom until he agreed to let her go.

Although she was not injured, she was sufficiently upset by the experience to be admitted a few days later to the university infirmary where she remained under sedation for several days.

That evening, another coed, whose job it was to greet visiting speakers, went to see Capp at his hotel. She said that he exposed himself to her and made suggestive comments. She, too, found she could not open the door, but she said Capp let her go when she threatened to open a window and scream. The next afternoon Capp was introduced in his room to another woman student who had just completed a taped interview with his staff for a planned broadcast called the "Now Morality." She said that Capp exposed himself to her and made suggestive comments. She immediately left.

> Late that night, he brought another coed to his room, coaxing her to come by saying that a party was planned. There was no party, however, and the girl said Capp made an unsuccessful pass at her. (Anderson 93)

The incident ended with local police running Capp out of town and college officials hushing the scandal so that the young women would not have to suffer any public notoriety or shame.

Capp's behavior, if considered in the context of the clubby, chauvinistic ethos that ruled the cartooning bullpens, the NCS, and old-boy cartoon networks for years, is easy enough to fathom. As described in the first chapter, Kelly was guilty, to a lesser extent perhaps, of similar womanizing. A significant difference, however, was that Capp's flirtations amounted to both criminal behavior and defiance of the core ethics of a poplorist. Rather than using one's art and position to address the social and psychological needs of his core readers, it became a platform for Capp to engage in self-focused congratulations and the coercive achievement of his own lustful desires.

Kelly's preoccupations with beautiful females also short-circuited certain aspects of his work. Side effects could have included a reductive treatment of female types in his strip and a reticence to challenge the clubby and sometimes misogynistic practices of the NCS. In Capp's case, a career-long run of womanizing did not seem to affect his ability to see and speak clearly about the ways that the NCS needed reformation, but it did infect his satire much more deeply than Kelly's case, amounting ultimately to a career-derailing obsession. Long before the campus escapades, Capp's strip seemed devoted to the task of featuring scantily clad, full-figured women making strained poses. Furthermore, he hired assistants, like Frank Frazetta, who made a career of illustrating fantasy-themed cheesecake, which underscores the centrality of this device in Capp's work. And although Capp was able to successfully defend himself against charges from Ham Fisher that he intentionally placed sexual imagery in his strips, this did not mean that he was completely innocent of those charges. Fisher had doctored Capp's cartoons to make them seem more explicitly pornographic than they actually were, but fellow cartoonists had long been aware that Capp suffused his strip with sexual innuendo, ribald imagery, or the occasional visual gag based on the appearance of sexual organs. Fisher, in other words, was simply amplifying and distorting what was already there. The most obvious sexual elements were evident in characters like Apasionata von Climax and Available Jones, with his long, penis-shaped nose. Other, more coded references included female anatomy drawn into the knots in trees, noses behaving as if they were the male organ in various states of arousal, the prevalence of the number 69 in many storylines, and the occasional comic, "wink-wink" use of some of Capp's most important satiric devices—the Shmoo, the Kigmy, and the Dogpatch Ham—as phallic symbols (Williams 76).

Figure 6.7: Al Capp, "Moonbeam McSwine."

Figure 6.8: Al Capp, a female participant in the Sadie Hawkins Day event.

Onto that racy imagery Capp added some layers of misogyny as well. In his strip, women are divided into two categories: the inaccessible sex goddesses and the accessible but ugly, aggressive, and shrewish females (Figures 6.7 and 6.8). There are echoes here of Kelly's own reductive treatment of Mam'sell Hepzibah and Miz Beaver, but in Capp's case those divisions are more exaggerated and the themes more pronounced. The crudeness in his approach to gender relations is especially pronounced in his episodes that feature the Sadie Hawkins races—carnivalesque romps when most of the women, with the exception of Daisy Mae and a few other rivals for Abner's affections, were drawn as ugly brutes with giant, phallic noses. Capp even held reader contests to see if amateur artists could beat him in drawing the ugliest woman in the world, Lena Hyena of Lower Slobbovia.

For Capp, this layering of sexual imagery and themes into his strip was a game; it both tickled and perplexed him that editors never complained about the name Apasionata von Climax and he was eager to see how far he could go before being attacked by cultural guardians. Even in his public comments he seemed to be flirting with the borders of propriety, making outlandishly sexist comments such as his claim that his primary goal in life was to be like the early cartoonist Bud Fisher, "who married a fresh Ziegfeld Follies girl every couple of years—and could afford them all" (Marschall 14). If Capp had used this racy art, comedy, and public commentary as an earthy, vulgar affront to repressive societal attitudes toward sex, one might be able to justify them as aspects of a brand of "liberating" Rabelaisian satire. But there was no such coherent objective at work. In fact, for many young male fans, the satire of the strip was less interesting than trying to decode the sexually charged material that Capp consistently layered into images and storylines (Williams 76). In sum, his gratuitous use of idealized cheesecake, his misogynistic categorizations of female types, the sexist prank-ing, and the real-life abusive behavior toward college coeds amounted to little more than a juvenile preoccupation that distracted him or prevented him from creating a brand of more coherent and principled satire.

In a final assessment of Kelly's and Capp's differing brands of poploric com-edy and satire, one could use the criteria of how each used their privileges and power as sateurs in the most ethical and socially progressive ways. Both of them achieved that auteur-like independence in similar fashion—creating a genre-defying comic strip set in the American South that featured folk characters and challenging satire. In Capp's case, there were moments of real integrity where he used his prominence in the field of cartooning to campaign for artists' rights and a reformation of the clubby practices of the NCS. But within his strip he engaged in punishing, Hobbesian satire; as one critic described it, "he did not observe the people and the life around him so much as he used the common stereotypes of broad low comedy" (Williams 75). And those stereotypes were warped by his own reactionary and self-congratulatory politics, as well as a sexism and misogyny that pervaded both his work and personal life.

Kelly's case is similarly marred by a few personal foibles: a clubby compla-cency at times when it came to advocating artists' rights or for sharing the re-wards of fame, and a hard-drinking lifestyle that sometimes degenerated into womanizing behavior—excesses that were less egregious, nevertheless, than Capp's. There is no evidence, for example, that he ever compromised his role as a campus-going poplorist to chase after vulnerable female fans. And within Kelly's strip, the worst by-product of his bad-boy behavior might have been a mildly reductive treatment of female stereotypes.

Kelly's essential comedy and satire, moreover, remained true to the demo-cratic heritage of its folkloric roots, and Kelly used his clout as an auteur to create a syncretic work of comedy that met the psychological needs of his core fans. In that respectful back and forth exchange, he also pushed and prodded his readers, encouraging them to embrace an ideological worldview that challenged dogmatism, intolerance, hypocrisy and scapegoating. The repercussions of the principled use of his position as a powerful poplorist—reaching into millions of homes across America through the comics page—are perhaps too difficult to quantify, as they shaped (and continue to shape) the sensibilities and politics of several generations of devoted readers.

NOTES

1. Notable exceptions to this silent complicity were Elmer Davis, Edward R. Murrow, Drew Pearson, and Herblock.

2. This succinct iteration of the maxim did not appear until July 1970.

3. In recent years scholars and fans have begun to reclaim the legacy of quality animal and kiddie comics. Those efforts include reprints of Kelly's *Our Gang* and *Animal Comics* series as well as the *Toon Treasury* collections put together by Art Spiegelman and Françoise Mouly, and various books edited by Craig Yoe.

4. Supporting this contention is the fact that so many of the iconic animal characters of early to mid-century comics and animation—Mickey Mouse, Krazy Kat, Felix the Kat, Bugs Bunny, and others—can trace their origins, like Pogo, back to comedic types that emerged from blackface and trickster tales (Soper 126).

5. Levine supports this point by tracing the form and functions of trickster tales from slavery times into the Harlem Renaissance, citing later variations that depicted Brer Rabbit embodying the "New Negro" ethic—behaving more confidently, setting up his feet on Brer Bear's table, turning the predator's shotgun back on its owner and demanding—rather than conniving—the rights and pleasures he is owed.

6. The emergence of the different layers of meaning often depended on the nature of the listening audience. Christie Davies, a scholar of ethnic humor, explains how the ethnic underdog in this genre of comedy uses language in complex ways to his advantage: "Jokers [or tricksters, in our case] may deliberately and cleverly misuse language and exploit error so that we laugh at the cleverness of the pseudo-foolishness. A person who makes a statement with an ambiguous or contradictory meaning may be regarded by his or her listeners as a silly fool who has made a risible mistake or as a subtle wit who has produced a clever joke. Either way, the audience may laugh, but their estimation of the speaker's abilities will differ greatly depending on how they interpret his or her intention or meaning. Also jokes, repartee, the pretense of error or stupidity can be used as a skillful means of manipulating other people, so as to evade responsibility, to avoid answering a question, to reduce anger to amusement, or simply secretly to mock the other party. To succeed in such a game requires a great deal of shrewd understanding and/or gift for language. Only the clever can play the fool."

7. Due to length constraints, this study does not discuss at length the ideological complexity of the blackface tradition, but it is informed by the rich scholarship in this area from the last two decades—scholarship that sees these forms, in David Krasner's terms, as a "liminal space of resistance, parody, and double-consciousness" (Krasner 2). Besides Bluestein's book—which discusses the syncretic quality of the genre—there are the following significant texts: David Krasner, *Resistance, Parody, and Double Consciousness in African American Theatre, 1895–1910* (New York: St. Martin's Press, 1997); Eric Lott, *Love and Theft* (Oxford: Oxford University Press, 1995); W. T. Lhamon, Jr., *Raising Cain* (Cambridge, MA: Harvard University Press, 2000); Dale Cockrell, *Demons of Disorder* (Cambridge: Cambridge University Press, 1997); and Gavin Jones, *Strange Talk: The Politics of Dialect Literature in Gilded Age America* (Berkeley: University of California Press, 1999).

8. According to Jones, black vernacular was considered by most cultural guardians in the late

nineteenth century to be a result of ignorance or carelessness or of racial deficiencies in organs of speech or hearing.

9. Dubois's conception of double consciousness reads as follows: "After the Egyptian and Indian, the Greek and Roman, the Teuton and Mongolian, the Negro is a sort of seventh son, born with a veil, and gifted with second-sight in this American world—a world which yields him no true self-consciousness, but only lets him see himself through the revelation of the other world. It is a peculiar sensation, this double-consciousness, this sense of always looking at one's self through the eyes of others, of measuring one's soul by the tape of a world that looks on in amused contempt and pity. One ever feels his two-ness—an American, a Negro; two souls, two thoughts, two unreconciled strivings; two warring ideals in one dark body, whose dogged strength alone keeps it from being torn asunder" (Dubois 8).

10. These are lyrics from the song *Zip-A-Dee-Doo-Dah*, featured in Disney's *Song of the South* (1946).

WORKS CITED

"About Pogo and His Pals." In Post Hall syndicate promotional booklet, 1950. Reprinted in *The Best of Pogo*. Selby Kelly and Bill Crouch Jr., eds. New York: Simon & Schuster, 1982. 105.

"The Art of an Unknown Future." the *Times Literary Supplement* (29 May 1953) 348.

Anderson, Earle. "Bridgeport Remembers Walt Kelly." *The Best of Pogo*. Selby Kelly and Bill Crouch Jr., eds. New York: Simon and Schuster, 1982. 69.

Anderson, Jack. "Capp On Campus." Syndicated article, January 1971. 1.

Andrae, Thomas and Geoffrey Blum. "Ward Kimball Remembers Walt Kelly." *Phi Beta Pogo*. Selby Kelly and Bill Crouch Jr., eds. New York: Simon & Schuster, 1989. 132–47.

Aristotle. "Poetics." *Art and Its Significance: An Anthology of Aesthetic Theory*. Stephen David Ross, ed. Albany: State University of New York Press, 1994. 66–76.

Astor, David. "Trudeau is 'Amazed' His Comic Endures." *Editor & Publisher* 133.43 (2000): 31–32.

Bagdikian, Ben. "Pogo Creator Kelly Spurs Fight for Survival of Ideas." the *Evening Bulletin, Providence* (20 February 1952) 1.

Bakhtin, M. M. *The Dialogic Imagination*. Austin, TX: Texas UP, 1981.

Bakhtin, Mikhail. *Rabelais and His World*. Bloomington, IN: Indiana University Press, 1984.

———. "Bard of Okefenokee." *Time*. 29 October 1973. 89, 93.

Barthes, Roland. "The Death of the Author," *Image, Music, Text*. New York: Hill and Wang, 1977.

Bates, Eric. "Doonesbury Goes to War." *Rolling Stone*. 5 August 2004, 62.

Becker, Stephen. *Comic Art in America*. New York: Simon & Schuster, 1959.

Beiman, Nancy. "Interview with Selby Kelly." *Phi Beta Pogo*." Selby Kelly and Bill Crouch Jr., eds. (New York: & and Schuster, 1989) 193–206.

Beiman, Nancy. "Walt & Selby Kelly." *Cartoonist Profiles* 60 (December 1983): 26–31.

Berger, Arthur Asa. *L'il Abner: A Study in American Satire*. Jackson: University Press of Mississippi, 1994.

Berry, Boyd M. "A Perusal of Pogo Possum's Politics." *The Best of Pogo*. Selby Kelly and Bill Crouch Jr., eds. New York: Simon & Schuster, 1982. 195–97.

Bickley, R. Bruce Jr., *Critical Essays on Joel Chandler Harris*. Boston, Mass.: G. K. Hall, 1981.

Blair, Walter and Hamlin Hill. *America's Humor*. New York: Oxford UP, 1978.

Block, Herbert. *Herblock: A Cartoonist's Life*. New York: Macmillan Publishing Company, 1993.

Bluestein, Gene. *Poplore: Folk and Pop in American Culture*. Amherst: Massachusetts UP, 1994.

Boatner, Barbara. "Pogo Returns to Harvard," *The Best of Pogo*, Bill Crouch Jr., ed., New York: Simon & Schuster, 1982.

Brandon, Henry. "London Calling: Kelly Interviewed by the Sunday Times." *Pluperfect Pogo*. Bill Crouch Jr., ed. New York: Simon & Schuster, 1987. 92–97.

Bremmer, Jan, and Roodenburg, Herman, eds. *A Cultural History of Humor*. Cambridge: Polity Press, 1997.

Candee, Marjorie Dent, ed. "Walt Kelly." *Current Biography Yearbook*. New York, 1956. 332.

Canemaker, John. *Felix: The Twisted Tale of the World's Most Famous Cat*. New York: Da Capo Press, 1991.

Caniff, Milton. "NCS newsletter, June 14, 1951."

————. "Cartoonists Complain." *The Cartoonist*. Spring 1954.

Capp, Elliot. "We called him Alfred. . ." *Cartoonist Profiles* 48, (December 1980): 79–81.

Chillino, Frank. "Syndicate Production Chief." *Cartoonist Profiles*. 88 (December 1990): 64.

Chute, David. "The Return of Pogo; and Not a Moment Too Soon." *Los Angeles Times*, 25 August 1991: 1BR.

Cohen, Karl F. *Forbidden Animation: Censored Cartoons and Blacklisted Animators in America*. Jefferson, NC: McFarland & Company, 1997.

Connery, Brian, and Combe, Kirk, eds. *Theorizing Satire*. New York: St. Martin's Press, 1995.

Coupiere, Pierre, and Horn, Maurice. *A History of the Comic Strip*. New York: Crown Publishers, Inc., 1968.

Cremin, Dorothy. "*Pogo's* Dad Raps Violence in People." *The Atlanta Journal*. 9 November 1953: A1.

Crinklaw, Don. "A Cult of Whimsy: Fans of Pogo and His Critters Are a Determined Bunch." the *St. Louis Dispatch*. 29 October 1972: 1–5.

Crouch, Bill, Jr. "Desegregation and Jack Acid." *Pogo Files for Pogophiles*. Selby Daley Kelly and Steve Thompson, eds. Richfield, MN: Spring Hollow Books, 1992. 147–58.

————. "Early Kelly." In *The Best of Pogo*. Selby Kelly and Bill Crouch Jr., eds. New York: Simon & Schuster, 1982. 157.

————. "George Ward Talks about Kelly, and Pogo and Times Past." In *The Best of Pogo*. Selby Kelly and Bill Crouch Jr., eds. New York: Simon & Schuster, 1982. 76–85.

————. "Interview with Selby Kelly on October 7, 1974." *Phi Beta Pogo*. Selby Kelly and Bill Crouch, Jr., eds. New York: Simon & Schuster, 1989. 188–93.

————. "Milton Caniff Talks About Walt Kelly." *Phi Beta Pogo*. Selby Kelly and Bill Crouch Jr., eds. New York: Simon & Schuster, 1989. 106–12.

————. "Ray Dirgo Remembers Walt Kelly." In *The Best of Pogo*. Selby Kelly and Bill Crouch Jr., eds. New York: Simon & Schuster, 1982. 70–71.

————. "Two Mavericks at the Disney Studio." In *Phi Beta Pogo*. Selby Kelly and Bill Crouch Jr., eds. New York: Simon & Schuster, 1989. 131.

————. "Walt Kelly's Editorial Cartoons and World Events of 1948." In *The Best of Pogo*. Selby Kelly and Bill Crouch Jr., eds. New York: Simon & Schuster, 1982. 38–39.

————. "Walt Kelly in High School." In *The Best of Pogo*. Selby Kelly and Bill Crouch Jr., eds. New York: Simon & Schuster, 1982. 65.

————. "What do you know about *The New York Star*?" In *The Best of Pogo*. Selby Kelly and Bill Crouch Jr., eds. New York: Simon & Schuster, 1982. 10.

Crouch, Bill Jr. "Two Mavericks at the Disney Studio," in *Phi Beta Pogo*. Selby Kelly and Bill Crouch Jr., eds. New York: Simon & Schuster, 1989. 131.

————. "Walt Kelly's Editorial Cartoons and World Events of 1948." *The Best of Pogo*. Selby Kelly and Bill Crouch Jr., eds. (New York: Simon & Schuster, 1982) 38–39.

cummings, e. e. "Introduction." *Krazy Kat*. New York: Henry Holt and Company, 1946. 1–8.

cummings, e. e. *Krazy Kat*. New York: Henry Holt and Company, 1946. 1–8.

Denney, Reuel. "The Revolt Against Naturalism." *The Funnies*. David Manning White and Robert H. Abel, eds. London: The Free Press of Glencoe, 1963. 61.

Dale, Alan. *Comedy is a Man in Trouble*. Minneapolis: University of Minnesota Press, 2000.

Davies, Christie. *Ethnic Humor Around the World: A Comparative Analysis*. Indianapolis: Indiana UP, 1990.

Dennison, Sam. *Scandalize My Name: Black Imagery in American Popular Music*. New York: Garland Publishing, Inc., 1982.

Dillard, J. L. *Black English: Its History and Usage in the United States*. New York: Random House, 1972.

Dubois, W. E. B. *The Souls of Black Folk*. New York: Vintage Books, 1990.

Dusser, Erik. "Subversion in the Swamp: Pogo and the Folk in the McCarthy Era." *The Journal of American Culture*. Volume 26 Issue 1, Winter 2003: 134–41.

Fabe, Marilyn. *Closely Watched Films: An Introduction to the Art of Narrative Film Technique*. Berkeley: UCP, 2004.

Fishkin, Shelley Fisher. *Was Huck Black?: Mark Twain and African American Voices*. New York: Oxford UP, 1993.

Friedman, Rick. "Journey Into Suburbia, Part III," *Editor & Publisher*. 13 January 1962: 50.

Geerdes, Clay. "Pogo in the Underground." *The Best of Pogo*. Selby Kelly and Bill Crouch Jr., eds. New York: Simon & Schuster, 1982. 91–93.

Gerson, Robert. "Pogo Learns Human Beans Nothin' At All; Nature's Screechers Just Have Fun," *News Workshop*, New York University (April 1958) 1–2.

Goldstein, Kalman. "Al Capp and Walt Kelly: Pioneers of Political Satire in the Comics." *Journal of Popular Culture* (Summer 1992): 81–95.

Gordon, Ian. *Comic Strips and Consumer Culture: 1890–1945*. Washington, D.C.: Smithsonian Institution Press, 1998.

Green, Daniel. "A World Worth Laughing At: *Catch-22* and the Humor of Black Humor." *Studies in the Novel*. Vo. 27, Summer 1995: 186–96.

Griffin, Dustin. *Satire: A Critical Reintroduction*. Lexington: The University of Kentucky Press, 1994.

Grimaldi, Lennie. *Only in Bridgeport: An Illustrated History of the Park City*. Northridge, California: Windsor Publications Inc., 1986.

Grove, Gene. "What's So Funny?" *New York Post*. 16 June 1963: 5.

Hajdu, David. *The Ten-Cent Plague: The Great Comic-Book Scare and How it Changed America*. New York: Farrar, Strauss and Giroux, 2008.

Harvey, R. C. *The Art of the Funnies: An Aesthetic History*. Jackson: University Press of Mississippi, 1994.

Harvey, R. C. "Joe Palooka and the Most Famous Food Fight of the Funnies." *The Comics Journal*. 168 (May 1994): 107.

Harvey, R. C. "Tales of the Founding of the National Cartoonists Society." *Cartoonist Profiles* 109 (March 1996) 48.

Horn, John. "A Memory of Walt Kelly." *The Best of Pogo*. Selby Kelly and Bill Crouch Jr., eds. New York: Simon & Schuster, 1982. 41–47.

Horn, Maurice. "Pogo 'Possum: A French View." In *The Best of Pogo*. Selby Kelly and Bill Crouch Jr., eds. New York: Simon & Schuster, 1982. 104.

Johnson, E. Patrick. *Appropriating Blackness: Performance and the Politics of Authenticity*. Durham: Duke University Press, 2003.

Jones, Gavin. *Strange Talk: The Politics of Dialect Literature in Gilded Age America*. Berkeley: U of California Press, 1999.

Jung, Carl Gustav. "Psychology and Literature." *Art and Its Significance: An Anthology of Aesthetic Theory*. Stephen David Ross, ed. Albany: State University of New York Press, 1994. 507–20.

Kelly, Walt. "Aesop Takes to the Swamp." *Pluperfect Pogo*. Bill Crouch Jr., ed. New York: Simon & Schuster, 1987.

———. "Autobiography, Circa 1954." *The Best of Pogo*. Selby Kelly and Bill Crouch Jr., eds. New York: Simon & Schuster, 1982. 41–47.

———. "I GO POGO Campaign Letter to Editors." Distributed by Post-Hall syndicate in July 1956. Reprinted in *The Best of Pogo*. Selby Kelly and Bill Crouch Jr., eds. New York: Simon & Schuster, 1982. 185–86.

———. "Letter to Donald Clarke." *Walt Kelly Papers*. Billy Ireland Cartoon Library & Museum, Box 8, Folder 9.

———. "Letter from Feb. 2, 1959." *Walt Kelly Papers*. Billy Ireland Cartoon Library & Museum, Box 8, Folder 9.

———. "London Calling: Kelly Interviewed by the *Sunday Times*." *Pluperfect Pogo*. Bill Crouch Jr., ed. New York: Simon & Schuster, 1987. 94.

———. "Memo to Post-Hall Syndicate, 1954" Official Pogo Website. 1.

———. "NCS Newsletter 1953." From a 1953 newsletter found in NCS Dossier in the Ohio State Library Cartoon Collection.

———. "Pogo Looks at the Abominable Snowman." In *The Funnies*. David Manning White and Robert H. Abel, eds. London: The Free Press of Glencoe, 1963. 291.

———. "Promotional Material, 1954." *Walt Kelly's Pogo*. www.pogopossum.com. Web. 21 July 2010.

———. "Promotional, mid-1950s." *Pogo Files for Pogophiles*. Selby Daley Kelly and Steve Thompson, eds. Richfield, MN: Spring Hollow Books, 1992.

———. *Ten Ever-Lovin' Blue-Eyed Years With Pogo*. New York: Simon & Schuster, 1959. 6.

———. "The Bunny Rabbit Strips." In *The Best of Pogo*. Selby Kelly and Bill Crouch Jr., eds. New York: Simon & Schuster, 1982. 198–99.

———. "The Land of the Elephant Squash: A Biography of Walt Kelly." *Pogo Even Better*. Selby Kelly and Bill Crouch Jr., eds. New York: Simon & Schuster, 1984. 49–50.

———. "Unpublished Autobiographical Sketch." Billy Ireland Cartoon Library & Museum, Box 5, Folder 16.

———. "Walt Kelly Views the Press with CBS-TV." In *Pluperfect Pogo*. Bill Crouch Jr., ed. New York: Simon & Schuster, 1987. 194.

Kelly, Walt. "Aesop Takes to the Swamp." *Pluperfect Pogo*. Bill Crouch Jr., ed. New York: Simon & Schuster, 1987.

Kelly, Walt. "Atlanta Letters." Billy Ireland Cartoon Library & Museum, Ohio State University, Walt Kelly Collection, Box 8, folder 10.

Kelly, Walt. "Autobiography, Circa 1954." *The Best of Pogo*. Selby Kelly and Bill Crouch Jr., eds. New York: Simon & Schuster, 1982. 9.

Kelly, Walt. "I GO POGO campaign letter to editors." Distributed by Post-Hall syndicate in July 1956.

reprinted in *The Best of Pogo*. Selby Kelly and Bill Crouch, Jr., eds. New York: Simon & Schuster, 1982. 185–86.

Kelly, Walt. "Ka-Platz: The Delight in the Unexpected." *Pluperfect Pogo*. Bill Crouch Jr., ed. New York: Simon & Schuster, 1987.

Kelly, Walt. "Letter, August 14, 1957." Billy Ireland Cartoon Library & Museum, Ohio State University, Walt Kelly Collection, Box 8, folder 10.

Kelly, Walt. "Letter to Al Capp, December 16, 1954." Personal correspondence of Walt Kelly, Billy Ireland Cartoon Library & Museum, Ohio State University, Walt Kelly Collection, Box 4, Folder 14.

Kelly, Walt. "Letter to the Editor." *Life*. June 1952. 3.

Kelly, Walt. "London Calling: Kelly Interviewed by the *Sunday Times*." *Pluperfect Pogo*. Bill Crouch Jr., ed. New York: Simon & Schuster, 1987.

Kelly, Walt. "Okefenokee." Walt Kelly Papers, Billy Ireland Cartoon Library & Museum. Box 8, folder 16.

Kelly, Walt. "Pogo and Creator Walt Kelly Are Both for the People." *Syracuse Journal*. 1952: 1.

Kelly, Walt. "Post-Hall Syndicate Promotional, 1954." www.pogopossum.com. 2010.

Kelly, Walt. "Senate Hearing Transcript on Comic Books and Juvenile Delinquency." Foley Square Federal Court House, Manhattan (21 April 1954).

Kelly, Walt. *Ten Ever-Lovin' Blue-Eyed Years with Pogo*. New York: Simon & Schuster, 1959.

Kelly, Walt. "The Bunny Rabbit Strips." *The Best of Pogo*. Bill Crouch Jr. and Selby Kelly, eds. New York: Simon & Schuster, 1982. 198–201.

———. "The Land of the Elephant Squash." *Pogo Even Better*. Selby Kelly and Bill Crouch, Jr., eds. New York: Simon & Schuster, 1984. 49–50.

Kelly, Walt. "Unpublished Autobiographical Sketch." Billy Ireland Cartoon Library & Museum, Ohio State University, Walt Kelly Collection, Box 5, Folder 16.

Kelly, Walt. *Ten Ever-Lovin' Blue-Eyed Years with Pogo*. New York: Simon & Schuster, 1959.

Kelly, Walt. "Unpublished Autobiographical Sketch." Billy Ireland Cartoon Library & Museum, Box 5, Folder 16.

Kelly, Walt. "Zeroing in on Those Polluters: We Have Met the Enemy and He is Us." *The Best of Pogo*. Selby Kelly and Bill Crouch Jr., eds. New York: Simon & Schuster, 1982. 224.

Kerouac, Jack. *On The Road*. New York: Penguin, 1957.

Kercher, Stephen. *Revel With a Cause: Liberal Satire in Postwar America*. Chicago: The University of Chicago Press, 2006.

Kimball, Ward. "W.K. Meets W.K." *The Complete Pogo Comics: Dreamin' of A Wide Catfish*. Mark Burstein, ed. Forestville, CA: Eclipse Books, 1990. 7–12.

Landay, Lori. *Madcaps, Screwballs, and Con Women: The Female Trickster in American Culture*. Philadelphia: The University of Pennsylvania Press, 1998.

Levine, Lawrence. *Black Culture and Black Consciousness: Afro-American Folk Thought From Slavery to Freedom*. New York: Oxford UP, 1977.

Lindvall, Terry and Ben Fraser. "Darker Shades of Animation: African-American Images in the Warner Bros. Cartoon." *Reading the Rabbit Explorations in Warner Bros. Animation*. Kevin S. Sandler, ed. New Brunswick, NJ: Rutgers UP, 1998.

Lockwood, Alma R. "Walt Kelly Visits Real Swamp; Pogo Insulted by Real Possum." the *Bridgeport Post*. 14 April 1955: A2.

Lockwood, George. "Walt Kelly." *Cartoonist Profiles* 67 (September 1985): 48.

Maltin, Leonard. *Of Mice and Magic: A History of American Animated Cartoons*. New York: Plume, 1987.

Marschall, Richard. *America's Great Comic Strip Artists*. New York: Abbeville Press, 1989.

———. "Walt Kelly Remembers Bridgeport." *Connecticut Sunday Herald* 28 October 1973: 8A.

Marschall, Richard. "Interview with Al Capp." *The Comics Journal*. 37 (March 1978): 15.

———. "National Cartoonists Society newsletter, July 15, 1954." Billy Ireland Cartoon Library & Museum, Ohio State University, Walt Kelly Collection,. Box 4, folder 15.

———. "National Cartoonists Society newsletter, May 14, 1955." Billy Ireland Cartoon Library & Museum, Ohio State University, Walt Kelly Collection,. Box 4, folder 14.

Marschall, Richard, and Groth, Gary. "Charles Schulz Interview." *The Comics Journal*. (January 1992) 9.

Mastrangelo, Joseph P. "Remembering Walt Kelly: A Last Hello From the Old Swamp Boat." *Washington Post*, 10 November 1973, B1.

Maule, Rosanna. *Beyond Auteurism: New Directions in Authorial Film Practices in France, Italy and Spain since the 1980s*. Bristol, UK: Intellect, 2008.

———. "Pogo's Campaign Launched While Crowds Yell Approval." the *Times-Picayune*. (21 October 1952) 1.

May, Elaine Tyler. *Homeward Bound: American Families in the Cold War Era*. New York: Basic Books, 1990.

Mendelson, Edward. "Possum Pastoral." *Phi Beta Pogo*. Selby Kelly, and Bill Crouch Jr., eds. New York: Simon & Schuster, 1989, 15–20.

McCloud, Scott. *Understanding Comics*. New York: Harper, 1993.

Nachman, Gerald. *Seriously Funny: The Rebel Comedians of the 1950s and 1960s*. New York: Pantheon, 2003.

O'Sullivan, Judith. *The Great American Comic Strip*. Boston: Little, Brown and Company, 1991.

O'Sullivan, Judith. The Great American Comic Strip: One Hundred Years of Comic Art. Boston: Little, Brown and Company, 1991.

"Over the Transom." Excerpts from fan letters. Billy Ireland Cartoon Library & Museum, Ohio State University, Walt Kelly Collection, Box 2, Folder 7.

Pells, Richard H. *The Liberal Mind in a Conservative Age*. New York: Harper & Row, 1985.

"Pogo Campaign Memorabilia." Reprinted in *The Best of Pogo*. Selby Kelly and Bill Crouch Jr., eds. New York: Simon & Schuster, 1982. 183–97.

———. "Police Seize 28 in Wild Harvard Riot." the *Boston Post*. 16 May 1952: A5.

"Possum Attack in Vancouver, British Columbia." A collection of news clippings reprinted in *Phi Beta Pogo*. Selby Kelly and Bill Crouch Jr., eds. New York: Simon & Schuster, 1989. 118–22.

Ritvo, Harriet. "Learning from Animals" Natural History for Children in the Eighteenth and Nineteenth Centuries," *Children's Literature* 13 (1985): 72–93.

Rodgers, Richard. "Pogo Genius Advises Clubmen On Merits of Chocolate Ducks." the *Evening Star*. Washington, D.C. 18 April 1952: A21.

Sampson, Henry T. *That's Enough, Folks: Black Images in Animated Cartoons, 1900–1960*. Lanham, MD: The Scarecrow Press, 1998.

Sanders, Allen. "The Comics from Pow to Wow!" *The Cartoonist*. (Spring 1957) 9.

Sandler, Kevin S. *Reading the Rabbit: Explorations in Warner Bros. Animation*. New Jersey: Rutgers University Press, 1998.

Sartwell, Frank. "America Needed a Possum, and That's Why We Got Pogo." the *Evening Star*. Washington D.C. (2 December 1953) 1.

Schickel, Richard. *The Disney Version: The Life, Times, Art and Commerce of Walt Disney* 1968.

———— . "Walt Kelly Insists Comic Strip Aims at Amusement." the *Times Picayune*, (22 October 1952) 1.

Schickel, Richard. *The Disney Version*. London: Michael Joseph, 1986.

Sewell, David. *Mark Twain's Languages*. Berkeley: University of California Press, 1987.

Silverman, Samuel J. "Legal document sent by Kelly and his lawyers to Governor Averill Harriman." Walt Kelly Papers, Ohio State Cartoon Library. (8 April 1955) 1–2.

Sito, Tom. "The Disney Strike of 1941: How It Changed Animation & Comics." *Animation World Network*. www.awn.com. 19 July 2005: 1–4. Web. 21 July 2010.

Snyder, Susan. "As You Like It: A Modern Perspective." *Folger Shakespeare Library: As You Like It*. Barbara A. Mowat and Paul Werstine, eds. New York: Washington Square Press, 1997. 231–42.

Solomon, Charles. *Enchanted Drawings: The History of Animation*. New York: Random House, 1994.

Soper, Kerry. "From Jive Crows in *Dumbo* to Bumbazine and *Pogo:* Walt Kelly and the Conflicted Politics of Reracinating African American Types in Mid-20th Century Comics" *The International Journal of Comic Art* (Fall 2010, Vol. 12, No. 2/3): 125–49.

Stewart, Bhob. "King Features Went Back to the Future on Its 75th Anniversary." *Witty World*. Summer/Autumn, 1991: 18–24.

————. "Students Claim Mishandling In Police Methods at Melee." the *Harvard Crimson*. 16 May 1952: A1.

Strausbaugh, John. *Black Like You: Blackface, Whiteface, Insult & Imitation in American Popular Culture*. New York: Penguin, 2006.

Swift, Jonathan. "Verses on the Death of Dr. Swift, D.S.P.D." *Jonathan Swift: A Critical Edition of the Major Works*. Angus Ross and David Woolley, eds. New York: Oxford University Press, 1984.

Thompson, Steve. "McCarthy, Krushchev, and Castro." *Pogo Files for Pogophiles*. Selby Daley Kelly and Steve Thompson, eds. (Richfield, MN: Spring Hollow Books, 1992): 87—94.

Thompson, Steve. "Pogo's Adolescence." At the Mercy of the Elephants: *The Complete Pogo Comics, Vol. 2*. Mark Burstein, ed. Forestville, CA: Eclipse Books, 1990. 7–10.

Thompson, Steve. "Returning to *Our Gang*," *Walt Kelly's Our Gang: 1945–1946*. Seattle: Fantagraphics Books, 2007. 3–11.

Tilton, John. *Cosmic Satire in the Contemporary Novel*. Lewisburg: Bucknell University Press, 1977.

Trudeau, Garry. "Introduction," *The Best of Pogo*, Bill Crouch Jr., ed., (New York: Simon & Schuster, 1982).

Turberville, Gus. "Pogo in the Fifties." *The Best of Pogo*. Selby Kelly and Bill Crouch Jr., eds. New York: Simon & Schuster, 1982. 94.

Vervain, Chris. "Performing Ancient Drama in Mask: the Case of Greek New Comedy." *NTQ* 20:3, August 2004, 245–60.

"Walt Kelly." *Walt Kelly Exhibition Guide*. Springfield, MA: Museum of Cartoon Art, 1973.

Ward, John. "About Walt and His Friends." *The Rhode Islander* (23 March 1958) 2–4.

Watkins, Mel. *On The Read Side: Laughing, Lying, and Signifying; The Underground Tradition of African-American Humor That Transformed American Culture From Slavery to Richard Pryor*. New York: Simon & Schuster, 1994.

Wadsworth, Philip A. "The Art of Allegory in La Fontaine's Fables." *The French Review*. Vol. 45, No. 6 (May 1972): 1125–35.

Watkins, Mel. *On The Read Side: Laughing, Lying, and Signifying; The Underground Tradition of African-American Humor That Transformed American Culture From Slavery to Richard Pryor*. New York: Simon & Schuster, 1994.

———. "Walt Kelly Insists Comic Strip Aims at Amusement." *The Times Picayune*. 22 October 1952: 1.

Watterson, Bill. "Some Thoughts on Pogo and Comic Strips Today," *Phi Beta Pogo*. Selby Kelly, and Bill Crouch Jr., eds. New York: Simon & Schuster, 1989. 10–14.

Weisenberger, Steven. *Fables of Subversion*. Athens: University of Georgia Press, 1995.

Wells, Paul. *Animation and America*. New Jersey: Rutgers University Press, 2002.

Wexman, Virginia Wright. "Introduction." *Film and Authorship*. Virginia Wright Wexman, ed. New Brunswick, NJ: Rutgers UP, 2003. 1–18.

White, David Manning, and Abel, Robert H. "Introduction: Comic Strips and American Culture." *The Funnies: An American Idiom*. White and Abel, eds. London: The Free Press of Glencoe, 1963.

White, Timothy R. "From Disney to Warner Bros." *Reading the Rabbit*. Kevin S. Sandler, ed. New Jersey: Rutgers University Press, 1998.

Williams, Martin. "The Hidden World of *L'il Abner*." *The Comics Journal*. 147 (December 1991): 76.

Woolacott, Janet. "Fictions and ideologies: The case of situation comedies," Popular Culture and Social Relations, Tony Bennet, ed. (Philadelphia: Open University Press, 1986).

Zwigoff, Terry. *Crumb*. Sony Classics Films, 1994.

INDEX

Page numbers in *italics* indicate illustrations.

CPSIA information can be obtained at www.ICGtesting.com
Printed in the USA
BVOW070914160512

290211BV00002B/4/P